PERSPECTIVES IN ECONOMICS

PERSPECTIVES IN ECONOMICS
Economists Look at Their Fields of Study

Edited by
ALAN A. BROWN   Indiana University
EGON NEUBERGER   State University of New York at Stony Brook
MALCOLM PALMATIER   The RAND Corporation

McGraw-Hill Book Company
New York   St. Louis   San Francisco
Düsseldorf   London   Mexico
Panama   Rio de Janiero
Singapore   Sydney   Toronto

**PERSPECTIVES
IN ECONOMICS**

Copyright © 1971 by McGraw-Hill, Inc.
All rights reserved. Printed in the
United States of America. No part of
this publication may be reproduced,
stored in a retrieval system, or
transmitted, in any form or by any
means, electronic, mechanical,
photocopying, recording, or otherwise,
without the prior written permission
of the publisher.

*Library of Congress Catalog Card
Number 77-126745*

0 8 3 1 1

1 2 3 4 5 6 7 8 9 0   MAMM
7 9 8 7 6 5 4 3 2 1 0

This book was set in News Gothic by
Monotype Composition Company, Inc.,
and printed on permanent paper and
bound by The Maple Press Company.
The designer was Edward Zytko; the
drawings were done by John Cordes,
J. & R. Technical Services, Inc. The
editor was Cynthia Newby. Les Kaplan
supervised production.

PREFACE

THIS BOOK is the collective effort of twenty-three specialists in various subject areas of economics. It is designed to give the reader—whether a student in an introductory college economics course, or perhaps someone casually interested in the subject—a broad sense of the textures and dimensions of current economic thought, as revealed both in the special concerns of individual areas and in the relation of these areas to the discipline as a whole. For the committed student, particularly, it can stand as a complementary text in economic principles or as a survey of economic fields to guide him in his career choices.

The first five essays deal with methodological approaches to economics, including economic history, econometrics, and microeconomic and macroeconomic theory. They provide the reader with an appreciation of some of the tools of professional economists and introduce him to the way in which economists think about and approach their special fields.

The next eight essays describe the application of these tools to selected economic subject areas. Some of these areas, such as monetary policy, fiscal policy, and industrial organization, are traditional ones, generally taught in every liberal arts college or university. Others, such as urban economics and the economics of employment, of the public sector, of national defense, and of health and education, represent the application of economic tools to important areas of modern public policy and are not always taught as separate courses.

The last six essays in the book discuss economic relations among countries and the process of economic development past and present. Here we deal with international trade and monetary reform, with economic growth and development, with changes and continuities in market and centrally planned economies, and with comparative economic systems.

This book had its origin in the observed need to give college students in elementary economics courses useful perspectives in the field. Most of the chapters are original essays written specifically for the book. In a few cases, where certain articles in the literature particularly matched the purposes of this book, we included previously published material with minor modifications. Differences in individual authors' coverage and approach were preserved in the interest of freshness of perception.

A preliminary edition has been tested in economics courses at selected universities from coast to coast. We are greatly pleased with this manifestation of student power—that economics students participated in the improvement of their own textbook. The comments of outside reviewers indicate that the approach to economics embodied in this book and the quality of individual contributions provide a much-needed aid to the study of economics.

On the basis of experience with the preliminary edition, the book suggests itself primarily as a supplementary volume for introductory economics courses at the college level. Specific chapters dealing with theory or policy have been used successfully in intermediate courses. The volume has also been tested as the major text for senior honors students at the high school level. The response of the students showed that most of the chapters were intellectually challenging and not beyond the grasp of able high school seniors.

We are grateful to the contributors, who agreed with our wish to further elementary education in economics and who devoted some of their scarcest resource—time—to the venture. We are indebted to the students and instructors whose criticisms helped to improve the book. We wish, as well, to acknowledge the loyal assistance of Mr. Akeel Hany Al-Sadi, who tirelessly coordinated the complex processing of the original copy, and of Mrs. Helen O'Connell, who typed it, as always, with great skill and accuracy.

ALAN A. BROWN
EGON NEUBERGER
MALCOLM PALMATIER

LIST OF CONTRIBUTORS

WILLIAM G. BOWEN
Provost, Princeton University

ALAN A. BROWN
Visiting Professor of Economics,
Indiana University; on leave from the
University of Southern California

RICHARD CAVES
Professor of Economics, Harvard
University

BENJAMIN CHINITZ
Professor of Economics and
Chairman, Department of Economics,
Brown University

ARNOLD COLLERY
Professor of Economics, Amherst
College

JOHN E. ELLIOTT
Professor of Economics, University
of Southern California

ALEXANDER GERSCHENKRON
Walter S. Barker Professor of
Economics, Harvard University

GREGORY GROSSMAN
Professor of Economics, University
of California at Berkeley

SEYMOUR E. HARRIS
Professor of Economics, University
of California at San Diego;
Littauer Professor Emeritus, Harvard
University

ROBERT W. HARTMAN
Research Associate, Brookings
Institution

ESTELLE JAMES
Associate Professor of Economics,
State University of New York
at Stony Brook

CHARLES C. KILLINGSWORTH
University Professor, Michigan
State University

ROBERT LEKACHMAN
Professor of Economics, State
University of New York at
Stony Brook

ABBA P. LERNER
Professor of Economics, University
of California at Berkeley

AURELIUS MORGNER
Professor of Economics, University
of Southern California

EGON NEUBERGER
Professor of Economics, State
University of New York at
Stony Brook

JEFFREY B. NUGENT
Associate Professor of Economics,
University of Southern California

MALCOLM PALMATIER
Editor, Economics Department, The
RAND Corporation

E. BRYANT PHILLIPS
Professor of Economics, University
of Southern California

THOMAS C. SCHELLING
Professor of Economics, Harvard
University

WARREN L. SMITH
Professor of Economics, University
of Michigan

ARTHUR SMITHIES
Professor of Economics, Harvard
University

ROBERT TRIFFIN
Frederick William Beinecke Professor
of Economics, Yale University,
and Master of Berkeley College

CONTENTS

Preface   v

List of Contributors   vii

1 **SCOPE AND METHOD OF ECONOMIC ANALYSIS**   1
Alan A. Brown and John E. Elliott

2 **ECONOMIC HISTORY AND ECONOMICS**   14
Alexander Gerschenkron

3 **ECONOMETRICS**   27
William G. Bowen

4 **MICROECONOMIC THEORY**   36
Abba P. Lerner

5 **MACROECONOMIC THEORY**   50
Arnold Collery

6 **MONETARY INSTITUTIONS AND POLICIES**   65
Warren L. Smith

7 **FISCAL POLICY**   83
Robert W. Hartman

8   **FULL EMPLOYMENT AND THE NEW ECONOMICS**   101
    Charles C. Killingsworth

9   **INDUSTRIAL ORGANIZATION**   120
    Richard Caves and E. Bryant Phillips

10 **ECONOMIC ANALYSIS OF THE PUBLIC SECTOR**   134
    Arthur Smithies

11 **ECONOMIC REASONING AND NATIONAL DEFENSE**   143
    Thomas C. Schelling and Malcolm Palmatier

12 **ECONOMICS OF HEALTH AND EDUCATION**   160
    Seymour E. Harris and Estelle James

13 **URBAN ECONOMICS: THE PROBLEM OF THE GHETTO**   173
    Benjamin Chinitz

14 **INTERNATIONAL ECONOMICS: THEORY AND POLICY**   186
    Aurelius Morgner

15 **INTERNATIONAL ECONOMICS: MONETARY REFORM**   198
    Robert Triffin

16 **ECONOMIC GROWTH AND DEVELOPMENT**   213
    Jeffrey B. Nugent

17 **CONTINUITIES AND DISCONTINUITIES IN ECONOMIC DEVELOPMENT**   225
    Robert Lekachman

18 **CONTINUITIES AND CHANGE IN CENTRALLY PLANNED ECONOMIES**   234
    Gregory Grossman

19 **COMPARATIVE ECONOMIC SYSTEMS**   252
    Egon Neuberger

PERSPECTIVES IN ECONOMICS

1
SCOPE AND METHOD OF ECONOMIC ANALYSIS

Alan A. Brown*
John E. Elliott**

THE SCOPE OF ECONOMICS

ALTHOUGH what we know as "reality" is a seamless whole, our approaches to the study of it are traditionally divided into parts or disciplines, such as economics, history, literature, and physics. This intellectual division of labor has proved generally beneficial, although at times it has been marred by gaps in our knowledge and failures in communication between different fields of study. At the same time, it is fruitless and even positively misleading to separate one discipline, such as economics, from another, where there may be no counterpart in reality. In its evolution and development as a discipline, the scope and boundaries of economics have not remained perfectly fixed.

Economics is an "open" system, in the sense that the number of variables that could potentially affect the behavior of the "economy" is indefinite. When economists place limits upon their studies by focusing upon selected variables and relationships, they typically assume *ceteris paribus* conditions—that is, conditions where one thing is allowed to change while "other things remain equal." As an intellectual device, this procedure contributes order and system to thinking about complex problems; however, economists are usually not in a position to "close" their systems of analysis by laboratory methods, nor to generalize easily from

---

* Indiana University.
** University of Southern California.

observation ("for all practical purposes"). Attempts to identify the scope and boundaries of economics are thus unavoidably arbitrary, and factors "outside" economics (such as politics, psychology, or technology) may have a profound effect upon the behavior of the economic system. Moreover, different economists may quite legitimately have different, but powerfully held, views as to the scope of the discipline.

Economics and Its Neighbors Because its boundaries are indefinite, economics encroaches on other disciplines and strikes pacts with them. This reciprocal behavior is illustrated by the growth of such hybrid titles as economic history, economic statistics, mathematical economics, economic psychology, economic sociology, economic anthropology, and, of course, political economy. During much of the nineteenth century, the term "political economy" was practically synonymous with what is now called economics, supplemented by social and political philosophy. Today, in fact, the older term is coming back into vogue, but with a twist, to mean issues and concepts pertaining to the interdependencies of politics and economics, as, for example, in the theory of collective choice, the determination of government economic policy, decisionmaking in large corporations, and so forth.

Economics both receives from and contributes to other fields of study in a mutually beneficial way. From mathematics, statistics, and history, for example, it receives methodological insights and empirical information to test its hypotheses. From psychology, sociology, politics, law, and technology it takes basic assumptions (about which more later) upon which to build economic theories. To other disciplines, economics contributes a logic for rational choice and comparison of alternatives, a healthy respect for reality and actual patterns of human behavior, a theory of exchange, an ethic of efficiency and economizing, and, perhaps above all, a useful distinction between "possibility functions" and "preference functions"—that is, between identification of alternatives and selection of the best alternative.

Scope by Definition? Economics has been defined variously as the study of (1) household management (Aristotle); (2) wealth (Adam Smith); (3) material welfare (Alfred Marshall); (4) avarice or self-interest (John Stuart Mill); (5) anything that can be brought within "the universal measuring rod of money" (A. C. Pigou); (6) markets, prices, and market exchange (Gustav Cassel); (7) the allocation of (given) scarce resources among competing (given) ends or uses (Lionel Robbins); and (8) the logic of rational human action (Ludwig von Mises).

These eight definitions represent two major points of view. Definitions (1) through (6) look at life as divided into parts, and identify economics as one of these parts; the last two definitions look at economics as an approach to or an interpretation of life.

In the past half-century, there has been a trend in the literature away from economics as a "part of life" and toward economics as an "interpretation of life." The major criticism of the first point of view is that it limits economic studies in unnecessary or misleading ways. Why, for example, should economists restrict themselves to the study of wealth or the material dimensions of human welfare? Economics is a social science, and as such is presumably concerned with relations among men, not merely relations among things or even relations between men and things. And what about services? Similarly, why should economics be restricted to the study of individual self-interest, money, or market exchange? What about community interests, barter, or central planning?

Economics defined as an interpretation of life has had a better reception; evidence of this may be found by consulting the first chapter of nearly any text on introductory economics. Economics defined as the allocation of scarce resources among alternative uses, or as the logic of rational purposive action, is more satisfying than economics defined as, say, material welfare. Yet, if we apply interpretation-of-life definitions too broadly, we encounter topics customarily regarded as beyond the scope of economics. If economics is literally the study of choice and resource allocation, then, as the early twentieth-century English economist and Unitarian minister Philip Wicksteed observed, questions such as the following fall within the province of the discipline: How high a cliff would you dive off to save your grandmother, drowning in the icy waters below? How short would you cut family prayers in order to speed a visiting relative to the railroad station?

A Pragmatic Solution: Economics Is What Economists Do A second trend in recent years has been to refrain from formal definitions in favor of informal descriptions of the major issues that have concerned economists. It is summed up in Jacob Viner's reputed definition, "Economics is what economists do." This approach is not very satisfying; if economics is "what economists do," then what is it that economists do? But it does reflect practical wisdom. First, any definition is arbitrary. Second, economics is not a "word to be defined," but a set of issues to be explored. Third, most definitions are only lightly concealed value judgments as to what an author thinks his professional colleagues *should* do.

A reasonably accurate list of the the issues studied in contemporary economics would include the following: (1) the allocation of scarce resources, (2) the distribution of income, (3) the rate of economic growth, and (4) the overall levels of (and short-run stability in) income, employment, and prices.

Macro and Micro An alternative way of describing what it is that economists "do" is to divide the subject into *macroeconomics* and *microeconomics*. Macroeconomics aggregates individuals and commodities for an entire economy (regional, national, or international) or for major subdivisions (total consumption, investment, or government spending) of the economy as a whole. Microeconomics studies individual units of economic decision, such as households, business firms, and resource suppliers (landlords, capitalists, workers), their interrelationships, and the behavior of particular aggregates (such as the market for coffee). By emphasizing individual units, microeconomics tends to focus upon relative prices or exchange relations (such as the price of tea relative to the price of coffee), and the allocation of resources and distribution of income, given their overall levels. By contrast, macroeconomics, by emphasizing the economy as a whole, tends to regard relative prices as given and focuses upon overall income, employment, and price levels, depressions and inflations, unemployment versus full employment, and the rate of economic growth.

Over the years, emphasis has shifted between the two major branches of the discipline. From Adam Smith in 1776 to Karl Marx in the mid-nineteenth century, economics was concerned with *both* macro- and microeconomic issues, making no clear or rigorous distinction between them. In the latter part of the nineteenth century, the Austrian, marginalist, and neoclassical economists (for example, Stanley Jevons, Carl Menger, Alfred Marshall, Leon Walras) shifted the attention of the discipline to relative prices and the microeconomic relations of supply and demand for particular commodities and services. In the depressed decade of the 1930s, the English economist John Maynard Keynes and others shifted emphasis back to such macroeconomic issues as national income, unemployment, and depression. In recent years, economists have increasingly emphasized the *interdependencies* between microeconomics and macroeconomics. This is especially evident in the study of economic policy and international and comparative economics, as succeeding chapters of this book show.

In sum, each body of economic analysis has an important contribution to make to solving real-life problems. The central insight of macroeconomics is its view of the economic system as a whole, while that of microeconomics is its view of the mutual interdependencies of the different units of the economic system. The major strength of each is also its major weakness. Manipulation of macroeconomic variables glosses over microeconomic problems of individual choice and behavior, while exclusive emphasis upon microeconomic interrelationships may blind the student of economics to the "fallacy of composition," that is, assuming that what is true for a part of the system is true for the system as a whole.

ALAN A. BROWN & JOHN E. ELLIOTT

THE METHODS OF ECONOMICS

Economics as Ethic, Art, and Science At various times in its historical evolution, economics has been an ethic, an art, and a science. For St. Thomas Aquinas and other medieval churchmen, for example, economics was essentially a branch of applied theology, an ethic of good conduct in this life as a member of an ideal Christian commonwealth in preparation for salvation in a life to come. For mercantilist writers in the sixteenth through eighteenth centuries, economics was essentially an art of advising rulers about means of augmenting the wealth and power of nations. In recent centuries, and particularly in the last quarter-century, economics, while retaining and even expanding and enriching its artistic and ethical dimensions, has become an increasingly sophisticated and exacting scientific discipline.

Like science in general, economics is an ordered body of knowledge, developed in terms of methods and procedures known to, and generally understood and accepted by, a group of specialists (economists in our case) for the purposes of the description, explanation, and prediction of reality. More particularly, economics is a social science; it studies the behavior of men in society as members of groups or as participants in the activities of the marketplace. Most particularly, economics is a *generalizing* social science, characterized by the advancement of theories that would describe, explain, or predict the unifying properties of economic experience. In addition, economic theories may help in the formulation of economic policies to achieve individual and social goals, and thus serve as a means of social control. In sum, economic theory contributes importantly to the practical task of helping solve human problems.

The Structure of Economic Theory The theoretical study of economic problems proceeds by three major steps: (1) specifying assumptions or underlying axioms, (2) formulating hypotheses or theories from the assumptions, and (3) testing the validity of the hypotheses or theories.

ASSUMPTIONS In the broadest sense, assumptions are those dimensions of a science which are taken as "given," in the sense that they are beyond the scope of the discipline, or of a specific problem, to explain. In short, they are taken as axiomatic and are used as underlying premises upon which other ideas (hypotheses) are built. Clearly, assumptions lie at the frontiers of a scientific discipline, for any change in them, given conventions for the formulation of hypotheses, may result in different hypotheses.

Most assumptions in economics may be classified as resource-technological, institutional, or psychological-motivational. (1) Assumptions regarding resources and technology specify relationships between resource inputs and outputs, and thus the resulting impact upon productivity (output per unit input, on the average or at the margin) under a given state of technology. (2) Institutional assumptions come in a large variety of forms, such as capitalism versus socialism; competition versus monopoly; the existence versus the nonexistence of a commercial banking system with power to create money in the form of demand deposits or checking accounts. (3) Psychological-motivational assumptions usually specify the goals that economic units are assumed to pursue, the principle that guides their conduct in such pursuit, and the relation between psychological variables, such as "utility" or satisfaction, and the magnitude of inputs and outputs. For example, the economic "theory of the household" generally assumes a desire to maximize utility under conditions where the relative marginal utility of two commodities varies inversely with the relative quantities consumed. The economic "theory of the firm" generally assumes a desire to maximize profits, or the difference between expected sales revenues and expected costs.

Questions frequently arise about the realism of assumptions. Assumptions can be unrealistic in the sense of being freed from factual details so as to focus upon unifying properties; this can be a useful device. Assumptions may also be unrealistic in the sense of introducing "pure" or "perfect" cases (pure or perfect competition, pure or perfect monopoly, perfect elasticity of demand, perfect flexibility of resources). These kinds of assumptions are simplifying and incomplete (because the world is more complex), but often analytically useful as end-points. Or an assumption may be unrealistic in the sense of being patently false. This is unfortunate because hypotheses consistent with and logically derived from false assumptions will also be false.

The proof of the pudding is in the eating. It is often tempting to reject economic theories out of hand for being oversimple or unrealistic. But if such assumptions yield explanatory hypotheses or predictions about the behavior of economic variables which correspond as closely to the real world as more complicated and more realistic assumptions, then more power to them!

HYPOTHESES Hypotheses or theoretical generalizations (the terms being for all practical purposes synonymous in economics)[1] provide a method for the systematic description, explanation, and prediction of

[1] It is fashionable in some disciplines other than economics to distinguish among hypotheses, theories, and laws, in terms of their (ascending) degree of explanatory or predictive value. In other words, a hypothesis is merely "hypothetical"; a theory is one step better, but for all that just a theory; but a law, watch out! Economists are generally content to say that *all* theoretical generalizations, whatever their names, are hypothetical *if . . . then* constructions, with varying degrees of explanatory or predictive value.

economic variables. An economic variable is anything of interest to students of economics which is subject to variation. One set of such variables might include such items as income, output, investment, consumption, and saving—variables measured as *flows* or rates of change over time. A second set might include wealth, capital stock, stock of consumer durable goods, and savings—variables measured as *stocks* existing at a moment in time. A third set of variables might include ratios *between* stocks and/or flows. A price, for example, is a ratio between a flow of expenditures and a quantity of output or resource input purchased or sold. Velocity, to give a second example, transforms a stock into a flow, as in the equation $MV = E$ (money times velocity of circulation or rate of turnover equals expenditures).

A hypothetical generalization regarding relations between economic variables has three central features: a dependent variable, an independent variable, and a *ceteris paribus* condition. The dependent variable is the one whose changes the hypothesis seeks to explain or predict. The independent variable is the one whose changes yield changes in the dependent variable. The *ceteris paribus* condition holds constant all factors other than the selected independent variable which could plausibly affect the dependent variable.

Equations (1-1) and (1-2) give examples of hypotheses, one for microeconomics and one for macroeconomics:

$$D_1 = f(P_1) \qquad (1\text{-}1)$$

$$C = f(Y_d) \qquad (1\text{-}2)$$

Equation (1-1) states that the demand for commodity 1 (D_1) by one or more consumers is some function f of—that is, depends upon—the price of commodity 1 (P_1). Equation (1-2) states that the aggregate or overall level of consumption in the national economy C is some function of the level of disposable national output or income Y_d (income actually available for disposition by households between consumption and saving after taxes, depreciation, undistributed corporate profits, and other items are added to, or subtracted from, the total gross national product). Typically, the form of the postulated relation between the independent and the dependent variable is also specified. For example, Equation (1-1) is typically accompanied by the proposition that D_1 varies *inversely* with P_1, rising (falling) as P_1 falls (rises); Equation (1-2), by the proposition that consumption varies *directly* with income, rising (falling) as income rises (falls). Either of these propositions may be derived *deductively*, as generalizations from underlying assumptions, or *inductively*, from particular experiences in various markets or countries. A general mathematical formulation of the hypothesis, as thus defined, describes the *direction* of change in the dependent variable caused by a change in an independent variable. An econometric model would hypothesize the expected *magnitude* of change as well, by specifying the value of the functional relation. For example, $C = 0.9Y_d$ says that consumption is 90 percent of disposable national income.

Equations (1-1) and (1-2) assume implicitly that "other things" remain equal. Some other things (such as Tibetan goat milk production) may remain equal, for all practical purposes, with changes in Y_d and P_1. Others (such as technology, social institutions, the stock of known natural resources) may remain relatively stable over short periods of time. Still others may vary in "countervailing" ways—for example, P_2 may decrease and P_3 may increase, leaving the overall price level roughly stable. Basically, however, the *ceteris paribus* method is a useful, indeed indispensable, analytical device. It enables one, in the conduct of intellectual experiments, to focus attention on specified functional relations in a simplified, rigorous, and precise way.

Changes in underlying *ceteris paribus* conditions may be made an integral part of a system of hypotheses by shifting the position of the functional relations themselves. For example, an increase in income would normally cause an increase in the quantity of commodity 1 demanded at every price in Equation (1-1); an increase in the general propensity to save (say, because of pessimistic expectations by households) would be accompanied by a decrease in consumption at all levels of income in Equation (1-2). In sum, the functional relationship itself may alter because of changes in factors other than the one selected for major emphasis as the independent variable.

TESTING HYPOTHESES Because economics can be regarded as both a theoretical *and* an empirical discipline, tests for empirical validity should supplement those for logical consistency. A good theory, then, yields good explanations or predictions of reality.

We shall mention here three common problems associated with empirical testing: appropriateness, correspondence, and practicality.

The problem of *appropriateness* is one of selecting the field of observation appropriate to testing a theory. For example, a generalization about an economic system "as a whole" should be tested against data for an entire economic system, not merely for some industry or market within it. Allied to this is the need to state clearly any special conditions that restrict the theory, and thus its real-world counterpart. For example, the hypothesis that an increase in the supply of money will cause inflation under full-employment conditions with a given labor force and given technology is not invalidated by a noninflationary increase in the money supply *if* the economy is initially at less than full employment or *if* technology improves.

The problem of *correspondence* is one of determining the degree of "closeness of fit" between the theory (or its associated predictions) and reality, once observations about reality have been identified. Naturally, the closer the fit the greater the confidence in the theory. But theories differ in scope and complexity, and determining how close is close may be arbitrary. The problem of correspondence is compounded by the fact that an economic theory ("classical theory," "Keynesian theory") is often a set of interdependent hypotheses, some significantly more valid than others. In addition, correlation between two variables, say, does not in itself demonstrate the direction of causation. The fact that income and consumption rise and fall together may demonstrate that income determines consumption. But in the absence of further reasoning and evidence, it may also demonstrate that consumption determines income. Lastly, because science is open-ended, today's good theory may be replaced by a better one tomorrow.

Practicality has a number of facets. The one that needs emphasis here is suggested by the popular expression, "That's a good theory, but it doesn't work out in practice." In one sense this is a tautological statement. If practice means explanatory or predictive value, then a theory is only good if it *does* work out in practice; if it does not, it cannot be called a good theory. In another sense, however, the statement may express the homely truth that a theory whose logical and empirical credentials are in order may not be put to practical use by policy- or decisionmakers. This may be because of the policymakers' failure to understand the theory or the economists' failure to communicate it. Often, it stems from the fact that economic policymaking is essentially an artistic rather than a scientific enterprise, drawing implicitly (if not explicitly) upon economic theory and intuitively and artistically upon a blend of many noneconomic factors and ideas.

THE POLICY IMPLICATIONS OF ECONOMICS

In closing this introductory section, we may gain perspective on economic theory by relating it to broader issues of normative economics, economic systems, and economic policy.

Normative versus Positive Economics Economic science, or *positive economics*, proceeds from assumptions to explanatory or predictive hypotheses to the testing of hypotheses (and thereby, in a loop, to the revision of assumptions and hypotheses). The purpose of this procedure is to make positive statements about *what is*. By contrast, the purpose of *normative economics* is to make and support, by reasoning and evidence, value judgments regarding *what ought to be*.

Normative economics, like positive economics, advances in three major steps: (1) specifying assumptions, underlying axioms, and conditions; (2) formulating desired objectives from the assumptions or conditions; and (3) testing the objectives in terms of their consequences or impact. Two striking differences can be noticed, however. First, the assumptions of positive economics are *descriptive* (for example, that consumers do in fact desire to maximize utility), while those of normative economics are *prescriptive* (for example, that consumers ought to get what they are willing and able to pay for). Second, if positive scientific theories do not correspond to reality, then so much the worse for them; they should be revised to provide better explanations or predictions of what in fact exists. If reality does not correspond to normative prescriptions, however, so much the worse for reality; it should be revised to correspond more closely to our value judgments of what ought to exist!

As social scientists, economists wish to minimize *bias* in their inquiries—that is, to avoid value judgments that interfere with scientific objectivity. At the same time, it is important to emphasize that the relation between human values and scientific enterprise in economics need not be biased, and indeed, that values may contribute to science and science to the better understanding of values. These potentially constructive interdependencies between normative and positive economics exist at three major levels of inquiry: prescientific, scientific, and postscientific. At the prescientific level, value judgments may profoundly affect the choice both of problems for investigation and of scientific criteria. At the scientific level, value judgments themselves exist as empirical phenomena, and as such are subject to scientific investigation. At the postscientific level, value judgments affect both the objectives of economic policies and the means of reaching them.

Prior to Adam Smith, the famous founding-father-figure of the discipline—and who could be more fundamental than Adam and more common than Smith?—economics was essentially a normative subject. From the late eighteenth until well into the mid-nineteenth centuries, economics was a blend of positive and normative elements. The nineteenth-century model of the atomistically and efficiently functioning competitive price or market system, for example, was both an explanation of the economic world and a normative rationale of an ideal economic system. With increasing sophistication as a social science in the late nineteenth and early decades of the twentieth century, emphasis began to be placed upon the testable character of scientific propositions as contrasted with value judgments. Recently, economists, especially those concerned with economic policy, have recognized interdependencies between positive and normative issues, and the need to deal more explicitly with value judgments and social goals. Perhaps the essence of bias in normative economics lies not in accommodating social values and judgments in economic theory, but in insulating them from the test of experience and excluding them from critical appraisal.

Economic Systems Economics emerged as a social scientific discipline simultaneously with the emergence and development of competitive market capitalism as an economic system. As a result, economics was (and to a significant degree still is) the analysis of the social processes of competitive markets in a capitalist economy. Even Marxian economics, popularly associated with socialist and communist movements and ideas, was primarily an analysis and critique of industrializing capitalism.

The correlation of the emergence and development of economics with that of the market system is probably no historic accident. Tradition and command, the premarket methods for coordinating decisions to resolve societies' economic problems, are (at least in the context of economic underdevelopment) singularly unexciting from the standpoint of economic analysis. But the market system poses an intellectual puzzle. How can a society's economic problems be resolved in a systematic way when the power to make economic decisions is dispersed atomistically among millions of individual independent firms and households, whose freedoms are unconstrained by tradition or command? The answer given by classical nineteenth-century economic thought was that inherent in the decision processes of individual firms and households seeking their own economic gain through market exchange is a social process—the competitive market system—which automatically and spontaneously coordinates decitions and resolves society's economic problems in a systematic way.

One of the important facts about capitalism as an economic system, yet at the same time a reality that is difficult, especially for Americans, to subject to dispassionate study, is that it, like other forms or systems of economic organization, is historically transient. It emerged, after several centuries of transition, out of a precapitalist past in Western society. It surged to dominance with the industrialization of England; spread throughout most of the Western world in the nineteenth century; and then, through a variety of devices, penetrated and expanded economic and political control over large areas of the economically underdeveloped world. By 1913, at the peak of its grandeur, it was in virtually unchallenged control of the world economy. A study of comparative economic systems was, for all practical purposes, an examination of capitalism, with perhaps some tangential attention to socialism as a theoretical, vaguely formulated, and utopian-sounding alternative.

In the decades following World War I, this situation was to change dramatically. Capitalism's position of dominance was challenged repeatedly and, in many instances, successfully. New forms of economic organization appeared in rapid and bewildering succession in Italy, Germany, and Russia between the first and second world wars. In the post-World

War II period, increasing numbers of underdeveloped countries emerged from a colonial past into political independence with a desire to embark upon rapid industrialization and economic growth and a hostility toward classic, nineteenth-century capitalism as the appropriate route to that objective. Within the former capitalist countries themselves, "capitalism" (as it was continued to be called) was changing, partly through its own internal dynamics, and partly through political and other forms of collective pressure, such as the growth of labor organizations. Capitalism was modified and reformed. By the mid-twentieth century, one thing was clear: The era of absolute capitalist dominance in the world economy had disappeared, and had been replaced with a confusing array of competing economic systems.

The study of comparative economic systems is more of an approach to than a separate part of economics, just as economics in recent decades has itself increasingly been regarded as an approach to rather than a separate part of life. The unifying theme of comparative economic systems is the use of methods of comparative analysis. Because these methods may be applied to the study of topics in *any* subfield within economics (for example, systems of taxation or labor unions in different countries) or to economics as a whole (for example, theories of socialism or the overall performance of selected national economies), comparative economic systems cannot be separated from the general principles of economics or from any of its branches.

Economic Policy The emergence of new forms of economic systems and modification of old ones in the twentieth century have heightened the interest of economists in the issues of economic policy and brought economics into a closer relationship to applied problems of public affairs. In all contemporary economic systems—"Stalinist" and contemporary communist countries, emergent underdeveloped nations, modified capitalist economies of Western Europe and the United States—collective control over economic decisions plays a substantially greater role than in old-style, nineteenth-century capitalism. Collective control, whether exercised by labor unions, private or public corporations, central banks, governments, or regulatory commissions, involves the formulation and execution of "policies" designed to affect selected economic variables and thereby to eliminate or at least reduce the gap between an actual and a desired state of affairs.

A schematic display of the major processes of economic policy is provided in Figure 1-1. Reading from left to right, the coordination of economic theories with factual data yields models of economic analysis for the purpose of making decisions. The coordination of objectives with economic models yields policies designed to attain objectives. The formulation of objective-oriented policies, combined with techniques of control

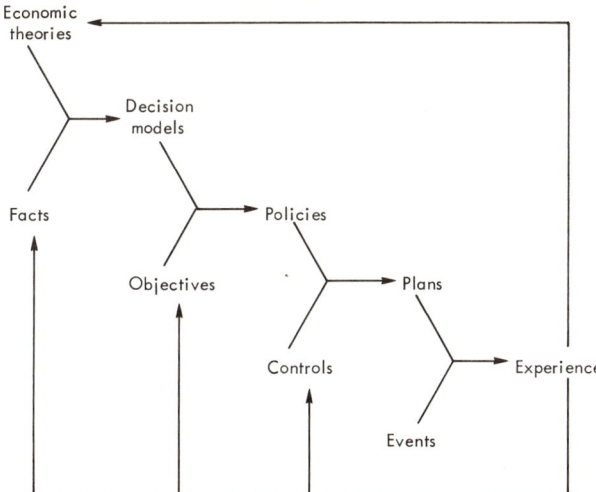

FIG. 1-1 The process of economic policy. Adapted from Richard Stone, "Models of the National Economy for Planning Purposes," in *Mathematics in the Social Sciences and Other Essays* (Cambridge, Mass.: M.I.T. Press, 1966), p. 69. Used with permission.

and thereby execution, constitutes a plan. The interaction of plans and events, many of which are beyond the control of any plan, yields experience. In the light of experience, successes or failures are evaluated and plans are revised (as illustrated by the lines leading back from experience to other parts of the diagram).

Three key points emerge from this synopsis. First, economic policy is a dynamic and continuing process involving the constant interaction of thought and action, with periodic revision or reformulation in the light of experience. Second, the dimensions of economic policy are far broader than any single "policy" itself, and involve theoretical analysis, factual investigation and measurement, model-building and applications, goals and objectives, plans, the development and application of methods and techniques of social control, and the interpretation of events often beyond the prediction and control of policymakers. Third, economic theory is an important, at times indispensable, contributor to the solution of policy problems. Theories provide an analytical basis for interpreting facts and identifying, comparing, and evaluating alternative ways of attaining objectives. At the same time, it should be emphasized that there is much more to economic policy than economic theory. The subtle interblending of theory, facts, goals, controls, plans, and events often makes economic policy as much an art as a science.

2
ECONOMIC HISTORY AND ECONOMICS

Alexander Gerschenkron *

ECONOMIC history has been defined as economic theory applied to the past.[1] There is an important core of truth in this statement. Yet any brief definition of this kind inevitably contains—and conceals—a number of problems which should be made explicit.

First of all, economic history like any other history does indeed deal with the past. But what is the past? Strictly speaking, the present is but a fleeting moment, and a sentence put on paper two seconds ago already belongs to the past. It is only by convention that we refer to the very recent past as the present, which means that the terminal point of the past is blurred, and "history" shades imperceptibly into the "present." In fact, all our knowledge of economic life is historical knowledge and all our empirical data are historical data. In this sense, every economist who is at all concerned with economic reality actually is an economic historian. Why then is there a special discipline called economic history? The obvious answer is that economic historians deal with more remote past. To say this, however, raises further problems. Is there anything special about the "more remote past?" How was it studied and how should it be studied?

If an economic historian embarks on a study, say, of the French

---
* Harvard University.
[1] This, despite some slight ambiguity in the phrasing, I take to be the meaning of Sir John Hicks when he wrote, "Economic history is just the applied economics of earlier ages" [4, p. 9].

glass industry between 1683 and 1685, he is not necessarily doing anything very different from an economist who has written on the development of the textile industry in the United States in the years 1967–1968. In principle, he has to ask the same type of basic questions. To be sure, in answering these questions he will have to take into account differences in what may be broadly called institutional environment. But a modern economist writing about contemporary industry in a country with a different economic system, say Soviet Russia, will have to face the same problem.

And yet, there is a more profound difference. It is the economic historian who is specifically concerned with the observation of very long periods. Accordingly, the study of processes of long-term economic change is the economic historian's special bailiwick. He is naturally treating developments that occupy many decades, and sometimes centuries, be they changes in the supply of precious metals and the resulting long periods of inflationary or deflationary pressures; or changes in the levels of output and the levels of consumption; or rise to predominance and subsequent fall of certain industries; or the effects of demographic changes upon the economy.

In dealing with these and hundreds of similar problems, the economic historian will be applying theoretical concepts in order to organize, and theoretical models in order to understand, his material. Thus, to give an example, in dealing with the price revolution of the sixteenth century, which was characterized by a fall in real income of wage earners, he will use the "inferior good" reasoning in order to explain the changes in the relative price structure. In explaining the vicissitudes of an industry over long periods, he will, among other things, try to understand as much as possible about the nature of, and changes in, its production function. In so doing, he will vindicate the definition of economic history as quoted in the first paragraph of this chapter. But the likelihood is that he will have to do a good deal more. And this raises further problems.

As we look at the history of economic history we find, perhaps surprisingly, that for a long time most of its adepts were not at all economists, but lawyers and historians. Both groups were able to make important contributions to the young discipline. The learned men of jurisprudence brought to it the discerning sharpness of juridical minds in studying laws and edicts, contracts and treaties. The historians unearthed many sources and applied to them the critical canons of historical research. But it was also the historians who injected into the discipline a host of methodological problems, most of them confusing and inhibiting rather than clarifying and facilitating the task of studying economic history. Some of these may be mentioned here, particularly as they affect the treatment of economic history by economists.

When modern economic historians try to understand past events and sequences of events by applying theoretical models, that is to say, with the help of abstract generalizations, they are told that history is "unique and individual," and that generalizations belong in science rather than in history. Under the influence of this view, even an otherwise very able scientist relatively recently presumed to say: "History is what is left over after the scientist has taken his pick" [1, p. 11]. Thus, history appears as some sort of a residual. The trouble with this view is that when we are finished with generalizations nothing at all remains, except that every event can be uniquely related to the coordinates of time and space, which, however, in themselves are in the nature of generalized systems. And the importance of the precise temporal and spatial determination may be the least important aspect for the *understanding* of a given event. In fact, the position is both biologically and logically untenable, because, as the brain biologists inform us, our "brain functions by fitting inputs against models" [6, p. 86]; and because all scholarly endeavor proceeds by abstraction and generalization. More than a century and a half ago, Goethe urged that "everything factual is already a theory," and a truer word was never spoken.

It is not surprising, therefore, that historians themselves, despite their basic predispositions, cannot remain altogether consistent and are forced to accept generalizations by letting them slip in through Max Weber's concept of "ideal types"; this means constructs involving a "one-sided accentuation of one or more points of view" and a "synthesis of a great many diffuse, more or less present and occasionally absent, concrete individual phenomena . . . arranged according to those one-sidedly emphasized viewpoints" [5, p. 90]. Use of such ideal types is then presented as something exceptional, rather ancillary in nature; but in reality all historical work consists of the formation of ideal types, and what customarily goes by the name of facts essentially is nothing but ideal types constructed at a very low level of abstraction. This is particularly clear in economic history where the basic material—that is, the facts—usually consists of generalized abstractions, such as time series of prices or wages, of incomes or outputs, which represent averages from which trends, or cyclical or seasonal variations, have been eliminated. At times, such data are described as "real types" rather than "ideal types," but actually they fit perfectly the definition of ideal types. The averaging and smoothing techniques constitute precisely the "one-sided accentuation" of which Max Weber spoke, and no point of a time series so obtained may actually ever represent a real occurrence, that is to say, coincide with anything contained in the primary statistical material. The time series, even though it pictures the "real world," is an abstraction, a generalization; it is an ideal type, if we wish to use that self-conscious, misleading expression. To repeat, therefore, the broad injunctions that are issued against application of theoretical models to economic history are methodologically ill-conceived and cannot be taken seriously.

It is only an emotional elaboration of the selfsame view when modern economic historians are charged with "dehumanizing" history, and what they produce is said not to be history at all in the proper sense of the term. This, however, is a statement rather devoid of meaning. Economic history is a study of past events, sequences of events, and interdependence of events in the realm of man's economic activities. As such it always deals with human motivations, sometimes in a more, sometimes in a less abstract and generalizing fashion. But there is no way of excluding those motivations, and accordingly there is no way of "dehumanizing" economic history. If you look at an empirically derived demand curve, say, for iron and steel in the United States between 1840 and 1860, every point at that curve represents nothing but human motivations, the result of economic calculations of individuals. Similarly, a series of wholesale prices over a certain period is the composite result of an immense number of human decisions and so is in an equally complex way an annual statement depicting a country's balance of payments.

Any such presentation of events in economic history can be more or less aggregative and, by the same token, more or fewer human motivations will be concealed behind the seemingly "lifeless" figures. In other words, there is an infinite variety in the degree of abstraction with which the study of problems in economic history can be approached. The actual way chosen will depend on the taste and special interest of the scholar, and the final judgment must depend on the adequacy of procedures used and the significance of the results obtained in terms of their contribution to our stock of knowledge about past economic phenomena. This is the crucial yardstick, and judged by it the outcome may be "rattling good history" or shockingly poor history, but economic history it will be, and authoritarian dictation which tries to tell us in advance what history is and what it is not is incompatible with the very essence of scholarship. For attempts of this sort, however much they may be draped in academic garbs, are in reality nothing else than a reflection of personal biases and preferences, an expression, that is, of camouflaged likes and dislikes.

And, finally, one more objection raised against modern economic historians must be mentioned. For some time, it was argued that application of economic theory to economic history implied an attitude of determinism because of the elements of "necessity" inherent in theoretical models. This was not much of an argument because the alleged determinism of the models was in reality just a set of expectations to be applied to empirical material. In other words, what necessarily follows from a model must not be confused with the unscientific notion that the concrete material was bound to be as it was. But then the critics changed their position and the line of attack very radically. For they had observed that economic historians, driven by the logic of analytical concepts, tried to assess the quantitative significance of a given event in a differential fashion, that is to say, by comparing it with a situation that would have obtained in the absence of that event. Let us assume, for instance, that we have determined the rate of industrial growth of a country during a certain period and want to measure the contribution of a given branch of industry to that rate. We must, therefore, find the weight of output of that particular industry in total output and the speed of its growth. But then it may be perfectly natural and useful to ask a further question, to wit, what would have happened if that given branch of industry had not come into being and another industry had developed instead. A problem that has attracted especial interest in recent years relates to attempts to measure the effect on gross national product of railroads by assuming that in their absence recourse would have been had to other less advantageous forms of transportation. Asking such questions has come to be known as "counterfactual history" or "history in the conditional mood." Obviously it is difficult to charge with determinism scholars who are willing to contemplate a course of events other than the one that actually took place.

Nevertheless, this way of looking at things has provoked considerable ire on the part of historians. It is claimed that the well-established historical canons require an historian to deal with things "as they actually were" (to quote Ranke's so famous and so misleading phrase), and not with what might have been. What actually happened, it is argued, can be established by the normal rules of historical evidence; by contrast, what might have been cannot be so ascertained. But the objection is not a valid one. First of all, most historians do in reality deal with counterfactual problems, as for instance, when they explore the errors that have been committed. To say that it was a mistake for Napoleon to fight in Spain, clearly implies an opinion on what would have happened, had he abstained from engaging in the Spanish adventure. How can an economic historian who deals with the economic policies of the Brüning government in Germany during the Great Depression of the 1930s emphasize the fatal nature of the deflation policies pursued, unless by placing them against the potentiality of fruitful reflationary policies? And, incidentally, it is only by putting the problem in this fashion that one can advance to the question of Brüning's motivations—the exquisitely "human" question in which the historians claim to be interested.

The truth of the matter is that there are no valid logical objections to the counterfactual method. The problem is an exceedingly pragmatic one. The adequacy or inadequacy of counterfactual explorations depends entirely on the plausibility of the results obtained. And this in turn will vary widely with the nature of the question at hand. If the question is a relatively simple one; if the period under consideration is relatively short; and if the number of factors that must be taken into account is relatively small, then an investigation of what would have happened under different circumstances may be altogether sensible and the results quite convincing. To give an example: If all we want to do is to measure the effect on domestic output of the introduction of a tariff on a single commodity during the following five years, we must try to ascertain what the course of output of that commodity would have been in the absence of the tariff; we would have to ask, for instance, whether in the absence of the tariff some cost-reducing and output-increasing technical progress would have occurred; or whether some of the increases in output were due to a growth of industry which was going on steadily, quite independently of the tariff because of a gradual increase in demand. Even in this limited case, the general trends of income within the economy could not be neglected. Still, these explorations are likely to leave us with a much better grasp of the effects of this particular measure. On the other hand, unduly ambitious projects are likely to lead to results that are so uncertain as to be incapable of satisfying our sense of reasoned adequacy. This will be especially the case, if in addition to economic variables, powerful noneconomic variables must be presumed to have affected the course of events. Thus counterfactual questions cannot be rejected a priori on any general grounds, but their value must be decided ad hoc in the light of the circumstances of each individual project.

We must conclude, therefore, that methodological considerations of the type discussed in the preceding pages are harmful rather than helpful. They tend to inhibit productive research rather than to promote it. At the same time, however, it must be recognized that there is a great deal that economic historians, however modern, can learn from the historians. Social sciences in general have tended to become more and more specialized; among those sciences, economics probably is the most specialized discipline. More and more, scholars tend to remain within the framework of their discipline, and transgressions into other areas are viewed with considerable distrust. It is only the historians who have preserved for themselves the undisputed right to roam fearlessly over the whole area of human action. No economic historian worthy of his salt can avoid doing just that.

It is clear that economic historians must at all times start by asking economic questions. They must explore the nature of economic situations and the facts of economic change. But when it comes to providing answers, that is to say, to interpreting the processes of economic change and looking for causes, it cannot be taken for granted that those answers will be primarily economic answers. The economy after all is an integral part of the total body social, and economic processes are naturally affected by factors which are not economic at all. This is the reason why a great economic historian, Eli F. Heckscher, once even defined economic history as a discipline that is interested "in the interplay of economic and other influences on the actual course of events" [3, pp. 30–31]. Economic theory can be "pure," but economic history cannot, and W. K. Hancock certainly was right when he stressed the basic "impurity" of economic history [2, p. 5].

Naturally, the degree of "impurity" in economic history varied from area to area and from period to period. At some times, the impact of political forces, and in general the role of power, was stronger than in others. No economic historian in dealing with the centuries that are usually described as the epoch of European mercantilism will be able to ignore the role of the state as the strong propelling force in the economic development of the period. Even more clearly, it would be impossible to write the economic history of Soviet Russia without it becoming predominantly a history of policies of the Soviet government. Whatever economic question one would ask, be it regarding the rate of industrial growth or the composition of output, the size of plants or the incidence of technological progress, the rate of investment or the standards of living—in every case the answer must be given in terms of the specific goals and actions, calculations and miscalculations of the government, and very often in terms of the general nature of the country's political system.

Other areas and periods present different situations. In an era of laissez faire policies, when the role of the government was small, there is less occasion for economic historians to concern themselves with questions of power; and such acts of the government as bear upon the economy as often as not can be largely explained in terms of economic interests of individuals and groups. Abolition of the corn laws in England in the 1840s is a good case in point, as, in general, England of the nineteenth century is one of the most suitable areas for the application of Marxian hypotheses, usually known as the materialistic conception of history, just as Soviet Russia is the least suitable area for the purpose. In other words, the primacy of the economic factor in England is counterpoised by the primacy of the political factor in Russia.

Yet one does not have to envisage an extreme situation, where the economy is the handmaiden of the dictatorial power, in order to discover a significant role of the government in shaping economic structures and directing the course of economic change. This is true of much of the nineteenth century despite its laissez faire reputation. In dealing, for instance, with the development of the French economy in the nineteenth century, explanation of its relative stagnation in the first half of that century must take due note of both the legacy of the Napoleonic administrative structure and the inept and irrational policies of the Restoration and the July Monarchies, particularly in the field of foreign commercial policies. Similarly, gold discoveries and a cyclical upturn are inadequate to explain the economic progress of the 1850s without placing a great deal of emphasis on the economic policies of Napoleon III, which in turn stemmed from the specific needs of his dictatorial regime. To give another example: In treating the agrarian reforms of the nineteenth century, the economic historian must first ask the question as to why agrarian structures were not reformed simply by the free play of the economic forces. In answering the question he will in some cases discover built-in self-perpetuating factors of stagnation which rendered profitable continuation of inefficient methods of production and obviated the pressure for raising the productivity of labor. Then having understood the needs for the reforming government interventions, their particular character and, by the same token, their effects upon the economy should not only be analyzed in economic terms but must also be related to the timing of the reforms and a scrutiny of the political forces that have originated them.

Nor is, obviously, exercise of political power the only noneconomic factor that economic historians must be concerned with. In studying entrepreneurial behavior or, for that matter, the qualities of the labor force, relationships pertaining to social, intellectual, or religious history are being transformed into integral parts of economic history. Whatever the empirical merits of Max Weber's celebrated hypothesis concerning the impact of Calvinism on the rise of modern capitalism, constructs of this sort are highly pertinent to economic history, even though they are outside the scope of economic theory. The point is precisely that they can supplement theoretical models in a meaningful and fruitful way, that is to say, by providing theoretical conceptions of things that must be taken as given in economic theory. If the economic historian studies the mode of financing economic development through investment banks of the German type, he has to operate with theoretical models involving credit creation by the banks and processes of forced savings. But such policies by the credit system can be carried out only where the standards of commercial honesty have attained a certain level. Thus, the process of formation of an entrepreneurial milieu within which punctual discharge of obligations has become customary is inseparable from the spread of credit-creating activities of the banks and indispensable for an appraisal of banking operations of this kind. Very similarly, studies of the formation of the modern labor force, its responses to incentives and the development within it of the qualities of reliability and efficiency are the natural appendix to investigations of changes over time in labor inputs as well as of determinants of investment and of decisions regarding substitution of capital for labor and technological progress.

There is one thing, however, that economic historians must not lose sight of in expanding the scope of their study beyond the narrow sphere of economics. At all times, the justification must be to provide more complete answers to *economic* questions; that is to say, the task is to construct models of changes in data that can be married to the theoretical models in which those data are used. If the so-called entrepreneurial approach to economic history has so far yielded less enlightenment than might have been expected, the reasons lie precisely in the inability or unwillingness of its adepts to extract economically significant data from the rich material at their disposal. Not entirely unlikely, intellectual history is used at times as though it were a substitute for economic history. This, for instance, is clearly the case with the tacit assumption that the doctrinal history of mercantilism is equivalent to the economic policies pursued in the era of mercantilism. The inevitable result is partly a distorted distribution of emphasis in dealing with those policies, and partly intrusion of material that is irrelevant from the point of view of economic policies.

At present, however, modern economic historians are not likely to fall prey to the dangers just mentioned, since it is precisely application of economic theory and of sophisticated quantitative analysis that stands in the forefront of their interests and preoccupies them to the exclusion of other approaches or amplifications. To appreciate this attitude, one has to see it against the background of doctrinal evolutions in economics and beyond it in the general spiritual climate of the times.

The so-called Keynesian revolution no doubt was crucial in this respect. To say this, however, should not mean that earlier use of economic theory in economic history would not have yielded significant results. To illustrate by a simple example: The catastrophe of the Black Death in the fourteenth century in its one horrible pandemic (to say nothing of the subsequent returns of the plague) must have destroyed about one-quarter of the population. It was observed that, in the event, rents fell and wages rose. The effect was generally attributed by economic historians to the resulting shift in the relationship between the decimated labor force and the constant number of manorial establishments. But guided by theoretical insights they would have been forced to ask further questions concerning the effects of the changed ratio of labor to land and to wonder whether before the plague land was subject to increasing or decreasing returns. Had they done so, they would have been led into studies of changes in land utilization and soon realized that the distributive effects alone could not have been more than a part of the story. In fact, with the help of modern electronic methods (age determination by carbon-14 in conjunction with pollen counts) it has been ascertained now that marginal lands of low productivity or lands located too far from the villages were either changed to pasture or allowed to revert to forest, while the planting of cereals was confined to the most fertile acres. This, incidentally, provides an additional explanation of the protracted decline of grain prices that followed in the wake of the plague. Thus, the lack of quite elementary economic sophistication has long prevented economic historians from addressing the appropriate questions to the material and from obtaining significant insights into the processes of economic change. An example of this sort incidentally demonstrates that, despite frequent assertions to the contrary, fruitful use of economic theory is by no means confined to modern history and can be effectively applied to rather remote periods. Nor was there more than application of traditional—although far from elementary—theory involved in a modern pioneering investigation of the profitability of the slavery economy in the antebellum South.

Nevertheless, there is little doubt that modern developments in economic theory immensely widened the area of productive application of theory to history. For macroeconomic analysis has proved to be more operational than the traditional theory in the pragmatic sense of being much more readily translatable into empirical data. Attempts to calculate totals of goods and services produced and their subdivisions have, of course, a century-long history, but it was only since the second half of the interwar period that trail-blazing work on the subject was begun, epitomized in the monumental contribution of Simon Kuznets. It is difficult indeed for the present generation, for whom macroeconomic statistics have become the daily bread of professional lives, to believe that only half a century ago or so national income was derided by an outstanding economist as an interesting toy, a mere plaything, not to be taken seriously. Naturally, the main impact was upon current statistics, but increasingly data for more and more remote periods have been assembled, and in the process difficult technical problems have been encountered and their solutions advanced.

Even more impressive have been the results attained with regard to statistics of output of manufacturing and mining. Walther Hoffmann's continuous series of British industrial output since 1700, the longest such series of existence for any country, demonstrated that with patience and ingenuity meaningful statistical series can be constructed for past periods for which no contemporaneously prepared aggregate data are available. The input-output approach which allows deep insights into the interdependence of the economy, too, has begun to be applied in historical analysis. While the sheer volume of information needed for extensive analysis along these lines may make it difficult to move too far into past times, effective use of the approach already has been made to investigate the role of exports in causing the retardation of British industrial growth in the second third of the nineteenth century (incidentally a fine example of successful counterfactual analysis), or to measure the extent of structural change in the American economy over a somewhat shorter period. Finally, modern economic history has benefited from the enormous improvement in statistical techniques that has taken place within the last few decades. Sophisticated methods of testing of hypotheses and safeguards against fallacious inferences have greatly increased the reliability of the results obtained.

And yet, it may well be surmised that progress in economic theory and statistics alone might not have sufficed to produce the great reorientation in economic history, if the spiritual climate of our time had not come to be dominated by the concern for economic development of backward countries. Since the end of the Second World War, economic development has become a powerful intellectual movement, comparable perhaps to the great intellectual movements of the nineteenth century—liberalism and socialism. Its effects upon economics have been profound. Faced with the problems inherent in the transformation of primitive agricultural countries into industrial economies, economists naturally turned to economic history in search for enlightenment from the processes of industrial change that had occurred in the past in the now developed countries. It was this intellectual impetus that caused young and able economists to direct their attention to a discipline which for such a long time had been neglected by the economic profession.

In appraising the effects of this profound change in attitudes and predispositions, it is useful to distinguish between the impact upon economic history and that upon economics. As far as the former is concerned, it would be futile to deny the existence of certain difficulties. Some of them are implicit in what has been said in the preceding pages. Precisely because of the rapid developments in both economic theory and quantitative analysis over recent decades, the study of economics has become more complex and time-consuming than ever before. This means that young economists who have developed an abiding interest in economic history often have had little opportunity to acquire competence in areas of knowledge that lie outside economics proper. Accordingly, problems that call for noneconomic answers to economic questions are at times ignored or dealt with inadequately. On the other hand, there has been a certain tendency in evidence to employ theoretical models that are more complex than is warranted and can be sustained by the available empirical material. The consequence is at best a disturbing diseconomy of means and the raising of promises that remain unredeemed, and at worst unconvincing and misleading results.

These are indubitable deficiencies. But it would be inappropriate to judge them too severely. To some extent, it must be kept in mind that the modern reorientation of economic history, even though it has its own history and modern economic historians have their predecessors, is still in its early stages. Much is being learned and more will be learned. But a certain one-sidedness no doubt will remain for a long time to come. And this is both natural and all to the good. Considering the great backlog of economic questions that should have been asked a long time ago and to which economic answers are possible, new economic historians have still a great deal to accomplish before diminishing returns will set in. They may never quite satisfy Heckscher's definition of economic history as quoted before. But Heckscher, who among great economic historians had done more than anyone else to marry economic history and economics, would have heartily approved of their efforts. And it is indeed encouraging to see how seemingly well-worked-upon areas of research suddenly reappear as virgin soils which are repaying the labor by a rich harvest. The recent studies in the history of American railroads are perhaps the most exciting instance of this transformation.

The other question concerning the impact of modern developments of economic history upon economics is more difficult to answer. For it raises the thorny problem of "lessons from history" and beyond it the even more fundamental problem of the purpose and value of economic history. One thing should be clear, however. Anyone who thinks that he can extract from past history ready-made propositions which can be instantly applied in the economic policies of today is likely to be sorely disappointed. Research in economic history naturally proceeds in such a way that hypotheses are formed and then the area of their validity is explored. This is so, because in economic history, as in general in the study of things human, no universal but only particular or existential propositions are formed. Accordingly, as likely as not, an economic historian, moving within a given area and period, will push against limits beyond which his hypotheses are no longer applicable and must be either reformulated or abandoned altogether. But if this be so, it is not surprising that results obtained from more or less remote past periods cannot be expected to hold when applied to very different economic, social, political, and cultural conditions of the present. This, however, does not mean that economic history has nothing to offer for the solution of modern problems. What it can contribute—and has contributed—are sets of highly relevant questions to be addressed to current material. And this is something that must not be undervalued. In fact, huge as the modern literature on economic development of backward countries has become, it has dealt with few questions that have not been raised in one way or another in the past processes of economic development. At any rate, modern economic history is able to offer a great deal more elucidation of current problems than could ever be expected from the earlier stages of its evolution.

And yet, important as it is, this pragmatic point of view cannot begin to do justice to the value and purpose of economic history. No creative work in a discipline is possible in continual subservience to utilitarian dictation by practical interest. This is as true of economic history as it is of economic theory. At all times, the true purpose of any discipline is the discipline itself. The exploration of a subject—be it the industrial transformation of a large country or changes in the system of cultivation in a small village—must carry its own rewards. But any discipline that has vitality and produces new insights is bound to receive strong stimulating impulses from what moves and excites the spiritual environment of the scholar. And at present this is precisely what the contemporary interest in economic development has done to and for economic history.

REFERENCES

1. BROWN, G. SPENCER. *Probability and Scientific Inference* (London: Longmans, 1957).
2. HANCOCK, WILLIAM K. *Economic History at Oxford* (Toronto: Oxford University Press, 1946).
3. HECKSCHER, ELI F. *Historieuppfattning, materialisk och annan* (Stockholm: 1944).
4. HICKS, JOHN R. *The Social Framework: An Introduction to Economics* (Oxford: Clarendon Press, 1942).
5. WEBER, MAX. *The Methodology of the Social Sciences*, translated and edited by Edward A. Shils and Henry A. Finch (Glencoe, Ill.: Free Press, 1949).
6. YOUNG, JOHN Z. *Doubt and Certainty in Science: A Biologist's Reflections on the Brain* (Oxford: Clarendon Press, 1951).

3
ECONOMETRICS

William G. Bowen[*]

ECONOMICS is a discipline in which analytical concepts and reasoning are not merely useful, they are absolutely essential. You will save yourself considerable difficulty if you recognize at the outset that common sense, helpful and necessary as it always is, is not enough in dealing with economic problems. I would venture to suggest that more nonsense is written about economics than about any other academic subject. Someone, many years ago, said, "Only one man in ten thousand understands the currency question, and I meet him every day." The paradoxes sometimes cited in freshman texts show how far astray common sense can lead. You may, as a student of economics, be able to explain cogently why, if everyone tried suddenly to save a higher percentage of his income, people might actually end up saving less. But this is not, I would suggest, intuitively obvious.

Once you do learn the basic concepts, you will, I think, be impressed by what a wide range of problems can be clarified by their use. Economics is fortunate in having a central theoretical structure of wide applicability, and this is, in fact, what makes economics such an aesthetically satisfying discipline for many of us.

A second characteristic of modern economics is the widespread use of quantitative methods. Quantitative methods are unusually appropriate to the subject matter of economics

[*] Princeton University.

because the central concepts—prices, quantities, manhours of labor—are, in principle, measurable. But this has, of course, been the case for many years, while it is only recently, really since the end of World War II, that quantitative analysis has been of such great importance in economics. What accounts for this development? It seems to me that there are several related explanations. First, we have much better data now than we formerly had. It may surprise you to know that before 1930 no regular unemployment series existed. Along with improvements in the data themselves have come more sophisticated techniques for analyzing existing data. Theoretical econometrics has made great progress in the postwar years. Third, and last, we now have the use of high-speed electronic computers. It is hard for me to exaggerate the difference that this technological development has made to the character of research in economics. Many problems are now investigated which before the advent of the computer would have been ruled out on the grounds of impracticability.

Since so much of modern economics does make use of quantitative methods and since quantitative methods are not explained in all texts, I am going to describe to you, step by step, the way in which some of us have investigated a particular research problem—namely, the relation between the *unemployment rate* and the *labor force participation rate* in the United States economy.

These are important terms to understand, so let us pause a moment and make sure of the definitions. The labor force participation rate L is the percentage of the population who are in the labor force. And being in the labor force means that one is either employed or looking for work (that is, unemployed). The remainder of the population (the group not in the labor force) consists of housewives, students, retired people, persons unable to work, and persons who for any other reason choose not to seek work. The unemployment rate U is the percentage of the labor force who are unemployed. To translate these concepts into real numbers, in the United States at the time of the 1960 census the civilian population fourteen years old and over numbered 125.5 million. Of these 125.5 million people, 64.5 million were employed during the survey week and 3.5 million were classed as unemployed. The total labor force, therefore, was 68 million. The labor force participation rate was 68 million divided by 125.5 million or 54 percent, and the unemployment rate was 3.5 million divided by 68 million or 5.1 percent.

Now, the central issue here is: *What relation would we expect to find between the unemployment rate, on the one hand, and the labor force participation rate, on the other?* Two conflicting hypotheses have been offered. The first hypothesis is the additional-worker hypothesis, which suggests that higher unemployment leads to increased labor force participation, because when the head of the household becomes unemployed, other family members, and especially wives, are forced to enter the labor force and to seek work in order to maintain family income. The additional-worker hypothesis, then, suggests a *positive* relation between unemployment and labor participation. It suggests that in areas where unemployment is unusually high additional workers will enter the labor force, and the labor force participation rate will therefore also be unusually high.

In the other corner, we have the discouragement hypothesis, which suggests that when unemployment is high and jobs are hard to find, people who would look for work if labor market conditions were better become discouraged and stop looking for work. It is asserted that they leave the labor force because of their discouragement. The prediction here is a *negative* relation between unemployment and labor force participation. In other words, the discouragement hypothesis asserts that in areas where unemployment is unusually high, some people will simply not expect to be able to find work, they will drop out of (or stay out of) the labor force, and therefore the labor force participation rate will be relatively low.

Which of these two hypotheses is right? A straw vote might favor the additional-worker hypothesis. Now, voting is a good way to settle many issues, but not issues of this kind. It is, of course, much better to look at the data, to use quantitative methods to examine the data, and then to draw conclusions.

Will Wives Work? There are any number of ways in which we could proceed. The way that I am going to describe involves comparing cities with high and low unemployment and seeing how their labor force participation rates compare. We shall work with figures for 1960, since data from the 1970 census are not yet available. But before actually collecting data and making calculations, it is necessary to refine our problem a bit. Instead of comparing unemployment rates in each of 100 cities with overall labor force participation rates in the same cities, it is better to examine labor force participation rates for a specific age-sex group, such as married women. What we shall do, then, is to compare unemployment in 100 cities with the labor force participation rates of married women in these same 100 cities.

Why is it desirable to work with a special group such as married women rather than with participation rates for the entire labor force? The answer is that labor force participation rates differ significantly among different age and sex groups. To take an extreme example, the labor force participation rate for fourteen-year-old girls is much, much lower than the labor force participation rate for thirty-year-old men. And, of course, the proportion of fourteen-year-old girls to thirty-year-old men is not the same in all cities. Some cities have more young girls relative to prime-age males than other cities, and if we compare overall labor force participation rates, we are likely to find the highest overall labor force participation rates in those cities with the (relatively) larger numbers of prime-age men. Because the demographic characteristics of the cities would largely determine overall participation rates, we would be unable to see the relation between unemployment and labor force participation. And this is, of course, the relationship that we want to examine. So, to avoid this problem we shall be comparing unemployment with the labor force participation of married women (a relatively homogeneous group).

We begin by plotting a "scatter diagram" of our 100-city observations (Figure 3-1). Is there a drift to this scatter? Well, yes, I would say. And, the drift seems to run from northwest to southeast. We would not want, however, to rely on visual inspection to answer a question such as this. Instead, we use one of a number of standard statistical techniques for fitting a line to these data—the method of least squares—and in this way obtain a more precise idea of the direction of the drift. This method consists of finding that line for which the sum of the squares of the vertical deviations from the line is a minimum. The mechanics of this operation are perfectly straightforward, and anyone who is interested can find a full explanation in any elementary statistics text.

The equation of the line which results from this "fitting process" is

$$L_{mw} = -1.4U + 38.7$$

with L_{mw} standing for the labor force participation rate of married women and U standing for the unemployment rate. This is what we call a regression equation. Now what does it tell us? Well, the fact that the line has a negative slope, as indicated by the minus sign in front of the $1.4U$, suggests that the discouragement hypothesis seems to fit this set of facts better than the additional-worker hypothesis. The relation between unemployment and labor force participation does appear to be negative. But the equation tells us more than the direction of impact; it also tells us something about magnitude. The slope of this line is -1.4, which in this context means that an increase in unemployment of 1 percent is associated with a reduction of the labor force participation rates of married women of 1.4 percent. On the basis of the equation of this regression line, we can predict the labor force participation rate of married women in any city in terms of the city's unemployment rate, the prediction being given by the appropriate point on the line.

But, one may—in fact should—ask: How good are these predictions going to be? How reliable? Again, there are standard statistical concepts

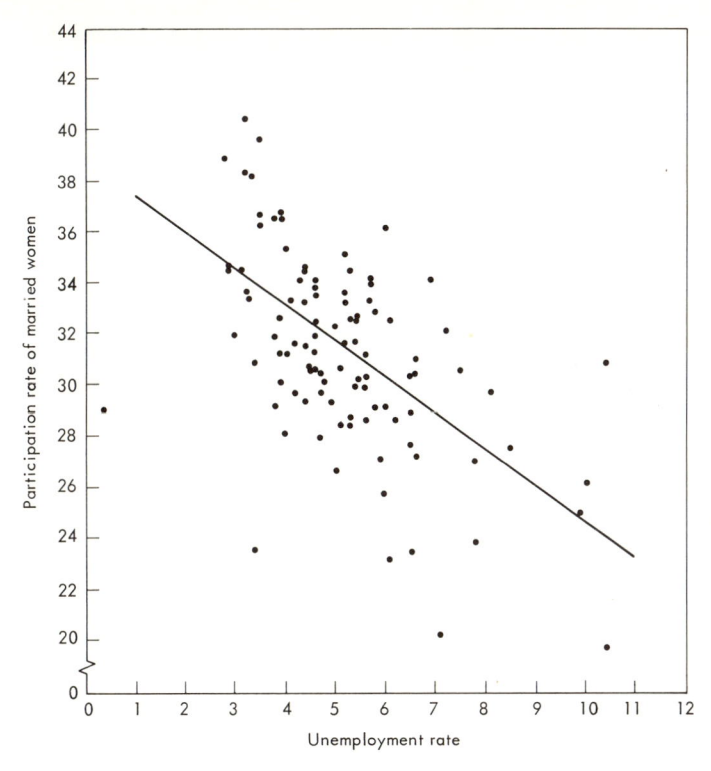

FIG. 3-1 Labor-force participation of married women and unemployment, 100 cities (1960).

designed to answer questions of this kind. One well-known concept is the coefficient of correlation (usually designated r), and it has the property of taking on higher values the better the regression line fits the scatter of points. What the correlation coefficient really tells us is how much better off we are predicting labor force participation by means of this kind of straight line than we would be by simply using the nationwide average as a prediction for each city. If the straight line predicted perfectly within the sample—that is, if all the city observations were right on the line—we would have an r of $\pm$ 1.0, the sign depending on whether the relationship between the variables was positive or negative. On the other hand, if the line were of no help at all we would have an r of 0. In the present case, the r actually is -0.58. Yet, you may ask, what does an r of -0.58 imply, anyway? Is this a meaningful result? How do we know? Well, on the basis of assumptions about the nature of the data and on the basis of what we know about the theoretical probability distribution of the coefficient of correlation, we can determine whether the value of r that we have obtained is large enough for us to be, say, 95 percent sure that there is indeed a negative relationship between U and L_{mw}, and that the relationship we have obtained is not just a chance happening. Let me simply assert that with a sample of 100 cities our r of -0.58 is large enough to pass this test easily.

From the standpoint of intuitive interpretation of what we have and have not accomplished so far, the *square* of the correlation coefficient r^2 is a very useful statistic. It tells us the percentage of the total variation of the individual city labor force participation rates around the average labor force participation rate which we have explained on the basis of the linear relation between unemployment and the labor force participation rate—34 percent in this instance. This r^2 tells us in statistical terms what our visual observation of this scatter and the line tells us: namely, that while some of the intercity differences in labor force participation rates are explained by the relation with unemployment, there is also much of the intercity variation that is *not* explained in terms of unemployment—in fact, about 65 percent.

A Further Danger So long as this is the case, there is the danger that our conclusion about the relation between unemployment and the labor force participation rate of married women is simply wrong. The negative relation that we found above may be the result of the fact that some other factor is causing low labor force participation rates for those cities in the bottom right-hand corner of our diagram, and that this other factor (or factors) just happens to be associated with relatively high unemployment. Hence, those who favor the additional-worker hypothesis could still argue that we have not really sorted out the *true* relation between unemployment and labor force participation, and that the true relation might still turn out to be positive if we succeeded in holding other factors constant.

What can we do to resolve these lingering doubts in the minds of the additional-worker-hypothesis people? The answer is that we can try to allow for the influence of other factors which might influence labor force participation. We can do this by means of what is called multiple regression analysis, "multiple" because now we shall make use of more than one explanatory variable. We ask ourselves, "What else besides unemployment might influence the labor force participation rates of married women?" and we compile a list of other variables, including:

Y_h = *the income of husbands (here we predict a* negative *relation, because presumably the higher the income of husbands the more the wife can afford not to work).*

Y_o = *other income of the family (again we predict a* negative *relation, since high other income also implies that the wife can afford not to work).*

Y_f = earnings opportunities for women (here we predict a positive relation, because the higher the wages that women can expect to receive, the stronger the incentive to work).

$C_{<18}$ = the number of children under 18 (a negative relation is predicted, because, of course, the more children one has the harder it is to get away from the house in order to take a job).

D = wages of domestic servants (here we predict a negative relation, because the higher the wages of domestic servants, the less likely the wife is to hire a domestic servant to take care of the house while she goes to work).

S_f = median years of schooling completed by females (we predict a positive relation here, since we suspect that one thing schooling does to women is to give them a stronger "taste" for work).

F_I = an index of job opportunities for women in particular cities (a positive relation is expected, because of the way the index is calculated).

$W\%$ = the relative number of women competing for the available jobs (a negative relation is predicted for this supply-side variable).

$N\%$ = the percentage of Negroes in the population of each city (here we predict a positive relation, since Negro women find jobs as domestics much more readily than white women).

Now that we have this list of variables, the next thing we do is collect data for each of them for all 100 cities, and then examine the interrelationships among all these variables, unemployment, and the labor force participation of married women. This is a multidimensional problem which cannot, of course, be graphed. But, what we can do is perform a number of calculations that will give us an equation expressing the labor force participation rate of married women as a function of all of the above variables. We did this, or rather Princeton University's computer did this (and in less than two minutes at that), with the following results:

$$L_{mw} = -0.8U - 0.2Y_h - 0.8Y_o + 0.5Y_f - 0.1C - 0.8D + 0.9S_f \\ + 0.9F_I - 0.8W\% + 0.1N\% + 67.8$$

The coefficient of each of the explanatory variables serves as an estimate of the effect of that variable on the labor force participation rate of married women when the effects of the other variables have been taken into account. If you look first at the signs of each of these coefficients, you will find that all the signs turn out as predicted, which is one reason why I have used this piece of research as an illustration. I hasten to add that things do not always work out this well. Let me next simply assert that all these regression coefficients are statistically significant—that is, it is very unlikely that they are the result of chance happenings.

We are, of course, especially interested in the sign of the coefficient that goes along with the unemployment variable, and we see that it is now -0.8. We therefore conclude that even after we allow for the influence of all these other factors, the relation between unemployment and the labor force participation of married women is still negative, but that the magnitude of the relationship is lower than it appeared before. The slope has gone down from -1.4 to -0.8. That is, when we allow for the influence of these other variables, a 1 percent increase in unemployment is associated with a reduction of 0.8 percent in the labor force participation of married women.

In an effort to answer the question of how much of the total intercity variation in participation rates we have now explained, we compute a multiple correlation coefficient which is similar to the simple correlation coefficient we calculated before—and we find that the multiple correlation coefficient is 0.86. Squaring this value, we find that we have now explained 75 percent of the total variance, and this is quite good. It is, I would think, good enough to convince any remaining supporters of the additional-worker hypothesis that their hypothesis is simply inconsistent with the facts, as of 1960 anyway.

So, we can conclude that the discouragement hypothesis appears to have won this contest, and that the true relation between unemployment and labor force participation of married women is negative. This conclusion has some rather important policy implications, but a discussion of them would take us beyond the scope of this chapter.[1]

Our equation should not conceal the fact that there is still much we do not know about economic behavior. Someone, for instance, might object vigorously to this labor force participation rate equation on the ground that I have left out of consideration some very important variable

---

[1] The most important policy implication is that as (if) overall unemployment declines, we should expect a larger percentage of married women to look for jobs. This implies that, to reduce unemployment from 5.6 percent to, say, 4 percent, new jobs will have to be found not only for the excess 1.6 percent of the labor force currently unemployed and for the net increase in new workers attributable to population growth, but also for the additional persons in the current working-age population who will be attracted into the labor force as labor market conditions improve. In short, reducing unemployment to any target level will require more of a net increase in jobs than one would think by looking only at the difference between the current and target rates of unemployment. Ignoring the tendency for potential workers discouraged by high unemployment to enlarge the pool of job applicants as unemployment declines will lead to a serious underestimate of the total number of new jobs needed.

that should be added. Scientific controversy of this kind is, of course, essential to progress in any academic subject and is a sign of life.[2]

REFERENCES

1. CHRIST, CARL F. *Econometric Models and Methods* (New York: Wiley, 1966).
2. CHU, KONG. *Principles of Econometrics* (Scranton, Pa.: International Textbook, 1968).
3. GOLDBERGER, ARTHUR S. *Econometric Theory* (New York: Wiley, 1964).
4. JOHNSTON, J. *Econometric Methods* (New York: McGraw-Hill, 1963).
5. KANE, EDWARD J. *Economic Statistics and Econometrics* (New York: Harper & Row, 1968).
6. MALINVAUD, E. *Statistical Methods of Econometrics* (Chicago: Rand McNally, 1966).
7. SUITS, DANIEL B. *Statistics: An Introduction to Quantitative Economic Research* (Chicago: Rand McNally, 1963).
8. TINTNER, GERHARD. *Econometrics* (New York: Wiley Science Editions, 1965).

---

[2] Readers interested in the research problem illustrated here may wish to consult William G. Bowen and T. A. Finegan, *Economics of Labor Force Participation* (Princeton University Press, 1969). Details of the equations and the results are slightly modified in the book.

4
MICROECONOMIC THEORY

Abba P. Lerner [*]

MICROECONOMICS consists of looking at the economy through a microscope, as it were, to see how the millions of cells in the body economic—the individuals or households as consumers, and the individuals or firms as producers—play their part in the working of the whole economic organism. Microeconomic theory facilitates the understanding of what would be a hopelessly complicated confusion of billions of facts by constructing simplified models of behavior which are sufficiently similar to the actual phenomena to be of help in understanding them. These models at the same time enable the economist to examine the degree to which the actual phenomena depart from certain ideal constructions that would most completely achieve individual and social objectives. They thus help not only *to describe* the actual economic situation, but *to suggest policies* that would most successfully and most efficiently bring about desired results, and *to predict* the outcomes of such policies and of other events. Economics thus has descriptive, normative, and predictive aspects.

Macroeconomics and macroeconomic theory look at the economy not through a microscope but through a telescope, and furthermore through the wrong end of the telescope. The purpose is not to magnify so as to see further detail (which is what both the

[*] University of California, Berkeley.

microscope and the telescope do in their normal use), but to reduce the image so that disturbing details disappear and only a few of the largest parts of the economy remain visible. These parts are aggregates of great numbers of smaller parts that are considered only in microeconomics. The macroeconomic view thus gives us a picture of a small number of inputs to the economic mechanism—land, labor, and capital—directed toward the production of a small number of outputs—consumption goods and investment goods, or food, clothing, and shelter, or perhaps merely guns and butter.

Such simplifications are useful for microeconomic theory too. They help to illustrate its basic economic principles.

The first of these principles is the *principle of scarcity*. It says that to have more of one thing (say, guns), one has to have less of something else (butter). Like all theorems in mathematics, some principles in economic theory are tautologies—statements that cannot logically be proved wrong—but they are nevertheless extremely useful in organizing our thinking. Cases where we *can* have more of something without having to give up (some of) something else are either disregarded as noneconomic because there is then no scarcity and no economic problem of deciding whether the unnecessary sacrifice is worthwhile or not, or they are condemned as uneconomic situations arising only from irrational or foolish conduct which has missed a golden opportunity. Such waste should be eliminated as quickly as possible by completely using up any possibility of getting more of anything that is scarce (meaning "of which we would like to have more than we have"), whenever this can be done without giving up any part of any other scarce item.

Macroeconomics concentrates mostly on a special uneconomic situation—the existence of involuntary unemployment—and on how this may be corrected or prevented. In microeconomics we are more concerned with the avoidance or elimination of waste, or with inefficiency arising from the fact that production is not organized in the most efficient possible manner. Such inefficiency means that it is possible, by rearranging the different ways in which products are being produced or consumed, to get more of something that is scarce without giving up any part of any other scarce item, or to replace something by something else that is preferred. Microeconomic theory spells out the conditions of efficiency (that is, for the elimination of all kinds of inefficiency) and suggests how they might be achieved. These conditions (called *Pareto-optimal* conditions) can be of the greatest help in raising the standard of living of the population. They are by no means self-evident, even though they are derived (again, like mathematical theorems) from simple postulates that few would think of questioning. Some of these will be illustrated later in some detail.

Another macroeconomic principle that is also basic for microeconomics is the *principle of increasing resistance* to the extension of any economic activity. For example, as resources are shifted, say, from the production of butter to the production of more and more guns (or vice versa), an *increasing* amount of butter has to be sacrificed for each additional gun (or in the converse case, an increasing number of guns have to be given up for each additional ton or thousand tons of butter). The general principle of increasing resistance here takes one of several forms in which it can appear—the form of diminishing transformability of one (potential) product into another. This may also be called the increasing cost of one product in terms of another. If we want to be more careful, we should call this increasing *marginal* cost, since it is the additional cost of getting additional units of the product (which economists find it convenient to call marginal cost) that goes up as more of the product is produced. It should be noted too that the cost we are discussing now is not the additional money paid out or sacrificed for the sake of getting additional units of the product, but the sacrifice of the opportunity of having more butter instead of more guns (or more guns instead of more butter). For this reason, it is appropriate to call the cost an *opportunity cost*. In this case, therefore, the principle of increasing resistance takes the form of increasing marginal opportunity cost.

The principle of increasing resistance is also a tautology and not a proposition about the nature of the natural universe. It is based on the assumption that whenever there is decreasing resistance to something people want to do they will keep on expanding the activity until they are induced to stop, either because they come up against increasing marginal opportunity cost later (when it finally does become necessary to give up larger and larger amounts of butter per additional gun, and vice versa) or because they come up against increasing resistance in another form (diminishing technical productivity of more guns, or increasing psychological objection to giving up more butter). The level of the activity thus stops increasing even though there might still be *diminishing resistance* (decreasing marginal opportunity cost, or unexhausted "economies of scale" in production). The tautology says in effect that any activity will be continued to some point where, for some reason or other, the actors find it worthwhile to stop. Once more (and again, as in mathematics), the tautological nature of the basic principle does not prevent it from being of great help in deducing criteria for economic action which are not obvious to everybody, even after economists have been pointing them out for decades and centuries.

The two basic principles—the principle of scarcity and the principle of increasing resistance—in their various forms, are seen in microeconomics to apply, not merely to the small number of aggregated items dealt with in macroeconomics, but to the behavior of the millions of individual producers engaged in the production of thousands of different goods and services out of millions of units of thousands of different kinds of inputs, most of which are in turn the outputs of thousands of other farms and factories, as well as to the behavior of millions of consumers in deciding how to choose among the final products. (The shipping of all the millions of intermediate and final products to the various points of production or consumption is included in "production.")

The macroeconomic "reversed telescope," essential as it is for rendering the trees invisible and permitting observation of the forest, has had the unfortunate effect of leading some people to deny the existence of the trees and the validity of the immensely complicated tasks required in getting them to produce their fruit.

It happened that until the 1930s, when John Maynard Keynes developed a "respectable" macroeconomics, economists were so occupied with the fascinating things they could see through their microscopes that they paid insufficient attention to the reversed telescope, and did not deal satisfactorily with the macroeconomic problem of maintaining full employment. This extremely important matter was left to critics of the economic system, who had little understanding of how it had managed to bring about much higher standards of living than had ever been achieved before, for much larger populations than had ever existed before. Convinced of the apparent inevitability of cycles of unemployment and depression in the "capitalist system," they came to believe that if they could only get rid of what seemed to them "the anarchy of the free market" they would be able to run the economy sensibly. Unhampered by considerations of markets and prices and the necessity of making profits for the owners of the means of production, they would "plan" the operation of the economy so that all the available productive resources would be put to work to make the things that were needed. This they called "production for use instead of production for profit."

The immense complexity of the task having been obscured by improper use of the "reversed telescope" (and by the conviction that the microscope was a malevolent invention of the capitalists, designed only to provide justifications for unjustifiable privileges), the running of the economy seemed a very simple affair. Lenin, for example, declared that the management of the economy could very well be left to the part-time attention of any cook. The attempt, soon after the civil war that followed the 1917 revolution, to take direct charge of the Russian economy and run it "sensibly" resulted in its complete breakdown. The economy (and the revolution) was saved in 1921 by the same Lenin's "New Economic Policy"—correctly described by his opponents as the restoration of a number of elements of the hated capitalist system. These elements enabled microeconomics to work again, so that the trees began to give forth fruits once more and the people of Russia were able to eat and live. But any economic lessons that might have been learned from this experience seem to have been lost in the excitements and sufferings of the early five-year plans, and microeconomics continued to be denied by the early socialist planners. In recent years, however, it has been accorded recognition by the socialist countries, who are now all (with the possible exception of China and Albania) gradually adopting the partial use of price and market mechanisms (with profits as a measure of economic efficiency).

Microeconomics teaches us that completely "direct" running of the economy is impossible—that a modern economy is so complex that no central planning body can obtain all the information and give out all the directives necessary for its efficient operation. These would have to include directives for adjusting to continual changes in the availabilities of millions of productive resources and intermediate products, in the known methods of producing everything everywhere, and in the quantities and qualities of the many items to be consumed or to be added to society's productive equipment. This vast task can be achieved, and in the past has been achieved, only by the development of a decentralized system whereby the millions of producers and consumers are induced to act in the general interest without the intervention of anybody at the center with instructions as to what one should make and how, and what one should consume.

What microeconomic theory has figured out is how such a decentralized system works. The explanation can be divided into three parts: *efficiency in consumption, efficiency in production,* and the integration of these into *overall economic efficiency.*

Efficiency in consumption involves an optimal distribution of different consumption goods (and services) among millions of different consumers. Once such efficiency has been achieved, it is no longer possible—by moving goods from consumers with relatively little need for them to consumers with relatively great need, and at the same time moving other goods in the opposite direction—to make some people better off without making others worse off. A central authority that would seek to bring about efficiency in consumption would have to know the quantities and qualities of all the different goods available, as well as how strongly each individual feels about having a unit more of any particular item (which would depend in turn on how much of the item he already had, or on how much he had of any other items that might be used together with, or as substitutes for, the item in question). Yet efficiency in consumption *can* be achieved by a decentralized system where every individual gets a money income that he can use to buy as much, or as little, as he wants of every item, provided that the prices (a) are the same for every consumer, and (b) are adjusted so that the quantity of each item that all individuals together want to buy is just equal to the total quantity available. (Otherwise, some of the individuals would not be able to buy as much as they want of the item, or some of it would be left unused—evidence of inefficiency or waste.)

Microeconomic theory demonstrates how each consumer, acting in his own interest, would so allocate his dollars among the different items that an additional dollar's worth of no available item is more eagerly sought by him than an additional dollar's worth of any other item that he is buying. If this were not so, he would reduce his purchases of the less desired item and use the dollars thus set free to buy more of the more desired one. Marginal dollars' worths of all the items will, consequently, have equal attractiveness for him.

This does not mean that one individual will not have a different level of desires than another individual for a dollar's worth of all the items. Such will, in fact, normally be the case for a poorer person as compared with a richer person. But for each individual an additional dollar's worth of any item will be exactly as desirable as a dollar's worth of any other item among his purchases. This being the case, it is not possible, by a redistribution of the items, to make anyone better off without hurting someone else.

It would, of course, still be possible to bring about what most people would regard as an improvement by transferring goods from persons who need them less to persons who need them more. But that is another problem altogether, touched on below, concerned not with the distribution of goods according to individual preferences, but with the division of the national *income* among individuals. This becomes obvious when one recognizes that such improvements could best be made by giving more money to those with greater need (possibly because they had less money to begin with) and less to others. But whatever the distribution of money among consumers, the procedure described above would bring about the ideal distribution of goods among consumers in accordance with their individual preferences.

This is not done by magic but by each individual's knowledge of his own relative preferences. Each consumer, in minimizing the sacrifice of money to buy things he prefers, refrains from buying things for more money than he feels they are worth. He thereby leaves unbought, and available for others, precisely those items for which they have a relatively greater need (which is why they are willing to buy them).

All this is discussed in microeconomics (in much greater detail, of course) under "consumer behavior" or "the household."

Efficiency in production consists of producing maximum possible amounts of various products from available resources. Or, expressed in negative terms, when efficiency in production is achieved, it is no longer possible, by rearrangement of the factors of production among their different uses, to increase the output of any product without decreasing the output of some other product. Achievement of efficiency by a physical central plan would involve an impossibly detailed collection of information by the center, a relaying of instructions to all the producers, and a reworking of the whole set of instructions whenever a change occurred in the availability of resources, in the knowledge of productive possibilities, or in the desired composition of the product.

This "impossible" task can be achieved, however, by the decentralized price mechanism. It is necessary that each productive unit be under the charge of a manager who buys the factors of production, sells the products, and tries to maximize the profit of the "firm." (Whether the profit is for himself or for shareholders or for the members of a cooperative or for a government unit is not relevant at this point. We are concerned here not with the issue of capitalism or socialism, but with the general condition for efficiency in production.) Furthermore, the prices must be the same for every manager, must be independent of the quantities he buys or sells, and must equalize demand and supply—otherwise, the managers will not be able to buy and sell as much (or as little) as they want of every item.

Every manager will then buy every one of his *inputs* and produce every one of his *outputs* in such quantities that an additional dollar's worth of each input will result in exactly one dollar's worth of additional output. Failing this, he will increase or decrease the input and the output, adding to his profit the difference between the value of the marginal input and the value of the marginal output, until this process is brought to a stop by "increasing resistance." After that, an extra dollar's worth of any output can be achieved only by the application of an extra dollar's worth of input. But this additional input can be made available only by taking it from some other place in the economy, where output would consequently be reduced by a dollar's worth. It is therefore impossible to increase output at one place without decreasing output someplace else at least as much. No net increase in output is possible, and so we will have achieved efficiency in production.

Here too the trick is done not by mirrors, but by each manager's special knowledge of the special conditions in his firm. In seeking to minimize his cost of production (so as to maximize his profits), the manager refrains from buying units of inputs when the price he would have to pay is more than he feels they are worth. He thus leaves for other managers those units of the factors of production which are more usefully employed by them than by him, since this is the only reason for their willingness, and his unwillingness, to buy.

Even if we have efficiency in consumption together with efficiency in production, we still may not have overall efficiency in the economy. The goods produced might not be those most preferred by consumers, from different possible combinations of products. By an analysis similar to that outlined above, microeconomic theory shows how this is put right if prices to consumers are the same as prices to producers.

The analogy of the microscope—used at the beginning of this paper—is likely to give the impression that microeconomics differs from macroeconomics in not being concerned with the economy as a whole. That this is not the case is indicated by its concern with overall economic efficiency. Actually, microeconomics is much more intimately concerned with the economy as a whole than is macroeconomics, and can even be said to examine the whole economy microscopically. We have seen how economic efficiency is obtained when the "cells" of the economic organism, the households and firms, have adjusted their behavior to the prices of what they buy and sell. Each cell is then said to be "in equilibrium." But these adjustments in turn affect the quantities supplied and demanded, and therefore also their prices. This price change means that the adjusted cells then have to readjust themselves. This change in turn upsets the adjustment of the others again, and so on. An important part of microeconomics is examining whether and how *all* the different cells get adjusted at the same time. This is called *general equilibrium analysis* in contrast with *particular equilibrium* or *partial equilibrium analysis*. General equilibrium analysis is the microscopic examination of the interrelationships of parts within the economy as a whole. Overall economic efficiency is only a special aspect of this analysis.

So far in this chapter, microeconomic theory has been expressed in language that would be appropriate for a socialist government that wanted to know how to achieve the efficiencies of decentralized decisionmaking. Indeed, these are among the problems with which the socialist countries of Eastern Europe are now struggling. Most of microeconomic theory was developed, however, not by the socialist economies recently seeking decentralization but by capitalist economies struggling a long time ago with mercantilist traditions and superstitions (from which they are still far from completely free). Many of the basic principles of microeconomics have had to be discovered again, and very expensively indeed, by socialist countries handicapped by ideological resistance to the use of "capitalistic" devices. It was as if the socialist countries were not able to make use of electricity, which had been developed under capitalism, until they had rediscovered it for themselves under other names, and only after they had executed several of its earlier rediscoverers for surreptitiously trying to introduce heretical capitalistic technologies.

The mercantilist regulations had grown up to protect an agricultural, traditional, feudal arrangement from disturbance by newfangled, free-trading innovations. In the debates on the possibility of managing without these regulations, it was only natural that the exaggerated claim should be made that with the removal of mercantilist restrictions the economy would be guided by the free market "as by an invisible hand."

The perfection of overall economic efficiency, as described above, would indeed be achieved by a *perfectly competitive* free market. This means a market where there are so many buyers and sellers—the market being large relative to the size of the households or firms buying or selling in it—that no single buyer or seller could influence market price by varying the amount he buys or sells, and where no combinations of buyers or sellers are permitted that would restrict trade so as to lower the price at which they are able to buy or to raise the price at which they are able to sell.

In perfectly competitive markets there is effective freedom of entry into any economic activity, as well as complete knowledge of productive possibilities and the true nature of available production and consumption goods, so that those who buy goods are not deceived as to their use.

A large part of microeconomics is therefore directed to the study of the nature of departures from the perfect market, some of them remediable and some of them not. The power of large firms, or of combinations of firms, over prices constitutes the problem of *monopoly* and provides many fascinating problems for microeconomists, attempted solutions to which have sometimes led to important and useful policy recommendations. Similar problems arise where buyers or combinations of buyers acquire power over market prices (*monopsony*), or where there are several large firms or combinations in a market, each having to take account of how the others will react to what he does (*oligopoly* or *oligopsony*). Here we shall refer to all such departures from the perfect market as monopoly.

Among other complications are cases where inputs or outputs are technically fixed in their proportions and problems arise as to what should be considered the marginal product or marginal opportunity cost. More important are cases where the production of a commodity affects people other than those who sell or buy it. The price mechanism then fails to achieve efficiency, because it does not take into account the benefits or the damages to those external to the buyers and the sellers. This is known as the problem of *externalities*.

An extreme case of externalities is where everybody in the community benefits as much as the person who buys the product—where, for example, a member of the community drains a mosquito breeding ground or provides some defense to the community from threatening outsiders. In such cases, called "common goods," each consumer will be tempted to wait for others to provide the service; it would thus never be provided under a pure market mechanism, and there has to be some arrangement whereby all are benefited by being forced to contribute to provide the service. This is what we call *government*. The intervention of government is also appropriate in less extreme cases of externalities and in other similar cases where it may be directed at correcting imperfections in the price mechanism. This may be called *corrective governmental intervention.*

A second kind of governmental intervention may be justified where the price mechanism has achieved complete and overall economic efficiency as defined above (or where externalities, common goods, and monopolies have been fully corrected by corrective governmental action), but where the resulting situation is still not considered satisfactory. There might be a greater (or a smaller) inequality of income than is considered desirable. Or it might be thought that more should be spent on exploring outer space or on providing help to the aged or invalid than individual members of society are willing to provide, or that people are spending more than they should on tobacco, on alcohol, or on meat. This may be called *substantive governmental intervention,* since it involves the overriding of consumers' preferences by those of the government.

In both types of governmental intervention, microeconomics is called upon to examine the effectiveness of alternative methods of achieving objectives. It then usually finds itself involved in struggles against powerful forces supporting inappropriate means, forces that are very similar in the socialist and the capitalist countries. This similarity should not be surprising, since they are both based mainly on antimarket prejudices, in the one case deriving from precapitalism, and in the other case from a confusion of capitalism with market mechanisms.

Central to such examination of policy proposals is the problem of avoiding or minimizing undesired side effects. Microeconomic analysis generally leads to the rejection of administrative prohibitions or commands and to the acceptance of taxes and subsidies carefully selected for their directness and effectiveness in producing desired results.

Almost identical with problems raised by governmental intervention are those raised by changes in the conditions in which the economy finds itself. This is because the effect of any change in production possibilities, in the available supplies of any input, or in the demand for any output can be closely simulated by a corresponding tax or subsidy imposed by the government. Thus, for example, a decrease in the demand for some output has the same effect on its production and on its suppliers as a tax on its purchase. Microeconomics therefore looks into taxes and subsidies in great detail for their effects on different parts of the economy, and it can use the results in a much wider field.

Of interest at this point is a special connection between microeconomics and macroeconomics. From macroeconomics we may learn that to maintain aggregate economic stability—that is, to prevent inflation or unemployment—it is necessary to decrease or to increase total spending in the economy. This may mean increasing or decreasing taxes, or decreasing or increasing government spending, or some combination of these measures. Microeconomics then assumes the task of considering how these overall measures could be translated into actions with the fewest undesired side effects.

The most important direct effect of a tax is that the taxpayer is made poorer; the opposite happens in the case of a negative tax, or subsidy. The most important indirect effect of a tax is that the price paid by the buyer of the taxed item is greater (by the amount of the tax) than the price received by the seller, and again conversely for a subsidy. This destroys the equality of prices for buyers and for sellers. Unless the tax (or subsidy) is an intended corrective or substantive governmental intervention, it causes an unintended departure from overall economic efficiency. (The raising of the price received for anything by a monopoly, or the lowering of the price paid by a monopsony, so as to increase profits, has all the effects of a tax and can be treated as if it were one, even though it is imposed not by the government but by the monopoly or the monopsony. This is one of the reasons for the unpopularity of such enterprises.)

An important microeconomic lesson concerns the importance of distinguishing between the *burden* of a tax (on the taxpayer) and the *damage* done by a tax (to the efficiency of the economy). The latter depends on the degree to which the tax causes production and consumption to be shifted from the taxed commodity to other items. The greater the shift, the greater the amount of damage done, since the shift is a measure of the degree to which consumers are induced to consume a less desired good and of the degree to which producers are induced to switch to a less profitable product. In the case of a subsidy, the shift in production and consumption is toward using *more* of the subsidized item. This benefits the producer and the consumer, but increases the burden on the taxpayer who has to provide for the subsidy. The increased burden on the taxpayer is greater than the benefits to the producer and the consumer, so that the shift still represents damage to the efficiency of the economy.

From this analysis we reach the very interesting and important result that the wider the area over which a tax is spread, the less the damage to the overall efficiency of the economy, because fewer other products remain to which consumers and producers can shift in efforts to avoid the tax. If there were a tax on *everything*, proportional to the price, nothing would be gained by shifting. The tax would transfer income from the consumers and producers to the government without interfering at all with efficiency. The same conclusion holds for a tax on an item whose consumers are unwilling to reduce their consumption, despite the higher price they have to pay (including the tax), or whose producers are unwilling to reduce their production, despite the lower price they receive for the product (net of the tax). In both cases, the economist likes to say that the tax does no damage to economic efficiency because it falls on *rent*.

The previous two paragraphs constitute an example of a kind of extreme and abstract argument that often makes economists unpopular. Economists like to argue in this way because it demonstrates their point dramatically, but such argument exasperates persons who are impatient to apply it to an actual problem and are disturbed at seeing the English language distorted to fit the convenience of the economist. Land rental happens to be the original case in economics where a tax does no harm to the efficiency of the economy. A tax on the rent on *all* land cannot harm economic efficiency, because the supply of land is fixed by definition and has nowhere else to go. It cannot be shifted in efforts to avoid the tax. The only result is the direct one—the burden on the owners. Rent, however, in the economics sense, is not restricted to its original meaning—payment for the use of land—and certainly does not refer to payment for the use of an apartment or a television set. Instead, it refers to any part of any payment that turns out, in this special sense, to be surplus over what must be received by the supplier of a productive service if he is to continue supplying it. No tax can be collected out of this *necessary payment*, since any such attempt would result only in withdrawal and transfer of the service to some other use where it avoids the tax. A tax can thus be collected only to the extent that it falls on rent. The damage done by taxes is caused solely by the practical impossibility of devising taxes that fall entirely on rent.

Rent may also appear in the equation that puts price equal to marginal cost for economic efficiency; wherever production takes place under conditions of increasing (average) cost, the marginal cost, and therefore the price, is greater than the average cost, and a surplus emerges over the payments necessary to the factors of production. In a capitalist economy, someone is always ready and able to absorb this surplus as a rent. When this rent is added to cost, there no longer appears to be a surplus, but any tax will fall on the rent. Economic efficiency requires that *someone* absorb the rent—in this case, it is the tax collector.

If an efficient unit of production is large in relation to the market, so that it has not yet encountered significant resistance to expansion (in the form of increasing cost), it may experience decreasing cost because of *economies of scale*. The average cost is decreasing with output, and the marginal cost is now below the average cost (pulling the average cost down). Economic efficiency, which calls for the price to be equal to the marginal cost, places the price below the average cost, and a deficit appears instead of a surplus. The rent is now negative, and there are no volunteers to absorb it. Economic efficiency therefore depends on governmental (or social) readiness to absorb the negative rent.

This payment may be regarded as a subsidy to correct an imperfection of the market. Here, perfect competition is not possible, because of the fact that firms in the necessary numbers would have to be too small to be efficient. Unless arrangements are made (by the government) to hold the price at the marginal cost (which involves absorbing the negative rent), the result will be either the emergence of a monopoly (making a profit by raising the price and reducing output below the efficiency level) or, worse still, the disappearance of the item from the market.

The reader may have formed the impression that microeconomics has cut-and-dried solutions to all microeconomic problems. This is far from the case. There is a long array of unsolved problems on which economists are breaking their heads. Attempts are being made to probe more deeply into the nature of communications and decisionmaking and the costs they involve, to examine the necessity and validity of interpersonal comparisons in converting the findings of *welfare* (normative) *economics* into policy recommendations, to explain more satisfactorily the very large "unexplained factor" in economic growth, to strengthen the rather rickety connection between microeconomics and macroeconomics, and to integrate economics more adequately with the other social sciences—and these are only a few, randomly selected problems on the frontiers of microeconomics.

Reference has been made earlier in this paper to what might be called a "leftist" ideological resistance to the analysis and use of the price mechanism. It is only appropriate to point out that there is a symmetrical "rightist" ideological resistance to the full recognition of the limitations and the inadequacies of the market mechanism. Some economists, blinded by the light surrounding the operation of the "invisible hand," seem unable to perceive its flaws. They appear to believe that the price and market mechanism is so far beyond human understanding and so wonderful a result of natural evolution that any attempt by mere man to improve on its operation can only result in making things much worse. It should therefore be approached only in fear and trembling. Some have even gone so far as to deny the usefulness of macroeconomic theory and policy in maintaining continuous full, or even high, levels of employment.

It is incumbent on the economist, and especially on the microeconomist, to avoid the ideological extravagances of both the left and the right. He must encourage the understanding of microeconomics and its use as a guide to the market and price mechanism, insofar as it can contribute to a better life for humanity. But he must also use his skills to describe its limitations; to develop possible measures for repairing its faults; to modify the use of macroeconomic tools for economic stability, full employment, and growth by microeconomic analysis of their side effects; and to identify situations and problems for which the market is an inappropriate tool. He must recognize that there is a third field for governmental or social action, one where man can be better served by nonmarket, administrative techniques like those found within every household where the father (perhaps after a family conference) tells the members what to do for the greatest welfare of the household; within every firm, where the manager (or possibly some committee) decides where and how the productive instruments and services are to be used for the greatest profit to the firm; or within every developed nation, where a regional or national body is required to plan and administer projects that require central coordination and management for their success.

This is neither microeconomics nor macroeconomics; nor is it governmental intervention of the kinds discussed above. It is household economics (the original meaning of the Greek word from which "economics" is derived), or managerial economics, or centralized economics, or administrative economics—or perhaps it is best called "plan economics." The economists of the West have tended to take it for granted, and so have neglected it. It belongs together with microeconomics and macroeconomics in a wider "metaeconomics."

REFERENCES

1. BREIT, WILLIAM, and HAROLD M. HOCHMAN. *Readings in Microeconomics* (New York: Holt, 1968).
2. FRIEDMAN, MILTON. *Price Theory* (Chicago: Aldine, 1962).
3. HEILBRONER, ROBERT L. (ed.). *Economic Means and Social Ends* (Englewood Cliffs, N. J.: Prentice-Hall, 1969).
4. HUTCHISON, T. W. *The Significance and Basic Postulates of Economic Theory* (London: Macmillan, 1938).
5. KEYNES, J. NEVILLE. *The Scope and Method of Political Economy* (London: Macmillan, 1891).
6. LERNER, ABBA P. "Macroeconomics and Microeconomics," in Ernest Nagel (ed.), *Logic, Methodology and Philosophy of Science* (Stanford, Calif.: Stanford University Press, 1962).
7. ———. "Consumer's Surplus and Micro-Macro," *Journal of Political Economy*, 71:1 (February 1963), pp. 76–81.
8. ———. *Everybody's Business* (New York: Harper & Row Torchbooks, 1964).
9. ROBBINS, LIONEL C. *The Nature and Significance of Economic Science* (London: Macmillan, 1932).
10. ROBINSON, JOAN. *Economic Philosophy* (Garden City, N. Y.: Doubleday, 1964).
11. ROSS, RALPH G., and ERNEST VAN DEN HAAG, *The Fabric of Society* (New York: Harcourt, Brace, 1957), chaps. 16–21, 27–30.

5

MACROECONOMIC THEORY

Arnold Collery*

THE first great economists were equilibrium theorists. David Ricardo and John Stuart Mill knew that the price of wheat could change with every transaction, but they did not make these fluctuations a part of their concern. What did interest them and what they thought deserved explanation was "normal" price—the price that would rule in equilibrium, when there was no tendency for change.

The classical economists' concentration on what would be true in a condition of long-run equilibrium prevented them from developing a body of analysis similar to modern macroeconomics. Consider how Ricardo and Mill would have answered the following question: What determines total output in a free-market economy? In modern terminology, they would have said that in a long-run equilibrium it would equal the productive potential of the economy, which would depend on the qualities and existing quantities of land, labor, and capital. They would have admitted that, at any given moment of time, some of the land, labor, or capital offered for use might be idle. But such a situation would be temporary, as would a situation with more supply than demand for wheat. In equilibrium, they would have argued, involuntary unemployment simply could not exist. Either men choose not to work, in which case they are *voluntarily* unemployed (thus not really unemployed at all), or they

* Amherst College.

offer their services for hire in the market at the going rate. If they cannot find employment, wages fall, tending both to increase the number of jobs available and to reduce the number of people looking for work. In equilibrium—and it was with equilibrium that they were concerned— everyone who was ready, willing, and able to work would find employment. Mill thought so little of the problem of unemployment that in the 979 pages of his great *Principles of Political Economy* the word never appeared.

There were nonetheless some economists who worried about unemployment. Thomas Robert Malthus and Karl Marx, contemporaries of Ricardo and Mill, are examples. But until the publication of John Maynard Keynes' *The General Theory of Employment, Interest and Money* in 1936, Ricardo and Mill were regarded as orthodox and Malthus and Marx as heretical. The arguments of the latter were simply unconvincing to the majority of economists. The depression in Great Britain in the 1920s and the prolonged world depression of the 1930s did much to increase the sense that something was wrong with the view that "prosperity is just around the corner." Economics was ready for a revolution, ready to reject Ricardo and Mill. Keynes led that revolution. Almost single-handedly he invented what we now know as macroeconomics.

How can we explain short-run fluctuations in output and employment? Is it possible that unemployment is not self-correcting, that an economy does not automatically tend to produce at its productive potential? In what sense were Ricardo and Mill right, and in what sense wrong? If involuntary unemployment is not automatically self-correcting, what can be done to prevent or eliminate it? These are some of the questions which macroeconomics attempts to answer and which will be treated in this chapter.

We begin with a concept that is central to contemporary macroeconomic theory: What is meant by the net national product?

The Real Net National Product An economy as complex as ours produces hundreds of thousands of different kinds of goods and services. Economists find it useful to sum up the quantities of all things produced, so that they can speak of the *net national product*, the output in an economy over a period of time. To make this summation—to add apples to books—it is necessary to express all quantities in the same units. By valuing each thing at the dollar price at which it has been sold or, if it has not been sold, at the dollar cost of producing it, the production of each good and service can be measured in dollars and then added to obtain a figure for the net national product.

There are two important reasons why the number representing the net national product may change, and it is essential to distinguish between them. Average prices may change in one direction with average physical quantities unchanged, or average physical quantities may change in one direction with average prices unchanged. While an increase in the net national product of the latter sort, more output with average prices unchanged, is desirable, an increase of the former sort is usually considered undesirable; the same output with higher prices is simply inflation. In macroeconomic theory it is changes in the net national product resulting from changes in physical quantities of output that are of primary interest; to secure information about this, the dollar figures for the net national product are adjusted for overall price changes—a complicated process that we shall not go into here. When the figures for the net national product are adjusted for price changes, we obtain information about the net national product in constant dollars, the *real* net national product.

In the discussion that follows we shall always be considering the net national product in constant dollars, the real net national product. When we say that the net national product increases by $40 billion, we shall mean that there is $40 billion more of physical output, not that prices have risen so that the same output now sells for $40 billion more.

The Central Concern and Premise of Macroeconomic Theory Macroeconomic theory attempts to explain why the real net national product is what it is and why it grows and declines, given the state of technology and the available supplies of land, labor, and capital. Typically in this theory, nothing is said about relative prices—the price of apples compared with the price of steel—or about relative outputs—the quantity of shoes produced relative to the quantity of pencils. The real net national product may have increased, even though some prices fell while other prices rose. The real net national product may also have increased, even though some components of it decreased; there is nothing inconsistent about saying that our economy is producing more goods and services, although less milk. Macroeconomic theory is based on the premise that predictions can be made about the behavior of the real net national product without considering individual prices or individual goods.

The central premise of modern macroeconomic theory is that the real net national product depends on the aggregate demand for it. So long as production is less than what it would be with resources fully employed—so long as there is unemployment—an increase in aggregate demand will lead to an increase in output. And if aggregate demand declines, production will decline. If a change in the direction of expenditures occurs without a change in aggregate demand—if, for example, there were an increase in the demand for housing coincident with an equal decrease in the demand for airplanes—macroeconomic theory would predict that the net national product would be unaltered, once a reallocation of resources occurred. This theory does not focus on the problems of reallocating resources but assumes that transfers occur smoothly and quickly.

Attitudes toward Aggregate Demand in Pre-Keynesian Economics It has only recently become the established view that the real net national product depends on the aggregate demand for it. The prevalent opinion from the eighteenth century until the Keynesian Revolution in the 1930s was that the aggregate demand for output could never be less than output itself; aggregate demand would always be sufficient to buy the real net national product. If the real net national product was $400 billion, then aggregate demand would be $400 billion. In this view, therefore, depressions and unemployment could not be explained by a deficiency of aggregate demand.

No one would have denied that, at existing prices, the supply of some particular good could be greater than its demand. This could occur, but earlier theory would insist that this would only indicate that elsewhere in the economy the demand for some other good was greater than its supply. All that was produced would be sold if the composition of output was appropriate to the composition of demand. And if the composition of output was not appropriate to the composition of demand, the real net national product would not change; only its composition would change.

The Equality of Output and Income One argument to explain why aggregate demand may be less than output is rejected by modern as well as earlier economists. It is the assertion that there is simply not enough income to buy all that is produced. Surely there would be a problem if this were the case, for even if everyone spent all of his income buying output, there would still necessarily be output left unsold.

Given the way income and output are defined, however, this situation is impossible. To see why this must be so, imagine, for example, that all output is produced by one giant firm and ignore the minor complication introduced by taxes. In the process of producing goods, the firm would hire labor and it might also rent property and borrow from the rest of the community. Assume, for example, that during a certain period of time it produced an output valued at $200 and it paid $120 to labor, $25 to landlords, and $15 in interest. These payments of wages, rent, and interest would represent income to those who received them. Thus the income payments to the factors of production would be $160. Clearly the sum of these income payments would be less than the output as a whole, but it does not follow that the total income would be less than the net national product. For we have said nothing yet about profits, which are another form of income. Since the firm produced $200 worth of goods and services at a cost to it of $160, it made a profit of $40. When this is added to the sum of the other incomes, we see that the national income would be precisely $200. Since, for the economy as a whole, profits are the difference between total output and the sum of wage and salary, rental, and interest incomes, then the sum of all incomes—wages and salaries, rents, interest, *and* profits—must exactly equal the net national product.

This fundamental accounting identity between output and income will be taken for granted in what follows. We shall use a single symbol (Y) to indicate the real value of the net national product as well as the national income.

Must Aggregate Demand Equal the Net National Product? But there were earlier economists who went much further than simply arguing that income must equal output. They also believed that all income would become demand, so that aggregate demand would necessarily equal the real net national product. It is this view, that aggregate demand will never be less than the real net national product, that modern economists reject.

To appreciate the difference between the pre-Keynesian and the modern view, we must say something about the nature of money. If money, that which is generally used as a medium of exchange, is simply a commodity that has been selected somehow to serve this function and if it can be produced by firms when they find it profitable to do so, then the earlier view would be correct and the modern view wrong. To understand this, assume that money consists of some commodity, say fountain pens. If, under these circumstances, people wanted to hoard part of their income, it would not follow that they would not demand output; aggregate demand would not be less than the real net national product. If people wished to hoard $20 billion out of a real net national product of $400 billion, there would be an excess supply of some goods, if no fountain pens had been produced. But the excess supplies of these goods would be matched by an excess demand for fountain pens. If $20 billion worth of fountain pens had been produced, the desire to hoard would not have resulted in a shortage of demand in any market. Hoarders would be demanders of commodities just as much as spenders.

But money has long ceased to be a commodity whose output can be assumed to increase when there is a demand for it. Money is not something that ordinary business enterprises can manufacture; its production has been taken over by the government and the banking system. One can accept the formal validity of the earlier view that aggregate demand necessarily equals the real net national product when money is a commodity, but deny its relevance to the world today. If the aggregate demand for things other than money falls short of their production because people want to hoard, the economy will experience difficulties that no rearrangement of resources could eliminate.

Is a Deficiency of Aggregate Demand Self-correcting? Earlier economists might have admitted the possibility of a deficiency of aggregate demand if money were not a commodity, but they would not have considered it a problem; such a situation would, in their view, be self-correcting. If aggregate demand were less than the net national product, forces would begin to operate to increase aggregate demand until it was equal to capacity output. Early economists could argue that if aggregate demand were less than output, the unspent income would not be hoarded; it would appear in the market as a demand for securities. The excess supply of funds in security markets over the demand for them would lower interest rates and, as a consequence, increase the desire to spend. To some extent the reduction in interest rates would reduce saving, increasing consumption, and to some extent it would increase the desire to invest, to add to the capital stock. In this view, then, interest rates would fall until the gap between output at full employment and aggregate demand disappeared.

Keynes challenged this analysis. He did not deny that the appearance of a deficiency of aggregate demand would reduce interest rates, but he did deny that the entire deficiency could be eliminated by this mechanism. Even if initially the part of income that was not spent was offered in the security markets, even if initially there was no desire to hoard, the decline in interest rates would induce some people to hoard more money. He argued that the reason savers are willing to lend rather than hold money is to earn interest. The lower interest rates become, the less incentive there is to hold securities rather than money, and the more people there will be who will hold some or all of their wealth in the form of money.

If the classical economists would be willing to accept this argument, they would still not have to give up. They could then argue that if aggregate demand fell short of output and if the entire deficiency were not eliminated by a decline in interest rates, firms would reduce their demand for labor and other factors of production. Competition among the factors of production would then result in a reduction in factor prices; wages would fall. With costs down, competition among firms guarantees that prices would also fall. Thus these economists could argue that the consequences of a continued deficiency of aggregate demand would be deflation. And, in the next step of the argument, they could insist that the deflation would not go on indefinitely, but would eventually cease, since it would raise aggregate demand.

If money consisted of pieces of paper issued by the government rather than some commodity and if there were a deficiency of aggregate demand for commodities because people wished to add to their money holdings rather than buy goods with their entire income, the market economy would automatically give them what they seek. For as prices fell, the value of the dollar bills they were holding would increase; the lower the price level, the more a dollar would buy. As prices got lower and lower, people would have more and more purchasing power in the form of money. They would not have more dollar bills, but each dollar would buy more. Thus people would achieve what they were seeking, more wealth in the form of money. When the purchasing power of the constant stock of money reached a certain level, because of the reduction in prices, people would cease trying to hoard part of their income and would spend all of it to buy output. The initial gap between aggregate demand and the real net national product would not result then in lower output, but would set up forces that would raise aggregate demand until it equaled output at full employment.

Again a modern economist might admit that this is a correct analysis, given its assumptions, but deny that it is relevant to the economy in which we live. Wages and prices simply refuse to behave as the theory assumes. When firms reduce their demand for labor, wages do not go down. In fact union leaders may argue for higher wages in order to increase purchasing power. And if wages will not fall, then the mechanism for increasing the real purchasing power of money through lower wages and prices will be inoperative, and the deficiency of aggregate demand will result in a smaller real net national product. Resources will be wasted, and men ready and willing to work will be unable to find employment.

The Modern Theory of Output and Employment We have seen that there are two important assumptions in modern macroeconomic theory which were not present in pre-Keynesian theory: that aggregate demand can be less than the real net national product; and that interest rates, wages, and prices are rigid downward. Our task now is to explain the determination of the total quantity of goods and services produced under these circumstances. We have argued previously that total production will tend to equal aggregate demand, so long as resources are not fully utilized. Although aggregate demand can be less than output, output would, under these circumstances, decline until it became equal to demand. Letting output equal Y and aggregate demand AD, this important generalization can be written as

$$Y = AD \qquad (5\text{-}1)$$

It must be remembered that this relationship will hold only so long as there are unutilized resources. When output becomes so great that resources are fully employed, an increase in aggregate demand would no longer be capable of leading to greater output. Equation (5-1) must be interpreted as an *equilibrium condition*. It is not something that is necessarily true, but rather something that tends to be true. Thus the predictions that result from this theory are predictions about what tends to happen.

Having established that output depends on aggregate demand, we must pursue the argument further. On what does aggregate demand depend? We shall simplify matters by ignoring government and foreign demand. Let us, therefore, consider a closed economy without a government. We can imagine that the economy consists of households and business firms. All output is produced in the business firms, and income precisely equal to that output is paid to the households. The households use their income primarily for purposes of consumption. It is possible that households will spend on consumption less than their income if their income is relatively large, and will spend more than their income if their income is relatively low. If consumption is less than income, then we say that households have saved, since saving is defined as income minus consumption. When households save, they can place their savings in financial intermediaries such as savings banks, lend directly to businesses, or, if they do neither, increase the amount of money they hold. If households consume more than their incomes (dissave), then they must have withdrawn funds from financial intermediaries, have sold their claims against businesses, or, if they did neither, have reduced the amount of money they hold.

If we assume that the relationship between consumption demand of households CD and national income Y can be approximated by a linear function, we can write the relationship as

$$CD = a + bY \qquad (5\text{-}2)$$

In Equation (5-2), a represents the amount of consumption that households would engage in if they had no income, and b represents the amount of consumption that would be induced by a dollar increase in income. Called *the marginal propensity to consume*, b is assumed, based on empirical information, to be a positive fraction.

In addition to the demand of households for consumption goods and services, business firms may themselves demand goods to add to their stocks of buildings, equipment, and inventories. Addition to buildings, equipment, and inventories is called *investment*, and the amount that firms wish to so add is *investment demand*. The word "investment" has many meanings in everyday usage, and it is therefore important that its technical use in economics be understood. If someone buys a stock or a bond, ordinary usage would allow us to say that he invests. But in macroeconomic theory this would not be investment. Only when the stock of capital (buildings, equipment, and inventories) increases is there investment. The purchase of stocks and bonds may result in some firm's investing, but it is not investment itself.

Let us assume that business firms wish to add a fixed amount to the stock of capital, so many billions of dollars. If we add this fixed amount of investment demand ID to consumption demand, we have aggregate demand.

$$AD = CD + ID \tag{5-3}$$

Equations (5-1), (5-2), and (5-3) can be solved simultaneously for equilibrium net national product Y.[1] The solution is

$$Y = \frac{a + ID}{1 - b} \tag{5-4}$$

Let us consider a numerical example. If a were $20 billion, ID were $40 billion, and b, the marginal propensity to consume, were 0.8, then equilibrium net national product would be $300 billion—that is, $60 billion divided by 0.2.

To help understand why equilibrium Y must be $300 billion in our example, consider what would be true if it were greater or less than $300 billion. If Y were $400 billion, then consumption demand would be $340 billion—that is, $20 billion plus 0.8 of Y. With investment demand fixed at a value of $40 billion, aggregate demand would be $380 billion. Thus, if the net national product were $400 billion, aggregate demand would be $20 billion less than that. Firms would be unable to sell all that they produce and therefore would reduce their production. The real net national product would decline.

Now consider what would happen if output were less than $300 billion, say $200 billion. With income equal to $200 billion, consumption demand would be $180 billion—that is, $20 billion plus 0.8 of $200 billion. Since investment demand is assumed to be $40 billion, aggregate demand would be $220 billion, which is greater than output. Firms would therefore hire more factors of production and expand their output. So long as output is less than $300 billion, aggregate demand would be greater than output, and output would expand.

If consumption demand were to increase, so that at every income level more was consumed, equilibrium net national product would rise by a multiple of this increase. Instead of assuming that a is $20 billion,

---

[1] It is obtained as follows. First, Equation (5-3) is substituted into Equation (5-1), yielding $Y = CD + ID$. Then, Equation (5-2) is substituted into this expression, eliminating CD and yielding $Y = a + bY + ID$. All that remains to be done is to bring bY to the left-hand side, factor out Y, and divide through by its coefficient. The result is Equation (5-4).

assume that it is $30 billion. Equilibrium net national product would rise by more than $10 billion; it would rise by $50 billion. If you check this result with Equation (5-4) by replacing a with 30, ID with 40, and b with 0.8, you will find that equilibrium Y becomes $350 billion.

If investment demand were to increase, it would also increase Y by some multiple, depending on the marginal propensity to consume. In the example we have been considering, the marginal propensity to consume is 0.8, and the multiple—called the "multiplier"—is therefore 5. Each dollar of increase in investment demand would increase equilibrium net national product by $5.

The reason why an increase in aggregate demand will raise output by a multiple has a simple verbal explanation. If aggregate demand increases by a dollar, output will rise by a dollar. We have assumed that consumption demand depends on income and that an increase in income by a dollar will raise consumption demand by the marginal propensity to consume. Thus, if the marginal propensity to consume were 0.8, consumption demand would increase by 80 cents. This, of course, would not be the end of the story. The 80-cent increase in consumption demand would lead to an increase in output of 80 cents, and this output implies 80 cents more of income. With the marginal propensity to consume equal to 0.8, consumption would again increase, this time by 64 cents. And so it goes. The initial increase in aggregate demand of $1 would raise income by $1 plus 0.8 times $1 plus 0.8 squared times $1 plus 0.8 cubed times $1 and so forth. The total effect would be 1 over 1 minus the marginal propensity to consume. With the marginal propensity to consume equal to 0.8, income would rise by $5.

Policy Implications If unemployment exists because of a deficiency of aggregate demand, then it can be reduced by increasing the level of spending. How can this be done?

In the previous analysis nothing was said about foreign trade or government activity; they were assumed away. If we now allow for the existence of government, it is clear that aggregate demand consists not only of consumption and investment demand, but also of government demand. If the government could increase its demand without private demand's falling, or with its falling as much as government demand increased, then aggregate demand would grow and, given unemployment, so would output and employment. Whether private demand would fall when government demand increased would depend on the method of finance chosen by the government. There are three possible methods of finance: the government could increase taxes, create new money, or borrow from the public. Let us consider each in turn.

If an increase in government spending was paid for by higher taxes, private demand would be falling at the same time that government demand was increasing, and the overall effect might be small or even zero. Higher taxes reduce disposable income and therefore reduce consumption. Furthermore, higher taxes reduce the profitability of investment and the funds available for that purpose, reducing investment demand. If a dollar increase in government spending reduces private spending by one dollar, nothing would happen to output and employment when the government increased its spending. If private spending falls by less than a dollar, then aggregate demand and output would rise somewhat.

If, instead of financing the new spending by increased taxes, the government paid with newly created money—either new paper money or new deposits created for it by the Federal Reserve banks—there is no apparent reason why private spending would fall. Thus aggregate demand would increase, and output would grow by a multiple of the increase, depending on the marginal propensity to consume and on the degree to which investment is stimulated by increased profitability and by increased availability of funds to undertake investment projects.

Finally, the government could finance the spending by borrowing from the public, borrowing money that already existed. In this case it would compete for funds in the security market with private borrowers. To some degree, private spending would fall, since funds would become more expensive and less available to private investors. If every dollar the government borrowed and spent reduced private spending by a dollar, aggregate demand would not change; increased government spending financed by the sale of bonds to the public would not reduce unemployment. But private spending is likely to fall less than the increase in government spending. The competition for funds in the security market would raise interest rates and induce people to economize on money holdings; to some extent money that would not have been spent, that would have been hoarded, would now be spent. In this case aggregate demand would increase somewhat and so would output and employment.

It should be clear from this analysis that the government, in increasing its expenditures in order to reduce unemployment, can be most certain of achieving its goal if it spends newly created money. But some people are alarmed at the suggestion that prosperity can be achieved by creating money. Isn't that simply inflationary? Many classical economists would surely have answered yes. They would have assumed that the economy was initially in a full-employment equilibrium. Under such circumstances an increase in aggregate demand could only be inflationary. But we are considering an economy in which there are people ready, willing, and able to work at the going wage who have not yet found employment. If there were more demand, more of them would find employment. Although it would be wrong to imply that an increase in aggregate demand, financed by the creation of money, would not be inflationary at all, it would be equally wrong to imply that the only effect would be higher prices. The increase in demand would encourage firms to hire more resources to meet the growing demand; prices might rise somewhat, but so would output and employment.

Instead of attacking the problem of unemployment by an increase in government spending, measures could be enacted that would increase private spending. One of them would be a reduction in taxes. With taxes down and disposable income up, consumption demand would increase and in all probability so would investment demand, since investment would be more profitable and investment funds more readily available. But again we must be careful to specify the method of finance. Both consumption and investment would increase if the tax cut were made possible by the creation of new money. If it were financed, however, by the sale of bonds to the public, then the net effect might even be to reduce investment demand rather than increase it, since the government would be competing with private investors for funds. But so long as higher interest rates speed up the velocity of money and reduce hoarding, the net effect of the tax cut, even when financed by the sale of bonds to the public, would be expansionary.

A tax cut is not the only means of stimulating private spending. We have yet to consider the instruments of monetary policy. The Federal Reserve authorities could stimulate private spending by making money cheaper to borrow or more easily available at existing interest rates. If, for example, the Federal Reserve banks bought government securities with newly created currency or deposits, investment demand would increase, raising output by a multiple of this amount.

Monetary Policy, Fiscal Policy, and the National Debt Monetary and fiscal actions may have implications for the national debt. Although many people exaggerate the burdens of an internally held national debt, most economists would agree that on balance a smaller debt is better than a larger one. Even an internally held debt is burdensome, since taxes must be collected to finance the payment of interest. Taxes in general reduce incentives and distort the allocation of resources. The question that shall now concern us is whether increased government spending, reduced taxes, or expansionary monetary policy to stimulate aggregate demand will cause the national debt to grow and impose a burden on the community.

We have argued that increased government spending or reduced taxes can be financed by the creation of new money. The new money may be new currency, or it may be demand deposits at the Federal Reserve banks given in exchange for government securities. Since it is the interest payments on the national debt that make the debt a burden, the government securities held by the Federal Reserve banks are not properly part of the national debt. The interest which the Treasury pays to the Federal Reserve banks, approximately two billion dollars a year, is returned to the Treasury. If new money is created, it should be clear that there is no reason why the national debt would grow if the government pursued expansionary policies. It could grow if the government chose to finance its expenditures by the sale of bonds to the public; in that case the government would be minimizing the expansionary effects of its action, since it would then compete for funds in the security market. The growth in the debt would be a choice, not a necessity.

If we need not create a larger national debt to finance deficits created to avoid unemployment, why would the government ever want the national debt to grow? There are two closely related situations under which it would be appropriate for the federal government consciously to increase the national debt. First, imagine that Congress decides on a level of spending that exceeds taxes at a time of full employment and inflationary pressures. Although one might suggest a reduction in spending or an increase in taxes under these inflationary circumstances, what if Congress is unwilling to do either? How then should the deficit be financed? Although it could be financed by creating money, clearly it would be better to sell bonds to the public. The sale of the bonds to the public—the increase in the national debt—would reduce private spending and minimize the inflationary effects of the deficit. Second, even if there were no deficit to be financed, the Treasury might wish to sell bonds to the public in inflationary circumstances. By permitting an increase in the national debt through the bond sales to the public and then keeping the money obtained idle, aggregate demand could be reduced and the inflationary pressures lessened. What should be noticed is that in either case the government might consciously increase the national debt, but it would do so to fight inflation, not to fight unemployment.

That a growing national debt should be associated with a fight against inflation rather than against unemployment becomes further apparent when we consider monetary policy. If the Federal Reserve authorities were to decide to stimulate aggregate demand by open-market purchases of government securities, the amount of debt in the hands of the public would fall; the bonds would be in the possession of the Federal Reserve banks and the interest returned to the Treasury. Thus, when the Federal Reserve authorities pursue policies to reduce unemployment, the national debt falls. If, on the other hand, the Federal Reserve authorities wished to contract aggregate demand they would sell bonds, permitting the national debt to grow. But they would do this to fight inflation, not to reduce unemployment.

To sum up: A growing national debt, contrary to popular opinion, is not one of the costs the nation would have to bear if the government engaged in deficit spending to achieve full employment. When lower taxes or higher government expenditures are called for to stimulate spending, new money can be created to finance the deficit. The new money may be either new currency or new deposits at the Federal Reserve banks. In neither case would the government have to pay any interest; if it pays some to the Federal Reserve banks, they will pay it right back. There may be other times when sound policy calls for an increase in the national debt, but they would be times of excessive spending and inflation, not deficient spending and unemployment.

The Importance of Economic Forecasting and Quantification of Relationships
Even if we accept the fundamental conclusion of modern macroeconomic theory that the equilibrium net national product depends on the aggregate demand for it and that employment and production can be controlled by the instruments of monetary and fiscal policy, many problems remain to be solved before we can be sure that unemployment due to insufficient demand can be prevented. Since any fiscal or monetary action must be debated before it is taken and since its effects once taken will not be felt until some time later, the achievement of economic stability requires us to know what the future has in store for us if *no* action is taken. If the main effects of a policy decision were not to be felt for three months, it would be necessary to know the unemployment rate three months from now in order to pursue the correct policy today. Thus, economic forecasting is of great importance. The better we learn to forecast the future of the economy, the more likely we shall be to prevent either deficient or excessive spending.

In addition, to stabilize economic activity we should be able to quantify the relationships between the variables of macroeconomic theory. If we could forecast so well that we knew that three months from now aggregate demand would be $15 billion too little, we would still have to know how much to increase government spending to prevent that deficiency. For example, what is the size of the multiplier? Will the Federal Reserve banks buy bonds if the government sells them? If so, how many? If taxes are reduced rather than expenditures increased, exactly how much should they be reduced to raise aggregate demand by $15 billion? Or if open-market purchases of government securities are to be made to raise aggregate spending by $20 billion, how many should be bought to do the job? Is it $1 billion or $5 billion? The answer will depend in part on the responsiveness of investment demand to changes in the cost and availability of funds. Just how responsive it is?

Economic forecasting and the quantification of relationships between macroeconomic variables are, therefore, of crucial importance in maintaining a prosperous and stable economy. Macroeconomic theory may show in principle how this objective can be achieved, but one must realize that it is only a beginning.

REFERENCES

1. COLLERY, ARNOLD. *National Income and Employment Analysis* (New York: Wiley, 1966).
2. DERNBURG, THOMAS F., and DUNCAN M. McDOUGALL. *Macroeconomics*, 3d ed. (New York: McGraw-Hill, 1968).
3. HANSEN, ALVIN H. *A Guide to Keynes* (New York: McGraw-Hill, 1953).
4. HICKS, J. R. "Mr. Keynes and the 'Classics': A Suggested Interpretation," *Econometrica*, 5 (1937), pp. 147–159.
5. KEYNES. J. M. *The General Theory of Employment, Interest and Money* (New York: Harcourt, Brace, 1936).
6. LERNER, ABBA P. *Everybody's Business* (New York: Harper & Row, 1964).
7. PATINKIN, DON. *Money, Interest, and Prices*, 2d ed. (New York; Harper & Row, 1965).

6

MONETARY INSTITUTIONS AND POLICIES

Warren L. Smith [*]

An important instrument of government in encouraging output and maintaining stable prices is *monetary policy*: adjusting the supply of money to the flow of production. I shall discuss this complex function in terms of the institutions created to implement it, the operational features that distinguish it, and some recent thinking with respect to relationships between money and income.

INSTITUTIONAL BACKGROUND

United States Financial Institutions
Monetary policy in the United States functions within the framework of a complex and highly developed financial system. There are about 13,800 commercial banks—that is, banks that accept deposits subject to withdrawal by check. These banks range in size from the Bank of America in California, which has total deposits of over $15 billion, down to nearly 1,000 banks having less than $1 million of deposits. Somewhat less than half of the banks are members of the Federal Reserve System, but member banks hold more than 80 percent of total deposits. Payment of interest on demand (checking) deposits is prohibited, but commercial banks also accept time and savings deposits on which they pay interest. Thus, besides serving as administrators of the nation's check-payment system and as the primary channel through which money—defined as demand

[*] University of Michigan.

deposits and currency—is injected into or withdrawn from the economy, commercial banks also form part of an elaborate system of savings institutions. In addition to commercial banks, United States financial institutions include a network of over 6,000 savings and loan associations, which provide savings facilities on a nationwide basis; mutual savings banks, which are important in a few states; and life insurance companies, which collect funds through the receipt of premiums from policyholders. Private pension funds, which invest amounts set aside for employee retirement benefits by business concerns, have become an increasingly important element in the capital market in recent years.

Major borrowers include households, which borrow on installment credit contracts for the purchase of automobiles and other consumer durable goods and on longer-term mortgages for the purchase of houses; state and local government units, which issue bonds to finance the construction of schools, highways and streets, sewage facilities, and other public improvements; and the federal government, which at times borrows substantial sums to cover budget deficits. Private business enterprises commonly finance much of their investment in inventories and plant and equipment through profits, but they also are heavy borrowers through loans and bond issues, particularly at times when economic activity is brisk.

The intermediation of financial institutions greatly increases the efficiency of the financial system in channeling saving into investment. The small saver is often reluctant to put his money into stocks, bonds, or loans. He usually does not possess the financial and business expertise required to make an adequate appraisal of the financial soundness and profit prospects of the borrower. Moreover, he often wants assurance that he can withdraw his funds quickly and without risk of loss if an emergency should arise; loans and securities are generally either not readily salable, or if they are, the day-to-day fluctuations in their prices create a risk of serious loss at the time of sale. By placing his money in a financial institution, the saver avoids having to appraise the quality of securities and loans himself, leaving this task to the professionally trained management of the institution. In addition, he is free to choose among a variety of financial assets—including time deposits, savings and loan shares, life insurance policies, and retirement annuities—designed to meet his special needs more effectively than direct investment in loans and securities. Funds placed in time deposits or savings and loan shares can be withdrawn quickly and without loss. Life insurance policies provide protection for his family. Investment in pension fund annuities provides an assured income at the time of retirement. The saver is often willing to accept a lower rate of return on such investments because of their other attractive qualities. Thus, even allowing for profit to the financial institution in the form of a differential between the interest rate charged to the borrower and that paid to the saver, borrowers are commonly able to raise funds at lower costs than would be incurred if they placed their securities and loans directly with savers.

The extent of competition in financial markets in the United States varies considerably, depending upon the type of borrower and his geographic location. For large business enterprises whose reputation is known throughout the country or throughout a major region, the alternative sources of funds are numerous and the degree of competition is high. For the household desiring to borrow on an installment loan or a mortgage, the situation varies from one city or community to another, but there is frequently a considerable amount of competition involving commercial banks, savings and loan associations, local agents of life insurance companies, and sales finance companies. The smaller business enterprise, however, is often limited in its sources of loan funds to commercial banks located in its immediate vicinity; these local markets may contain no more than two or three rival banks, with the result that competition is quite limited. The geographical area within which a particular commercial bank is permitted to operate varies greatly from one part of the country to another. In some states, notably California, commercial banks are allowed to establish branches throughout the state. In a few states, branch banking is completely prohibited, while, in the majority of states, branches are permitted but on less than a statewide basis.

The Federal Reserve System The Federal Reserve System is organized on a regional basis, with twelve Federal Reserve banks located in major cities throughout the nation. Member banks carry their reserves in the form of either cash in their vaults or deposits with the Federal Reserve bank of the district. Insofar as the member banks have occasion to deal with the Federal Reserve, their contacts are primarily with the district Reserve bank. In the conduct of monetary policy, however, the trend for many years has been toward greater centralization of authority in the hands of the System's central governing body, the Board of Governors of the Federal Reserve System, located in Washington, D.C. The Board is composed of seven members, appointed by the President of the United States for terms of fourteen years, with one member serving as Chairman for a term of four years. However, perhaps the most important body involved in the administration of monetary policy is the Federal Open Market Committee, which is composed of the seven members of the Board of Governors, together with the President of the Federal Reserve Bank of New York and the presidents of four of the other Reserve banks serving on a rotating basis. From a formal standpoint, the discount rate at which the System lends to member banks is determined by the individual Reserve banks; the percentages of their deposits that member banks must hold as cash in their vaults or as deposits at the Reserve banks are determined, within limits set by statute, by the Board of Governors; and the System's purchases and sales of United States government securities in the open market are determined and supervised by the Open Market Committee. In practice, however, the Committee is responsible for overall coordination of the instruments of monetary policy.

A variety of devices may be employed to achieve economic stability—that is, to keep the economy operating close to full employment without undue inflation. Monetary policy is one such device. The other major one is fiscal policy, which involves adjustments in tax rates and in government expenditures as a means of regulating the flow of purchasing power through the economy. In addition, the policies employed by the Treasury in managing the public debt may be of considerable importance. These include decisions on the types of securities to issue to finance budget deficits and to refund old securities as they mature. For success in stabilizing the economy, it is important that the monetary policy of the Federal Reserve System be carefully coordinated with the fiscal, debt management, and other policies that are primarily the responsibility of the President and his administration. However, there is no formal institutional arrangement designed to provide such coordination. As a practical matter, close and cordial working relations normally exist at the administrative and staff levels between the Treasury and the Federal Reserve System in the conduct of monetary and debt-management policy, and, during the past few years, in the conduct of certain operations in the foreign exchange markets which have been the joint responsibility of the two agencies.

The Federal Reserve Act, under which the System was established in 1914, emphasized the maintenance of a smoothly functioning banking system and the prevention of banking crises and made no reference to the use of monetary policy to maintain overall economic stability. The act has never been amended to provide guidance to the System for the conduct of monetary policy as that term is now understood. However, the Federal Reserve authorities have repeatedly declared their acceptance of responsibility for the promotion of the objectives of the Employment Act of 1946. That act established the responsibility of the federal government "to use all practicable means consistent with its needs and obligations and other essential considerations of national policy . . . for the purpose of creating and maintaining, in a manner calculated to foster and promote free competitive enterprise in the general welfare, conditions under which there will be afforded useful employment opportunities, including self-employment for those able, willing, and seeking to work, and to promote maximum employment, production, and purchasing power." This statement in the Employment Act is accordingly now recognized by the System as its basic guide in the conduct of policy.

THE CONDUCT OF MONETARY POLICY

Policy Instruments The three main instruments used by the Federal Reserve System in the conduct of monetary policy are open-market purchases and sales of United States government securities, adjustments in the discount rate at which the System will lend to member banks, and changes in the percentages of their deposits that member banks must hold in cash reserves either in their own vaults or on deposit at their district Reserve banks. Of these, open-market operations are by far the most important. In addition to their use for countercyclical purposes to affect interest rates, credit conditions, and the money supply in the interest of economic stability and growth, open-market operations are conducted on a day-to-day basis to offset factors affecting member bank reserves which are not subject to the direct control of the Federal Reserve.[1] Policy with respect to open-market operations is established by the Open Market Committee, which normally meets every three weeks, and is actually carried out by the Federal Reserve Bank of New York acting as agent for the System. The Federal Reserve executes its purchases and sales through regular government securities dealers.

At times, changes in the discount rate have been used as a signal of changes in monetary policy, but many adjustments in the discount rate are designed to keep that rate in line with interest rates prevailing in the short-term open market. The System does not rely entirely on the discount rate to control member-bank borrowing; by means of administrative regulations it attempts to discourage banks from borrowing except to meet temporary reserve needs, and the member banks are generally inclined to respect this limitation. Changes in reserve requirements have seldom been used in recent years. While potentially a powerful weapon of monetary control, they are of less practical importance than open-market operations under present System procedures.

The System has the power to establish ceilings on the interest rates that member banks can pay on time and savings deposits. Changes in these ceilings under the Federal Reserve's Regulation Q have been used several times in the past few years as a supplementary monetary policy instrument.

---

[1] These factors include changes in the gold stock held by the Treasury, changes in the Treasury's deposits in Federal Reserve banks, changes in foreign deposits in Federal Reserve banks, changes in the public's holdings of currency, and so on. For a systematic explanation of the factors that create and destroy member bank reserves, see [1, chap. 9].

Little use is made by the Federal Reserve itself of selective credit controls designed to affect particular credit markets. Indeed, at the present time the only instrument of this kind available to the Federal Reserve is the control of margin requirements in connection with stock transactions. This control is designed to give the Federal Reserve a means of dealing more or less directly with stock-market speculation financed through credit; it is of minor significance as an instrument of monetary policy. At times, particularly during World War II and in the immediate postwar period, the Federal Reserve has been given authority to fix minimum downpayments and maximum maturities on consumer installment loans for the purchase of durable goods. The System's authority to use such controls lapsed in 1952, and since that time no use has been made of them. However, the restitution of these controls, at least on a standby or emergency basis, is advocated from time to time in some quarters.

An important and distinctive feature of United States monetary policy is an almost exclusive reliance on regulation of the aggregate supply of bank reserves and on relatively free capital and money markets as the channel through which changes in bank reserves produce effects on the total supply of money and credit and the general level of interest rates. No use is normally made of such devices as direct control of bank loans or rationing of credit for specific purposes, which often play an important role in monetary policy in other countries. One major reason for the heavy reliance on markets as a means of transmitting the effects of monetary policy is the unique structure of the United States commercial banking system. Direct regulation of bank credit through such means as loan quotas for individual banks is feasible in countries like the United Kingdom or Canada, which have highly concentrated banking systems with most banking resources under the control of a handful of large institutions; but such regulation is clearly much less feasible in the United States with its more than 13,000 individual banks of widely varying sizes. In addition, there is, on the part of both the private financial community and the Federal Reserve authorities, a strong distaste for direct intervention by the government in the financial markets.

Impact of Monetary Policy on the Domestic Economy It is useful to distinguish between the automatic stabilizing effects of monetary policy in the absence of deliberate countercyclical actions on the part of the authorities, on the one hand, and discretionary action deliberately taken by the authorities, on the other.

THE AUTOMATIC ELEMENT IN MONETARY POLICY If a weakening of private demand for goods and services leads to a fall in income and employment, credit conditions will ease, and interest rates will decline to some extent, even in the absence of expansionary action on the part of the Federal Reserve. The reason is that there is a clearly established positive relationship between the level of income and the demand for money balances. As income declines, money is released from balances required to finance transactions, increasing the demand for securities and causing interest rates to decline. The fall in borrowing costs stimulates additional spending. Since the automatic easing of credit conditions is caused by the decline in income and employment, it can hardly restore the economy to the previous level of activity, but it will serve the useful function of checking the decline and making it less severe. Conversely, if a strengthening of private demand for goods and services generates an increase in income, employment, and perhaps price level, the increased demand for money to meet expanded transactions will cause interest rates to rise; this will automatically retard spending, thereby slowing the expansion to some degree.

DISCRETIONARY MONETARY POLICY   If the economy is suffering from an unduly high rate of unemployment, the Federal Reserve can take positive action to accelerate economic activity by speeding its purchases of United States government securities in the open market. This action will serve directly to bid up the prices of government securities and bring down their yields and, in addition, provide the commercial banks with additional reserves with which they can carry out a multiple expansion of loans and investments, increasing the money supply in the process. If the member banks are in debt to the Federal Reserve, a fall in short-term market interest rates with the discount rate unchanged will reduce the profitability of such borrowing and may cause the banks to repay some of their indebtedness to the Federal Reserve, thereby reducing bank reserves and offsetting a portion of the expansionary effect of the initial Federal Reserve open-market purchases. For this reason, the System may accompany the open-market purchases with a reduction in the discount rate to discourage the repayment of member-bank borrowings. There can be little doubt that by vigorous use of its instruments of credit control, particularly open-market operations, the Federal Reserve can produce a sufficient decline in interest rates to impart a substantial expansionary effect to the economy in periods of recession. As will be explained below, however, vigorous use of monetary policy to counter recessionary tendencies may be impracticable if the nation is suffering from a severe balance-of-payments deficit at the same time, since a sharp decline in interest rates under these conditions may cause investors to shift money out of the country in search of higher interest rates abroad, thereby increasing the deficit.

Monetary policy must be viewed in the context of a growing economy.

Productive capacity, defined as the total output that can be produced by the economy at full employment, increases each year as a result of growth of the labor force, improvement in the quality of labor through education and training, increase in the size and quality of the stock of capital resulting from investment, and advances in technology. Productive capacity appears to have been growing at a rate of 3½ to 4 percent per year in recent years. To maintain full employment, aggregate demand must expand in pace with the growth of productive capacity. To satisfy the additional demand for money associated with the expansion in economic activity, bank reserves and money supply must grow from year to year. Discretionary countercyclical monetary policy therefore involves acceleration of the rate of growth of bank reserves and the money supply in periods of recession to reduce interest rates and stimulate business activity. On the other hand, when the economy is operating at full employment but demand is rising more rapidly than productive capacity, a restrictive monetary policy is needed to prevent inflation; the Federal Reserve may implement such a policy by slowing the growth of bank reserves so that the supply of money and credit will expand less rapidly than demand. This will cause interest rates to rise and credit conditions to tighten and thus will serve to check the excessive growth of demand, helping to bring it into line with the growth of capacity. It is important to understand that a restrictive policy is seldom applied with such vigor as to result in an actual reduction in bank reserves and money supply for any substantial period of time. Rather, it normally involves a slowing down in the rate of increase of reserves and money.

Available empirical evidence indicates that monetary policy affects the demand for goods and services primarily by producing changes in interest rates and other terms of lending. The effects of changes in interest rates and credit conditions are not uniformly distributed over all components of demand. The elements of demand most likely to be affected by monetary policy appear to be the following: residential construction; business investment in plant and equipment and inventories; demand for consumer durable goods such as automobiles and home appliances; and capital outlays for schools, highways, and the like by state and local governments. Despite an increasing amount of econometric and other research in recent years, there is still considerable uncertainty about the magnitudes of the effects of monetary policy on these various types of expenditures. Such effects as are present are due in part to the fact that rising interest rates increase the cost of obtaining borrowed funds to finance spending, in part to imperfections in capital markets and institutional arrangements that make particular types of expenditures sensitive to credit conditions. For example, because of the existence of usury laws and customs relating to loan interest rates, together with the fact that loan markets, especially for smaller business enterprises, are frequently dominated by a small number of commercial banks, loan rates are relatively inflexible and the impact of monetary policy on bank loans partly takes the form of changes in the availability of loans at given interest rates.

Residential construction is clearly more sensitive to monetary policy than any other component of aggregate demand. This sensitivity can be attributed primarily to certain institutional peculiarities of the mortgage market. One is that interest rates on mortgages are sluggish and do not readily adjust to changes in monetary conditions. As a result, when credit conditions tighten and interest rates rise, some important lenders in the mortgage market (such as life insurance companies) rechannel their flows of investment funds away from mortgages and into corporate and other securities whose yields have risen relative to the interest rates on mortgages. As a result, households desiring to purchase houses may be unable to obtain mortgage loans, even though they would willingly pay the going interest rate. The sluggishness of mortgage interest rates is partly due to ceilings imposed by the federal government on interest rates that can be charged on mortgages insured by the Federal Housing Administration (FHA) and guaranteed by the Veterans Administration (VA). In addition, the fact that there is no well-developed secondary market for mortgages—where old mortgages can readily be bought and sold at prices that vary with market conditions—probably reduces the flexibility of mortgage interest rates.

In the past few years, it seems clear that investors have become increasingly sensitive to interest rates in allocating their savings among different types of financial assets. For example, when interest rates on time deposits in commercial banks or on marketable securities rise relative to returns obtainable from savings and loan shares, many investors will withdraw funds from savings and loan associations and place them in the higher-yielding assets. Since savings and loan associations invest almost all their funds in mortgages of long maturity, only a small portion of which is repaid and therefore available for reinvestment in any given short period of time, they derive relatively little immediate benefit from a rise in interest rates. As a result, it is difficult for them to raise the interest rates they pay on shares without encountering operating losses. They therefore find it difficult to compete with commercial banks and marketable securities during periods of sharply rising interest rates. Thus, in a period of restrictive monetary policy, the net flow of funds into savings and loan associations may fall sharply, and because they are the most important mortgage lenders, the volume of funds available to finance housing construction may contract abruptly. This occurred during the period of tight money in 1966 and was probably the chief cause of the decline of $6 billion in the annual rate of residential construction expenditures from the first to the fourth quarter of that year.

The sensitivity of *business investment in plant and equipment* to changes in interest rates is considerably blunted by the extensive risks involved in such investment. To illustrate, a business firm may not be willing to take the risk involved in building a new plant unless it expects a return of 25 or 30 percent on the investment. If it is expecting a return of this magnitude, why should its decision to invest be significantly affected by an increase from 5 to 6 percent in its borrowing costs? In addition to the basic factor of risk, the response of investment to changes in interest rates is further reduced by such institutional peculiarities as the tendency of United States business concerns to finance a large portion of their investment from retained earnings and depreciation allowances rather than by borrowing in the capital markets, and the fact that interest costs are deductible in computing business income tax liabilities. In spite of these considerations, recent research indicates that business investment does respond to changes in monetary policy and interest rates, although it takes a long time for the response to make itself felt.

Demand for consumer durable goods is no doubt sensitive to changes in the terms on which consumer installment credit is available, but the elaborate institutional arrangements for providing consumer credit serve to shield it effectively from changes in general credit conditions, with the result that the impact of monetary policy on this particular component of demand is not great. *Capital expenditures by state and local government units* are sensitive to changes in interest rates on security flotations of these units, partly as a result of statutory limits on the interest rates they can pay.

The initial impact of monetary policy on expenditures of various kinds is magnified through the operation of the *multiplier*. For example, an easing of monetary policy in a period of excessive unemployment will produce an initial impact on investment, broadly defined to include residential construction, state and local government outlays, and so on. This will stimulate production and create income, thereby leading to further consumption expenditures and further production and income creation, in a series of rounds. Empirical studies indicate that the multiplier is approximately 2 for the U.S. economy—that is, that through consumption effects alone the initial impact of monetary policy on investment will ultimately be magnified into an increase in gross national product equal to about twice the impact. Beyond this, the increase in sales and production may increase business profits and narrow the margin of idle plant capacity, thereby stimulating additional private investment demand. Such induced investment may add substantially to the effects on GNP produced by the multiplier, but this element of the magnification is difficult to judge and undoubtedly varies from one situation to another.

There are substantial *time lags* in the effects of monetary policy. There is a lag between Federal Reserve action and the appearance of a change in interest rates and credit conditions sufficient to affect expenditures significantly. The length of this lag undoubtedly depends on the environment in which the action is taken. For example, if commercial banks and business concerns possess large stocks of liquid assets such as short-term United States government securities at a time when the Federal Reserve is attempting to apply a restrictive policy, it may be possible for the economic units involved to dispose of these liquid assets in the market to obtain funds to lend or spend, and, as a result, some of the effects of monetary policy will be postponed until these stocks of liquid assets have been worked through. After interest rates and other credit terms have been changed to a sufficient degree to influence spending decisions, there will be a further lapse of time before these altered decisions have produced their effects on production, income, employment, and prices. The lags in the impact of monetary policy are undoubtedly distributed lags—that is, the impact is not felt all at once after a discrete delay but rather is spread out over time, probably building up gradually to a climax and then declining. Precise estimation of the lags by econometric or other techniques is difficult, and research on the subject is in its early stages. The lags are undoubtedly different for different types of expenditures, and they may well vary substantially from one situation to another. Although there is considerable uncertainty—and even controversy among students of United States monetary policy—concerning the lags, it seems likely that two to four quarter-years may elapse before a change in monetary policy produces the major part of its impact on demand. Of course, still further time lags are involved in the secondary multiplier and induced-investment effects on consumption and investment, referred to above.

The existence of lags in the effect of monetary policy is a source of serious practical difficulties. Some American monetary theorists believe that the lags are so long and erratic that any attempt to conduct a discretionary monetary policy is likely to introduce another element of instability—or at least of erratic random variation—into the economy, thereby decreasing rather than increasing overall economic stability. Those who hold this belief have advocated the complete abandonment of discretionary monetary policy and the adoption by the Federal Reserve of a policy of increasing the money supply at a steady rate in accordance with the long-term-trend rate of increase of GNP, after allowance for secular movement of the velocity of money circulation. The majority of United States monetary experts, however, feel that discretionary monetary policy, even though handicapped by the existence of lags, can make a net contribution to economic stability. The existence of lags clearly means that policy decisions must be based on implicit or explicit forecasts of future economic conditions and must be adjusted as these conditions change.

Monetary Policy and the Balance of Payments   Prior to the restoration of currency convertibility in Western Europe in 1958, capital did not move freely across international borders. Moreover, the United States had a very large gold reserve, and foreign central banks were glad to accept dollars in settlement of our deficits to build up reserves depleted during World War II. Under these conditions, the Federal Reserve was able to direct its policies almost entirely toward achieving the domestic goals of full employment and reasonable price stability without worrying about the balance of payments. Under a regime of convertible currencies such as now exists, however, money moves readily from one country to another. As a result, there is now a vast and growing quantity of money capital whose owners are constantly seeking the highest possible returns and shifting investments from one country to another in response to relatively small differences in interest rates. Moreover, many large business enterprises finance investment in plants and machinery by borrowing on bond issues or bank loans in the country where interest rates and other credit terms are the most favorable. At the same time, the countries of Western Europe have rebuilt their monetary reserves in the form of dollars and gold; consequently, foreign holdings of dollar claims that are convertible into gold have greatly increased, while the United States gold stock available for redeeming them has been reduced. The result is that foreign central banks are much less willing than formerly to accept dollars in settlement of United States balance-of-payments deficits.

Under these conditions, the Federal Reserve has to conduct monetary policy with one eye on the domestic economy and the other on the balance of payments. If an easy monetary policy causes interest rates to be appreciably lower or credit more readily available in the United States than in other countries with reasonably well-organized capital markets (such as the United Kingdom, Canada, and countries of Western Europe), investors are likely to shift existing money capital out of the United States, and foreign business enterprises can be expected to raise more new capital in the United States.

In addition to capital flows, monetary policy affects exports and imports of goods and services. An easing of monetary policy that stimulates aggregate demand will increase domestic income and employment and may also cause prices to rise. Rising income and production will stimulate the demand for imported consumer goods as well as imported materials. If prices rise, this will make home-produced goods more expensive relative to goods produced in other countries, thereby further stimulating imports and discouraging exports.

Thus, an easing of monetary policy will affect both the capital balance and the trade balance in such a way as to move the overall balance of payments toward a deficit. Conversely, a tightening of monetary policy which raises domestic interest rates will reduce the outflow of capital, reduce imports, and increase exports, thereby moving the balance of payments toward a surplus.

If the country is simultaneously suffering from unemployment and experiencing a balance-of-payments surplus, an easing of monetary policy may be doubly desirable: it will help to raise income and employment and also reduce the surplus through its effects on both capital movements and trade in goods and services. Likewise, if inflation coexists with a balance-of-payments deficit, a tighter monetary policy will help to solve both problems.

Under some circumstances, however, the authorities responsible for monetary policy are faced with a dilemma. Suppose, for example, that the country is experiencing heavy unemployment while at the same time the balance of payments shows a substantial deficit. An easier monetary policy would help correct the unemployment, but its effects on both current trade and capital flows would make the balance-of-payments deficit even larger. On the other hand, a tighter monetary policy would improve the balance-of-payments position but would accentuate the domestic unemployment problem.

In such a situation, it is better strategy to rely on fiscal than on monetary policy to correct the domestic unemployment. A reduction in tax rates or an increase in government expenditures would increase the flow of purchasing power and set in motion an increase in income and employment. The rise in income would lead to an increase in imports, thereby increasing the deficit on trade account. Indeed, the effect on trade in goods and services would probably be about the same as it would have been if the same expansion of income had been brought about by easier monetary policy. However, the effect on the capital account of the balance of payments would be quite different. The government would have to borrow to finance the deficit produced by the increase in expenditures or cut in taxes, and its borrowing would drive up interest rates. Moreover, the demand for money by households and businesses would increase as income rose and the volume of transactions increased, and this would also raise interest rates. Thus, expansionary fiscal action would cause interest rates to rise (unless, of course, the Federal Reserve were to prevent the rise by expanding the reserves available to the banks), and the rise in interest rates would reduce the capital outflow. Expansionary *fiscal* policy would worsen the trade balance and improve the capital balance, thereby having a less unfavorable effect on the balance of payments than would an equally expansionary *monetary* policy, which would worsen both the trade balance and the capital balance.

The opposite situation arises when a country is simultaneously experiencing domestic inflation and a balance-of-payments surplus. Under such circumstances, a restrictive monetary policy would help check the inflation, but it would affect both current trade and capital flows in such a way as to increase the balance-of-payments surplus. An easier monetary policy, on the other hand, would reduce the surplus but would accentuate the inflation. Under such conditions, the preferred strategy would be to employ a restrictive fiscal policy—implemented by reducing government spending or increasing tax rates—to check inflation. Although such a policy would be likely to increase the trade surplus, it would at the same time reduce the government's need to borrow to cover its budget deficit and reduce private credit demands, thereby lowering interest rates and reducing the surplus on capital account. That is, a restrictive fiscal policy would be likely to increase the balance-of-payments surplus less than would an equally restrictive monetary policy.

Under present conditions, the balance of payments may, under some circumstances, impose severe constraints on the ability of the United States to use monetary policy vigorously for the achievement of domestic goals. It would probably be impossible to pursue a vigorous expansionary monetary policy in time of recession without permitting short-term interest rates to fall to the levels (about 1 percent) that prevailed at the bottoms of the recessions of 1953–1954 and 1957–1958. If the balance of payments was in serious deficit, such a drastic decline in short-term interest rates would clearly be intolerable. As this is being written, the United States is experiencing inflationary pressures while the balance of payments is still in deficit. Under these circumstances, there is no conflict between the objectives of external and internal stability—tighter monetary policy and higher interest rates will, within limits, help both to check inflation and to reduce the deficit. However, if at some future time the country should experience domestic inflation when the balance of payments was in surplus, a conflict would again be present. Under such conditions, a restrictive monetary policy would help check inflation but would increase the surplus. While the limit on the size and duration of a balance-of-payments surplus is much less rigid than that imposed on a deficit by the limitation on the available supply of international monetary reserves, the adoption of a restrictive monetary policy when the balance of payments is in surplus has the effect of increasing the deficits of some other countries and may cause serious difficulties for them. Thus, responsible membership in an international monetary system of the kind now existing may, under some circumstances, impose constraints on a country's freedom to use monetary policy vigorously to counter unemployment or inflation. Recognition of these constraints clearly points to the importance of increased flexibility in the use of fiscal policy for domestic stabilization purposes, not only in the United States but in other countries as well.

INTEREST RATES OR MONEY STOCK?

The reader should be aware of the fact that there is some controversy regarding monetary policy. Indeed, it can be said that there are two schools of thought on the subject: the *money school* and the *credit school*.[2] The money school, whose views descend directly from the historic quantity theory of money, emphasizes a direct relation between money and income, paying relatively little attention to interest rates or credit availability. The credit school, of which the author may be counted a member and whose views are reflected in this chapter, emphasizes the detailed linkages—primarily involving interest rates and credit conditions—through which Federal Reserve action affects spending, attaching relatively little importance to the money supply as a causal factor. The credit school also pays considerable attention to the institutional arrangements by which credit is channeled to particular sectors of the economy, such as housing, and to changes in financial practices, on the ground that such institutional features of the financial system may significantly influence the way monetary policy works. Members of the money school, on the other hand, assign relatively little importance to such institutional and structural factors, apparently on the ground that they do not significantly affect the responses of the economy to changes in the money stock.

The money school attaches much weight to the relation that can be shown to have long existed between changes in the money stock and changes in income. Historically, a rapid growth of the money stock has tended to be associated with a rapid growth of money income, and vice versa, although the relationship is ragged and imperfect.[3] Of course, the credit school recognizes that the kind of Federal Reserve action which would reduce interest rates and make credit more readily available would also ordinarily cause the money stock to increase. Thus, the existence of a somewhat loose but positive relation between changes in money and changes in income should not come as a surprise to a member of the credit school. However, he would not attach causal significance to this relationship per se, but would prefer to look behind the relationship in his search for the detailed links through which Federal Reserve actions affect spending and income.

---

[2] Any effort to split students of monetary policy into two schools of thought, as I have attempted to do, necessarily involves some oversimplification. In particular, there are differences among economists whom I would classify as members of the credit school concerning the channels through which Federal Reserve action is transmitted to the real sector of the economy. Nevertheless, in my opinion, there is sufficient similarity in spirit among members of this group to justify classifying them as advocates of the same general approach.

[3] See [2, pp. 241–256]; also see Friedman's monumental study [4]. For a perceptive critique of Friedman's work, see [8, pp. 464–485].

Members of the credit school generally look upon demand deposits and currency—which together make up the money stock as usually defined—as simply financial assets inherently no more or no less important than other kinds of financial assets, such as time deposits, savings and loan shares, and United States government securities. Econometric studies of the determinants of expenditures on final output have consistently shown that several categories of such expenditures are affected by interest rates or credit availability.[4] To my knowledge, no such study has shown that the money stock has a significant effect on any category of expenditures. Nor is there any a priori reason to think that the money stock will have any more significant effect on spending than will any other of a considerable variety of financial assets. A good deal of current research in the monetary field is directed along lines favored by the credit school—that is, it is designed to uncover the detailed links through which specific Federal Research actions affect particular forms of spending, such as business expenditures for plant and equipment and inventories, residential construction expenditures, consumer spending on durable goods, and capital outlays by state and local governments.[5]

Some members of the money school hold the view that fiscal policy has relatively little independent influence on overall economic activity. If there is a rigid link between money and income, as members of the money school often believe, income cannot be changed significantly except by changes in the stock of money. An increase in government expenditures would then draw resources from the private into the public sector, but, except to the extent that it was accompanied by an increase in the money stock, would not significantly affect *total* demand. The need by the government to increase its borrowing (or decrease its debt retirement) to cover increased expenditures in the absence of a tax increase would raise interest rates enough to depress private spending by about as much as public spending had increased.[6] Members of the credit school, on the other hand, generally believe that fiscal policy has a substantial effect on aggregate demand independently of changes in the money stock. Increased government spending unaccompanied by a tax increase would

---

[4] Perhaps the most comprehensive econometric work on the effects of monetary factors on different types of spending is that incorporated in the model of the economy now being developed by a team of economists at the Federal Reserve Board and the Massachusetts Institute of Technology. The preliminary results of this study are summarized in [6].

[5] This is the objective of the Federal Reserve–M.I.T. study referred to in the previous footnote. The paper by de Leeuw and Gramlich [6] contains some simulations designed to trace the economic effects over time of certain monetary (and fiscal) policy actions. Other comprehensive models designed for analyzing the economic impact of monetary policy include [5] and [7].

[6] See [3, pp. 79–84].

increase the government's need to borrow, and thereby would cause interest rates to rise. However, the rise in interest rates would induce economization of money balances, thereby releasing money to finance additional economic activity without depressing private spending as much as public spending had increased.

In my opinion, the bulk of the available theoretical reasoning and empirical evidence supports the view that interest rates and credit availability rather than the stock of money are of primary importance, and that both monetary and fiscal policy are capable of exerting independent effects on income, employment, and prices.

CONCLUDING COMMENTS

I have attempted to explain the working of monetary policy in the United States and to summarize some of the recent thinking concerning it. In conclusion, I would like to point out two things. First, there has been much theoretical and empirical research concerning monetary policy in the United States in the past few years, and more research is now in progress. We may thus hope to achieve a more precise knowledge of the effects of Federal Reserve policy. Second, the United States banking and financial system is a dynamic one, which is constantly generating innovations that change the financial environment and may influence the functioning of monetary policy, making it difficult to arrive at durable truths in this field. An example of this kind of financial innovation is the development and increased use of the negotiable time certificate of deposit, which has occurred since 1961. The so-called CD has enabled the banks to compete more effectively with other financial institutions and with marketable securities through the payment of interest on deposits, and, in the process, has added a new complication that must be taken into account in the analysis of financial markets and the study of monetary policy. We can be sure from experience that further innovations will occur in banking and finance, and that theoretical and empirical research concerning monetary policy will have to be continually modified to take account of these innovations.

REFERENCES

1. CHANDLER, LESTER V. *The Economics of Money and Banking,* 4th ed. (New York: Harper & Row, 1964).
2. FRIEDMAN, MILTON. "The Supply of Money and Changes in Prices and Output," U.S. Congress, Joint Economic Committee, *The Relationship of Prices to Economic Stability and Growth* (1958), pp. 241–256.
3. ———. *Capitalism and Freedom* (Chicago: University of Chicago Press, 1962).

4 ———. *A Monetary History of the United States 1867–1960*, National Bureau of Economic Research, Studies in Business Cycles, No. 12 (Princeton, N.J.: Princeton University Press, 1963).

5 GOLDFELD, STEPHEN M. *Commercial Bank Behavior and Economic Activity* (Amsterdam: North-Holland, 1966).

6 DE LEEUW, FRANK, and EDWARD GRAMLICH. "The Federal Reserve—M.I.T. Econometric Model," in *The Economic Outlook for 1968*, Papers Presented to the Fifteenth Annual Conference on the Economic Outlook of the University of Michigan (Ann Arbor: University of Michigan, Department of Economics, 1968), pp. 51–109; reprinted in the *Federal Reserve Bulletin*, January 1968, pp. 11–40.

7 TEIGEN, RONALD L. "An Aggregated Quarterly Model of the U.S. Monetary Sector, 1953–1964," Paper Presented at a Conference on Targets and Indicators of Monetary Policy, held at the University of California at Los Angeles, April 1966 (to be published).

8 TOBIN, JAMES. "The Monetary Interpretation of History: A Review Article," *American Economic Review*, 55:3 (June 1965), pp. 464–485.

7
FISCAL POLICY

Robert W. Hartman *

IN its most general sense, fiscal policy is the study of how government income and spending actions affect the economic behavior of the nation. Under the heading "fiscal" are included:

TAXES   Since we deal exclusively with the federal government in this chapter, the major taxes considered are the individual income tax, the corporation income tax, and the employment (payroll) tax. These constitute 80 percent of federal tax receipts. The remaining tax receipts are made up of excise taxes, unemployment insurance taxes, estate and gift taxes, customs receipts, and numerous minor items.

EXPENDITURES   The expenditures of the federal government consist of two major components: purchases of goods and services, and transfer payments. In recent years, purchases of goods and services accounted for about 55 percent of total federal spending. The key characteristic of these expenditures is that they directly absorb goods and services; an additional one dollar of expenditures on goods and services immediately diverts one dollar's worth of resources from the private sector (or from the ranks of the unemployed). Far and away the largest category of purchases of goods and services is national defense. Transfer payments are government outlays that do not directly absorb output but rather redistribute income to various

* Brookings Institution.

persons and institutions; an increase of one dollar in transfer expenditure, thus, does not constitute a claim on one dollar's worth of resources in the private economy, but rather adds to someone's purchasing power. The largest component of these expenditures is transfer payments to persons, including social security and unemployment compensation payments. Additional major components are the interest on the federal debt and grants to state and local governments.[1]

These three broad elements of fiscal policy are the instruments that the federal government can use to affect economic activity. Although it has an impact on many national economic goals, fiscal policy is of major importance in influencing the fundamental goal of full employment. In the first part of this chapter, we will discuss the impact of fiscal policy on the attainment of full employment.

FISCAL POLICY IN THE SHORT RUN

The modern economic theory of employment[*] runs as follows: At any point in time, the government must establish a "target rate of unemployment," on the basis of its assessment of the social and economic costs and benefits of too high an unemployment rate (recession) versus too low an unemployment rate (inflation). Suppose the target unemployment rate is 4 percent. Then "full employment" exists whenever the labor force is 96 percent employed. Associated with this level of employment is a rate of national production or "full-employment GNP." That is, at any point in time there is some level of gross national product that will just fully employ the labor force. That level is full-employment GNP or "potential output." Actual GNP, on the other hand, depends on the level of *aggregate demand* in the economy. The three major components of aggregate demand are consumption expenditures, private investment expenditures, and government expenditures on goods and services. At any point in time, actual GNP will be determined by the strength of these three expenditure components.

The unemployment rate depends on the gap between full-employment GNP and aggregate demand. If aggregate demand is below full-employment GNP, the unemployment level will exceed the target rate (4 percent). If aggregate demand exceeds full-employment GNP, unemployment will fall below 4 percent, producing an undesired rate of inflation. Only if

---

[1] The federal budget also includes the lending activity of the federal government. These loan disbursements and repayments are similar in their economic effects to the monetary policies pursued by the Federal Reserve System and are beyond the scope of this chapter.

[*] This topic is discussed at greater length in Chapter 5, "Macroeconomic Theory."

aggregate demand and full-employment GNP are equal will unemployment be "on target" without undesired inflationary pressure.

If fiscal policy is to be used as a major instrument in achieving full employment, its job can be summarized as follows: fiscal policy should be adjusted to equate aggregate demand with full-employment GNP. Fiscal policy's role, in the short run, is through the aggregate-demand side of this equation. That is, given potential output, fiscal policy's purpose is to regulate the level of aggregate demand so that full employment results.

How do the three components of fiscal policy enumerated above—government expenditures on goods and services G, taxes T, and transfers R—affect the level of aggregate demand? In a rough sense the answer to this question is obvious. G is a component of aggregate demand, and therefore an increase in G obviously raises demand; a lowering of G reduces demand. T affects the incomes of households and firms, and an increase in T, by lowering after-tax income, reduces spending; a reduction in T raises after-tax incomes and thus raises demand. An increase in R adds to purchasing power and thus raises demand, while a reduction in R lowers spendable incomes and demand. It is tempting to put these facts together in this way: Define the federal budget surplus S to be equal to T-R-G. In a rough way, we could then say that as S rises, aggregate demand falls (since an increase in S means that T rises, or R falls, or G falls), while a reduction in the federal surplus would indicate that fiscal policy is increasing demand (since a fall in S is equivalent to a reduction in T, or a rise in G, or a rise in R). This kind of analysis was quite popular among Keynesian economists until recent years. It is the basis for such statements as, "If the economy is suffering from unemployment, the budget deficit should be increased" (that is, S must be lowered so as to raise aggregate demand).

Unfortunately, the budget surplus as a measure of fiscal policy suffers from a critical flaw, and fiscal economists today do not use it to represent the economic impact of the budget. The flaw is this: changes in the budget surplus are caused not only by purposive changes in fiscal policy *but also by an automatic response to the level of income in the nation.* Thus, even if Congress passes no new tax or spending programs, the actual budget surplus will fall as the economy declines, mainly because tax revenues will drop. This type of "passive" reduction in the budget surplus does not stimulate aggregate demand, but only moderates the size of the decline in GNP. It is this responsiveness of the tax system to swings in the economy (sometimes called the automatic fiscal stabilizer) that has necessitated the development of a new gauge of the economic impact of fiscal policy.

The "New Economics"[2] uses as its gauge of fiscal impact the full-employment surplus (FES)—the surplus that would accrue in the federal budget if the economy were at its full-employment level.[3] To calculate this measure we would estimate total tax revenue at full-employment GNP and subtract government expenditures on goods and services and transfer payments at full employment. The key to the usefulness of the measure is that it is independent of the level of GNP itself; the only way that the FES can change is if Congress uses its discretionary powers and alters tax *rates* or alters the level of transfer payments or government expenditures. Thus, the FES, unlike the actual budget surplus, is an unambiguous measure of discretionary fiscal policy. Expressed in terms of the FES, the rules for fiscal policy in attaining the full-employment objective are simple to state:

> *If the economy is less than fully employed, the FES should be lowered.*[4]
> *If aggregate demand exceeds full-employment GNP and there is inflationary pressure, the FES should be raised.*[5]

Suppose, for example, that the economy were operating at a level of unemployment of 7 percent. A large federal budget deficit might exist at the time. Our analysis indicates, nevertheless, that the FES should be cut—through tax reductions or spending increases. Suppose that spending is increased by $10 billion. Then the FES is reduced by $10 billion, but the *actual budget deficit is not reduced by $10 billion.* The reason for this is that the expenditure increase raises the level of GNP, and, as GNP rises, tax receipts rise. Thus, part of the expenditure increase generates income (tax revenues) to the government.

Now that we have an idea of the direction of change in the FES under various circumstances, it is time to ask how large a change in the FES is necessary to close a gap of given size between aggregate demand and full-employment GNP. Let us assume, for example, that aggregate demand is $10 billion below full-employment GNP.

The first point to make is that the FES should be reduced by less than $10 billion. This follows from the fact that changes in government spending and taxing have a multiplier effect on GNP. For example, an

---

[2] This is the name given to the macroeconomic policies pursued by Presidents Kennedy and Johnson in the 1960s. The intellectual foundations of the New Economics were laid in the 1930s by John Maynard Keynes. Those who oppose the New Economics probably don't trust anything over 30.

[3] If the FES is negative—that is, if, at full employment, taxes fall short of G and R— we might refer to the "full-employment deficit." These concepts are sometimes referred to in the literature as the "high-employment" surplus or deficit.

[4] At any point in time, the FES can be lowered only through a reduction in tax rates or an increase in G or R.

[5] At any point in time, the FES can be raised only through increased tax rates or a reduction in G or R.

increase in G of $10 billion would immediately increase GNP by $10 billion (since G is a component of GNP), but the GNP would rise more in subsequent periods. The reasons for this are:

1 Consumer incomes will rise as a result of higher employment and earnings in those industries supplying the government with $10 billion of new goods and services. As consumers' incomes rise, they spend more, thus generating new consumer-goods production and incomes.

2 Business profits will rise in the industries supplying the government with the new goods. Higher business profits may induce higher expenditures on capital goods and inventories, thus generating new investment output and income.

3 State and local governments will find their tax receipts rising from these newly generated incomes, and they too may expand their spending.

4 There is a possible offsetting factor to these three items. It is that as the federal government spends more, it will have to finance the spending through the sale of newly issued government bonds ("deficit spending"). The sale of these bonds will increase interest rates in the economy, and this increase in interest rates may reduce certain types of spending—for example, home-building. Such offsetting factors are likely to be of small importance when unemployment is very large, but they may be more important as the economy approaches full employment.

These reasons suggest that the change in the level of federal spending or taxing need only make up part of the spending gap when unemployment exists. The rest of the $10 billion gap will be induced by the change in the FES in the form of new demand by consumers, businesses, and non-federal governments.

Beyond this we cannot go in this chapter. The exact size of the multiplier effect depends on what type of government fiscal action is taken. In general, government expenditures on goods and services have a high multiplier effect because all the spending directly affects aggregate demand. Tax reductions and transfer-payment increases, however, do not directly affect demand but instead increase the incomes of recipients. If these recipients *save* part of their increased income, GNP will not "multiply itself up" as much as in the case of increased G. But generalizations in this area are dangerous. For example, if the federal government makes a grant to a state government on the condition that the state government match the federal grant, spending might go up immediately by $2 for every $1 of increased federal transfer payment.[6] The safest generalization, for a change of a given size in the FES, is that the larger the marginal propensity to spend of the recipients of the new incomes, the greater the effect on aggregate demand.

[6] And GNP will rise even more, of course, as consumer and business income rises.

FISCAL POLICY

The decision as to the form the change in the FES should take, however, depends only in small part on the differences in multiplier effects. Far more crucial are the questions of public-private mix and of lags in effect. When there is excess unemployment, the required reduction in the FES can take the form of increased government spending or increased private spending (via a reduction in taxes or an increase in transfers to persons). The federal government must decide whether the public's welfare is better served through an expansion of public or private goods. There is no general way to show that emphasis on one of these categories is always preferable to emphasis on the other. A value judgment is required to weigh the public's marginal utility from each type of good.

Our discussion of multipliers has ignored the fact that the various expenditure and tax changes that compose the change in FES affect aggregate demand with varying time lags. That is, the period between the decision to spend more (or tax less) and the actual occurrence of the spending may vary greatly among federal programs. Suffice it to say here that a program to reduce unemployment (or reduce inflation) immediately must include some items with very short time lags. A road-building project may have a very large multiplier effect, and it may be needed on public versus private grounds; but it may take a very long time to realize. By contrast, an increase in transfer payments to unemployed workers may not have so large a multiplier effect, but it would get the expenditure level up quickly.

The Relationship between Fiscal Policy and Monetary Policy in the Short Run

Fiscal policy is not the only instrument available to the government for affecting full employment in the short run. The operations of the central bank (in the United States, the Federal Reserve System) also influence the level of spending in the economy.* Thus, the fiscal policy (level of FES) appropriate at any point in time depends in part on what role monetary policy is taking. The interdependence of fiscal and monetary policy can best be shown on a "policy mix" diagram (see Figure 7-1).

On the vertical axis we plot various levels of the FES. As we move up in the diagram, fiscal policy becomes tighter and more restrictive— the FES is getting larger. Downward movements represent more expansive fiscal policy, as the FES is lowered. On the horizontal axis, it is sufficient for our purposes here to think of movements to the right as representing tighter (more restrictive) monetary policy, while movements to the left represent easier (more expansive) monetary policy.[7]

---

* See Chapter 6, "Monetary Institutions and Policies."
[7] Movements to the right involve higher interest rates and a slowly growing money supply, while movements to the left represent rapid money supply growth and lower interest rates.

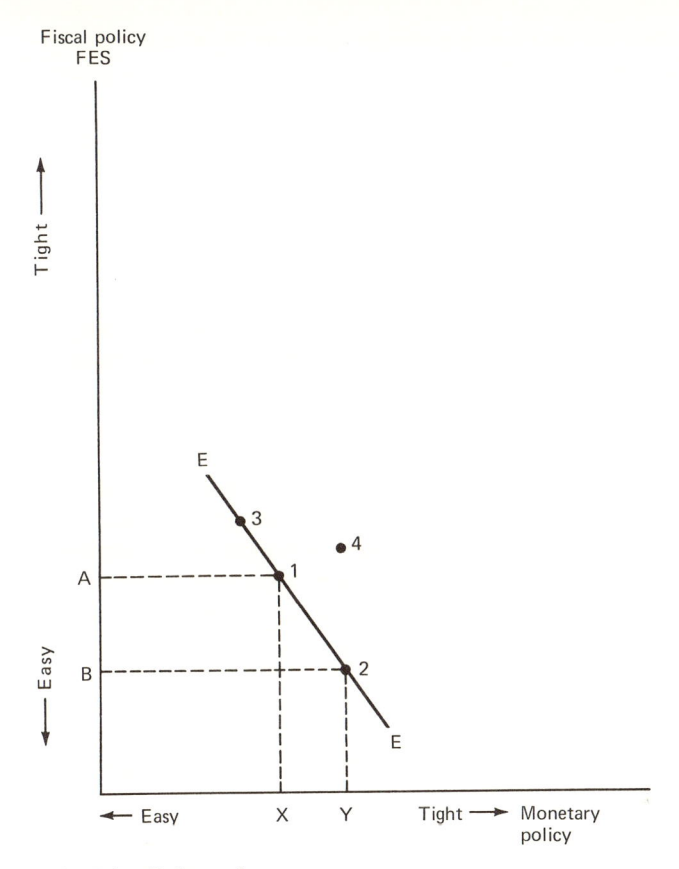

FIG. 7-1 Policy mix.

We can summarize our discussion up to this point as follows. Given the level of monetary policy at X, the FES that will lead to full employment in the economy is A. Thus, point 1 on Figure 7-1 represents a combination of policies, fiscal and monetary, compatible with full employment. If monetary policy, alternatively, were at the level Y, the FES would have to be reduced to B in order to generate a fully employed economy, because the tighter monetary policy at Y will discourage some spending. Thus, point 2 is another combination of monetary and fiscal policy compatible with full employment. It is obvious that an infinite variety of policy mixes compatible with full employment can be found. We show these as the line $E\ E$. All policies inside this line will overheat the economy, driving aggregate demand above full-employment GNP. All combinations of policy to the right of $E\ E$ will result in excessive unemployment: aggregate demand will fall short of full-employment GNP.

FISCAL POLICY

EE can thus be used as a guide to full-employment fiscal policy at various levels of monetary policy.

In the simple world with which we have been dealing, the role of fiscal policy is quite clear. As long as the nation is concerned with only one goal—full employment— and as long as two broad policy instruments— the full-employment surplus and monetary policy—are available, there is an infinite variety of combinations of instruments that will achieve the full-employment goal. The real world of economic policy is not so simple. It is complicated, on the one hand, by goals that compete (and conflict) with full employment and, on the other hand, by constraints on the rapidity with which full employment can be attained. Let us consider these one at a time.

Competing Goals Although all points on the EE policy-mix line result in an identical level of aggregate demand and employment, the level of interest rates will be vastly different as we move along the line. Such differences in interest rates have implications for the balance-of-payments position of the nation and for the rate of growth of potential output. To understand this, consider the economy to be at point 1 on the policy-mix diagram. Suppose that monetary and fiscal policy were coordinated in such a way as to move the economy to the right along the policy-mix line (to point 2). This change would involve a reduction in the full-employment surplus (stimulating aggregate demand) along with a tighter monetary policy (raising interest rates and lowering aggregate demand). This alternative policy mix would leave aggregate demand unchanged, but would raise interest rates in the domestic economy. While there is no reason to expect the volume of exports or imports to significantly change as the economic policy moves from 1 to 2, it is reasonable to expect some change in the capital accounts of the balance of payments. In particular, if domestic interest rates were to rise relative to interest rates in the rest of the world, some of the consequences would be as follows:

> *Some Americans who previously placed funds abroad would bring them back home.*
> *Foreigners who contemplated borrowing from Americans would divert their quest for funds to cheaper sources abroad.*
> *Foreigners who sought maximum return on idle funds would shift their funds to United States securities and banks.*

The upshot of these reactions is that movements to the right along the policy-mix line will improve the United States balance-of-payments position by causing an inflow of dollars from world capital markets.

It may seem tempting at this point to suggest that the "best" point on the policy-mix line is whichever point produces the desired balance-of-payments position along with full employment. However, a careful consideration of the domestic effects of movements along the policy-mix line suggests that the answer is not quite so simple. As the policy mix is changed from point 1 to point 2, the *composition* of aggregate demand is changed. Specifically, the higher interest rates of point 2 will in most circumstances lower the rate of investment in the economy (this reduction in demand is offset by higher consumption or government demand). Although such changes in the composition of aggregate demand are irrelevant for employment in the economy, they may have profound effects on the *rate of growth* of potential output. For a country to sustain a satisfactory increase in its ability to produce goods and services over time, it must provide an increased stock of capital goods. Investment in new plant and equipment must, in other words, be sufficiently large to provide for a growing labor force and for improvements in productivity.

As indicated above, the change in policy mix from point 1 to 2 improves the balance of payments, but we can now also say that the change slows up the rate of investment and reduces the economy's future potential output. Obviously, a move to the left along the policy-mix line, say to point 3, will worsen the balance-of-payments position, although it will quicken the rate of growth of potential output.

The necessity for a real-world economy to pay attention to its balance-of-payments position and growth rate as well as to its employment level poses one of the more intractable dilemmas in real-world policymaking. Under most circumstances (that is, barring some very good luck), it is impossible to manipulate fiscal policy and monetary policy in such a way as to achieve full employment, desired balance-of-payments position, and a satisfactory rate of economic growth.

In the post-1958 period, the United States has attempted to deal with these competing goals in essentially two ways. In the early part of the period, fiscal and monetary policies were regulated in such a way as to maintain a relatively high level of unemployment,[8] presumably in the hope that the United States balance-of-payments position could be kept under control (and also to prevent inflation). These policies, which amounted to abandoning the full-employment objective, did not work very well. The high rates of unemployment were a very high price to pay for the balance-of-payments objective; moreover, the balance-of-payments deficit during the period did not show a sizable trend toward improvement. The continuing slack in the economy, furthermore, held down the rate of growth of productivity.

In the early 1960s, the policies of stagnation were reversed on both the fiscal and monetary fronts. The full-employment surplus was slashed

---

[8] The policy mix was above the line $E\ E$.

from almost $15 billion in early 1960 to zero and less after 1965. The money supply grew rapidly during this period. As might be expected, the quickening rate of growth of demand posed a potential conflict with growth and balance-of-payments goals. The response to this threat was an attempt to supplement fiscal and monetary policies with new instruments of control. Among these new policies were:

The investment tax credit and new guidelines for depreciation of capital. These were changes in the tax law designed to spur investment through other means than an easier general monetary policy.

The interest equalization tax; curbs on lending and direct investment abroad; curbs on tourism. These were policies to improve the balance of payments despite the maintenance of a high rate of growth of demand in the United States.

Operation twist. This was an attempt to hold down interest rates on long-term securities (aiding growth) while allowing short-term interest rates to rise (helping the capital account in the balance of payments).

The verdict is not yet in on whether these measures supply enough added flexibility to fiscal and monetary policy to make feasible the simultaneous attainment of the goals of full employment, growth, and balance-of-payments equilibrium.

Speed of Attainment of Goals Our analysis has so far paid very little attention to the dynamics of adjusting the economy to changes in policy. In the real world of stabilization, how fast the economy tries to achieve its goals does make a difference. Two examples of the difficulties faced in the United States in recent years when policies changed too fast are the inflation of 1965–1966 and the disintermediation crisis of 1966. We shall use these to illustrate the problem.

INFLATION Between mid-1965 and mid-1966 the unemployment rate was driven down from almost 5 percent to less than 4 percent, largely as a result of a fiscal- and monetary-policy-induced expansion of aggregate demand. Defense expenditures, especially, increased rapidly, and monetary policy supported the expansion in demand; in terms of Figure 7-1, the policy mix was moving from the unemployment point 4 to the full-employment point 1 very quickly. The result of this rapid expansion in demand was a significant increase in the price level, the full impact of which was still working its way through the economy by early 1968. Why should increases in the price level be so dependent on the speed of expansion in aggregate demand? There are a number of reasons:

1 All sectors of the economy are not able to adjust their output quickly to a rapid expansion in demand. The "bottleneck" sectors respond to the rapid rise in demand by raising their prices. Moreover, if the out-

put of these sectors is widely used as an input elsewhere in the economy, the initial price increase will spread throughout the economy in the form of higher costs. A fast rate of growth of aggregate demand greatly increases the risk that some sectors will respond in this way. A slower rate of advance of demand would give industries time to expand their capacity and greatly reduce the risks of inflation.

2 There is a similar effect in labor markets. Even if overall demand is not excessive, some labor markets will have reached "full employment." As demand expands to the full-employment level, these tight labor markets are put under pressure and wage increases become excessive. Once again the wage increases may spread to other sectors of the economy. If demand were to advance more slowly toward the full-employment level, it would be possible that tight labor markets would be "cured" through new entrants into the labor force or through training programs. These responses cannot be counted on when demand expands rapidly.

3 A quickening of the rate of growth of demand may lead firms to mistakenly extrapolate this rate of growth into the future. The result of such expectational changes is that firms accelerate their orders for inventories and fixed capital goods and these changes worsen an already tight capacity situation. All kinds of artificial excess demands, and price increases, can be set off by such a process. Moreover, firms with latent market power, who have not used their power because of slack market conditions, are much more likely to exercise control over prices when demand expands rapidly than when it expands slowly.

In short, when economic policy moves too rapidly in instituting full employment, the dangers of inflation are virtually unavoidable. Although some economists express hope that wage-price guideposts (discussed below) can moderate the price increases, it is hard to see how the basic forces just described can be overcome through any policies short of wage-price controls. If there is a lesson to be learned from our recent fiscal and monetary policy experience, it is that to avoid inflation requires that the ascent to full employment be a slow and steady one. An even better lesson is that fiscal policy should not permit the economy to fall substantially below full employment in the mistaken belief that such policies conduce to price stability. They just postpone the day of reckoning and make the problem tougher at a later stage.

Part of the post-1965 inflation in the economy is attributable to the speed of adjustment factors just discussed. To stop the wage-price spiral from continuing would have required doses of both monetary and fiscal tightness in the 1967–1968 period. Increases in military expenditures and the requirements of new social welfare programs prevented the required tightness, and by late 1968 it was clear that the federal government was fanning inflation by moving inside line EE in the diagram above.

DISINTERMEDIATION AND ADMINISTRATIVE LAGS   The price inflation set off in 1965–1966 could have been avoided by fiscal policies designed to offset the booming military expenditures of the government. As we have seen, a reduction in government non-defense spending or an increase in federal taxes would have offset (or partially offset) the expansionary effects of rising defense outlays. Why were such offsets not introduced?

There was, first of all, some delay in *recognizing* what was happening to the economy. Economic forecasts are not perfect and the rise in military spending was unanticipated. However, by early 1966, there is reason to believe that most economists recognized that demand was expanding too rapidly. But even so, the federal non-defense budget was not notably restrictive in the following period. There are many reasons for this. First, drastic cutbacks in federal expenditures are almost impossible to make quickly. Expenditures today result from commitments made in the past, and unless an administration is willing to take the political consequences of welshing on past commitments, it cannot turn off the pipeline drastically. Moreover, federal taxes, given our present legislative process, cannot quickly be varied. Recent experience has shown that passage of a major tax change is an extremely time-consuming process.[9]

Here is a major flaw in our ability to regulate the economy through fiscal policy—it takes too long to adjust either side (expenditure or tax) of the budget. In 1966, the inability of fiscal policy to make a significant contribution to economic stabilization shifted the responsibility to monetary policy.

As we have seen, a reduction in the rate of growth of bank reserves and money can slow the rate of expansion of demand. By mid-1966, the Federal Reserve was engaging in just such a policy. There was an abrupt curtailment of bank reserves and the money supply began to drop. This turnaround in monetary policy was very severe compared to the expansionary policy during 1965. The rapidity of the change caused interest rates on government and corporate bonds to climb to their highest rate in decades. In response to the higher yields available in bond markets, households began to buy these securities instead of depositing funds with financial intermediaries such as savings and loan associations. This channeling of funds into direct security-purchase is called "disintermediation"; it stems from the inability of intermediaries to raise sufficiently rapidly the rates they pay their depositors. Given a gradual move to higher interest rates and tighter money, the savings and loan associations

---

[9] The income tax cut of 1964 was introduced to Congress in 1963, although the decision to lower taxes was made in 1962. See [8, chap. 1]. Similarly, the income tax surcharge of 1968 was over a year in the making.

could probably adjust their rates and remain competitive with government and corporate bonds. In the short period of rapidly rising rates in 1966, they could not compete effectively.

The result of "disintermediation" is very clear. The residential construction industry, which depends heavily on lending from intermediaries (especially savings and loan associations), was made to bear an enormous burden. Private housing starts fell by 50 percent (!) between December, 1965, and October, 1966. While this enormous reduction in construction activity contributed to moderating the inflationary tendencies in 1966, the inequitability of the impact of tight money was manifest. As the Council of Economic Advisers summarized the period, "The credit squeeze of 1966 had an impressive and beneficial restraining effect on overall demand. Its side effects were equally impressive but far less beneficial" [4, January 1967, p. 60].

The lesson of 1966 is that rapid changes in monetary policies have very uneven, and unfair, impacts on the various sectors of the economy. If monetary policy must be tightened, there is a limit on how fast the tightening should proceed. Moreover, it now seems evident that neither fiscal policy nor monetary policy should be made to bear the entire burden of achieving an adequate level of demand. The risks of too rapid a change in either instrument are considerable. Some of the proposals now under study in this area are:

Presidential power to vary tax rates without Congressional action.
New controls over the banking and intermediary system designed to diffuse the effects of tight money.
New federal programs to alleviate the problem of bottleneck sectors in the economy.

The rudiments of the economic theory of fiscal policy in the short run are by now well understood by economists. But the fiscal and monetary instruments now available to us may not be adequate in a world of competing objectives. Moreover, delays in varying the FES may overburden monetary policy and reduce the freedom of economic policy.

FISCAL POLICY IN THE LONGER RUN

Up to this point we have discussed the problem of fiscal policy as it might be viewed at a single point in time. We have discussed the effects of fiscal policy on bringing aggregate demand up to the level of a given potential output. As we look at the economy over time, however, we must consider the fact that potential output does not stand still. A growing labor force and productivity advances enlarge the size of full-employment GNP. Economic growth offers both a challenge and an opportunity to fiscal policy.

The Challenge As the potential output of the economy grows, with *given tax rates*, the total tax revenue of the federal government will increase as personal and corporate incomes rise. These automatic increases in federal revenues, unless offset by new government programs (see below), will create a "fiscal drag" and prevent the economy from achieving its potential over time. Another way of looking at this fiscal drag is to consider what happens to the full-employment surplus as potential output grows. If Congress does not pass new tax or spending legislation, the full-employment surplus rises. As we have seen, a larger full-employment surplus tends to restrain the growth of aggregate demand. Thus, once full employment is reached, unless the automatic growth in the full-employment surplus is offset, the economy will drift back into recession.

The job of fiscal policy, over time, is thus to declare "fiscal dividends" of sufficient size to offset the tendency toward stagnation that accompanies economic growth. A fiscal dividend may consist of a reduction in tax rates, or an expansion in federal spending on goods and services, or new transfer-type expenditure programs. As a rough approximation the federal government may undertake new programs in a volume equal to the automatic growth in tax revenues, *without imposing any extra inflationary pressure on the economy*. For example, if tax revenues at full employment were growing at $10 billion per year and the federal government introduced $10 billion worth of new spending programs, there would be approximately no net stimulus to aggregate demand relative to potential output. If the economy were initially at full employment, the new government programs would just offset the fiscal drag, leaving the economy at its initial state of full employment.

The Opportunity The prospect of declaring a sizable fiscal dividend year in and year out greatly broadens the choices available to fiscal policy in the longer run. In the short period, room for new federal programs must be made by squeezing out other programs or by raising tax rates. In the long run, the "room" is provided by growing tax revenues at given tax rates. This is not the place to discuss all the possible uses of fiscal dividends, but a short list should indicate the types of alternative programs available.

> Programs to alleviate poverty. *The fiscal dividend may be used in part to broaden present transfer programs in the welfare area, or to provide guaranteed incomes to the poor, or to subsidize housing for the low-income population.*
>
> Programs to remove structural barriers to economic growth. *One of the consequences of inadequate manpower training, health, and education facilities is poverty; another consequence is stunted economic growth. Fiscal dividends may be declared by the federal government in this*

area to broaden and expand the small existing expenditures on such programs. These new programs can be viewed as investments in the nation's future.

Aid to state and local governments. *State and local governments have suffered from inadequately expanding tax bases in the postwar era. The federal government has preempted the best (that is, income) tax sources. One proposal, the Heller-Pechman plan, suggests that the federal government turn over a share of its receipts to the lower units of government, thereby supplementing their revenue sources.*

Private spending. *To the extent that programs in the above areas are thought to be inferior to larger private spending, the federal government may declare its fiscal dividend in the form of reductions in tax rates. Such a fiscal dividend would result in larger consumer (and, perhaps, business) spending as an offset to the fiscal drag.*

Stimulus to private investment. *The federal government could allow growing tax revenues to take place, creating a surplus in the federal budget. This demand-depressing surplus could be offset, without any further fiscal action, by having the Federal Reserve System rapidly expand the money supply and thereby lower interest rates. The effect of such a policy (which would, incidentally, lower the national debt) would be to supply the needed demand-stimulus through private investment spending.*

In summary, then, some stimulus to the economy is needed to offset the fiscal drag of rising tax revenues. The choice of appropriate stimuli depends on the priorities assigned to present consumption versus providing for the future through government or private investment. Much of the recent research in fiscal policy has been directed toward assessing the effects of various specific programs that will compete for available capacity in the economy.

Other Aspects of the Long Run Unfortunately, the setting of an appropriate annual rate of fiscal dividend will not guarantee that all the macroeconomic objectives will be reached as the economy grows. As we have seen earlier, price inflation and balance-of-payments objectives can impose important constraints on fiscal policy in the short run. This is no less true in the long run.

As the United States economy moves along its full-employment growth path, the balance-of-payments position will depend on such forces as the rate of change in United States technology, prices, and real income vis-a-vis the rest of the world. If, in full-employment growth, American prices rise faster than world prices, or if American incomes rise faster than world incomes, there will be a growing tendency toward deficit in the United States balance of payments. Fiscal policy alone cannot prevent this occurrence unless it abandons the full-employment goal.

Policymakers in Western societies have been trying to find suitable supplements to fiscal policy for these longer-run problems. One recent innovation in the United States is the "Guideposts for Non-inflationary Wage and Price Behavior."[10] These guideposts, which stipulate that money wage rates should rise at the rate of growth of labor productivity in the economy, are designed to set the course for price levels over time in the economy. As the guideposts point out, if money wages rise in accord with productivity, costs per unit of output for the whole economy will remain constant and the general price level will not rise. Although individual product prices may rise (or fall), the general trend of prices will remain level. A perfectly functioning competitive economy would produce this result as well, given suitable fiscal and monetary policies; but in a modern oligopolistic economy some form of government guidance may be necessary to ensure price stability over time. The framers of wage-price guideposts intended them to be primarily educational (to clarify the issues in the minds of the general public, business, and labor) rather than coercive. Although it is too early to judge whether the guideposts have been effective, some economists argue that in the (slack) years of the early 1960s the guideposts were responsible for some moderation in wage and price increases.

After 1965 the rapid movement of the economy to full employment set off a wage-price spiral. By 1967 wage-price guideposts were abandoned, and as fiscal and monetary policy failed to stem inflation in 1968–1969, little was heard of the rules of responsible wage-price behavior. By late 1969, as inflation continued despite some evidence of a slowing-down in the economy, the Nixon administration (while disavowing wage-price guideposts) began to "educate the public" as to responsible wage and price behavior. This cycle in use of the guideposts, portrayed as a move from the "jawbone" to the "backbone," probably has several more anatomical stops before long-run price stability is achieved.

As indicated above, a stable price level (or a situation where United States prices grow more slowly than the rest of the world's prices) would aid considerably in correcting a long-standing United States balance-of-payments deficit. But even if price-level movements were to move in pace with international prices, the long-run United States balance-of-payments position could suffer. Rates of growth of real income may differ from country to country; there may be technological changes that impair a country's competitive position; long-run interest rate levels may move in a divergent fashion. All these can contribute to slowly growing, or secular, balance-of-payments problems. Fiscal policy, even with

---

[10] See [4, January 1962, pp. 185–190].

effective wage-price guidepost supplementation, may not be able to deal with such trends.

In response to these international financial problems, economists have begun to turn their attention to two potential avenues of solution. One possibility is greater international cooperation and coordination in making fiscal and monetary policy. As we have seen on the domestic level, coordination of monetary and fiscal policy is necessary to achieve a given set of goals; so, internationally, coordination between countries may be necessary to preserve the goal of balance-of-payments equilibrium with fixed exchange rates. The form that international cooperation might take is still a topic of great debate. The debate may never be resolved, because any world body that can govern the previously autonomous policies of member states will obviously wield tremendous power in setting the course of both economic and political developments in the world.

The major alternative solution to the coordination problem is to free exchange rates. That is, the system of (mostly) fixed exchange rates would be abandoned in favor of letting the forces of supply and demand determine the relative price of national currencies. Although this "market solution" to the balance-of-payments problem has long been favored by economists, all efforts to free exchange rates have been blocked by policymakers. Increasingly, as the alternatives to free exchange rates (protectionism in various forms) come into the foreground, interest in the market solution has heightened. Although a regime of free exchange rates would not entirely free fiscal and monetary policy to pursue domestic objectives, it would measurably improve the range of policies open to decisionmakers.

CONCLUSION

Let us now sit back and ask what this chapter means in terms of the reader's study of fiscal policy. We have tried in the first part of the chapter to outline the major features of what might be called "fiscal policy proper"—the impact of fiscal institutions and policy on the economy. We emphasized the role of fiscal policy in achieving full employment and then broadened our scope to consider other goals and other instruments. In the final section, we dealt with fiscal policy in the longer run—its problems and prospects. Advanced study and research in this field are mainly concerned with two needs. One is the need for a more precise, quantitative understanding of the effects of taxes and spending programs on full employment and other goals. The other—and this will be a matter of growing concern in the future—is the need for coordination and flexibility in fiscal policy in a complex world.

REFERENCES

1. BURNS, ARTHUR F., and PAUL A. SAMUELSON. *Full Employment, Guideposts and Economic Stability* (Washington, D. C.: American Enterprise Institute for Public Policy Research, 1967).
2. COMMITTEE FOR ECONOMIC DEVELOPMENT. *Fiscal and Monetary Policies for Steady Economic Growth* (New York: Committee for Economic Development, 1969).
3. ECKSTEIN, OTTO. *Public Finance*, 2d ed. (Englewood Cliffs, N. J.: Prentice-Hall, 1967).
4. *Economic Report of the President* (Washington, D. C.: Government Printing Office, annual).
5. FRIEDMAN, MILTON. *Capitalism and Freedom* (Chicago: University of Chicago Press, 1962).
6. ——— and WALTER W. HELLER. *Monetary vs. Fiscal Policy* (New York: Norton, 1969).
7. HANSEN, ALVIN H. *The Dollar and the International Monetary System* (New York: McGraw-Hill, 1965).
8. HELLER, WALTER W. *New Dimensions in Political Economy* (New York: Norton, 1967).
9. LECHT, LEONARD A. *Goals, Priorities and Dollars: The Next Decade* (New York: Free Press, 1966).
10. MUNDELL, ROBERT A. *Man and Economics* (New York: McGraw-Hill, 1968).
11. OTT, DAVID J., and ATTIAT F. OTT. *Federal Budget Policy*, Revised ed. (Washington, D. C.: Brookings, 1969).
12. SCHULTZE, CHARLES. *National Income Analysis*, 2d ed. (Englewood Cliffs, N. J.: Prentice-Hall, 1967).
13. STEIN, HERBERT. *The Fiscal Revolution in America* (Chicago: University of Chicago Press, 1969).
14. THUROW, LESTER C. *American Fiscal Policy: Experiments for Prosperity* (Englewood Cliffs, N. J.: Prentice-Hall, 1967).
15. TOBIN, JAMES. *National Economic Policy* (New Haven, Conn.: Yale University Press, 1966).

8
FULL EMPLOYMENT AND THE NEW ECONOMICS[*]

Charles C. Killingsworth[**]

MUCH attention, both at home and abroad, has been attracted to the so-called "New Economics" in the United States. One point of discussion is whether there is really anything new about the New Economics. A widely quoted quip has it that what is new is not economics, and what is economics is not new. I disagree. It is true that, in a broad sense, the core of the New Economics is simply the conscious use of fiscal and monetary policy to achieve and maintain full employment—in other words, the application of Keynesian ideas which have long been familiar, at least to economists. Nevertheless, considering practice as well as rhetoric, the New Economics goes beyond Keynes in several important respects.

My discussion is divided into four parts, as follows:

1 I shall discuss the ways in which the New Economics goes beyond Keynes.

2 I shall review a controversy that has developed concerning the validity of this enlargement of Keynesian doctrine (and as a participant in the controversy, I must warn you that I do not present a wholly disinterested viewpoint).

---

[*] The text, somewhat revised, of a paper presented to the Economics Seminar of the University of Glasgow on May 16, 1968. First published in the *Scottish Journal of Political Economy*, 16 (February 1969), pp. 1–19.

[**] Michigan State University.

3 I shall summarize some of the empirical evidence bearing on this controversy.

4 Finally, I shall consider the implications of this controversy and this evidence for employment policy in the United States, especially in the post-Vietnam period.

I.

We may conveniently begin with a little-noticed passage in the *General Theory* in which Keynes explicitly sets forth some of the limitations of his system—that is, those elements of the economy that he takes as "given."[1] Among the "givens" are the following:

The existing skill and quantity of available labor
The existing quality and quantity of available equipment
The existing technique
The tastes and habits of the consumer

Keynes assures the reader that he is not assuming that these elements never change; he is simply not considering the effects of changes in them. His reason is that changes in them are generally so slow that they have "only a small and comparatively negligible *short-term* influence" (emphasis added) on the levels of employment and unemployment. We should note here that these elements are among those that are commonly said to make up "the structure of the economy."

The New Economics developed in the United States during the Kennedy administration largely as a response to what appeared to be a secular rise in unemployment levels in the United States economy. The official national unemployment rate was below 3 percent during and immediately after the Korean war period in the early 1950s; in the next prosperity period, 1955–1957, the unemployment rate stayed above 4 percent; then, in prosperous 1959, the rate held above 5 percent; and when the Kennedy administration took office in January 1961, the rate was at a recession high of almost 7 percent—about three times the rate of ten years before. Even after recovery was well advanced in 1963, the rate remained above 5.5 percent.

There had been suggestions that a substantial part of this increase in prosperity-period unemployment must be due to long-run changes in some of the structural factors mentioned above—that is, to a secular rise in structural unemployment. This was a viewpoint that was sharply and totally rejected by the newly appointed Council of Economic Advisers in 1961. The Council argued that there was no reason to believe that there had been any increase in the structural component of unemploy-

---

[1] The reference is to the first section of chap. 18 of [7].

ment in the entire period since World War II. We should note that this position does not deny that structural changes had occurred, nor does it deny the presence of some structural unemployment; the argument rather is that structural unemployment had remained at some constant level during the postwar years. The real cause of the secular rise in unemployment from cycle peak to cycle peak, the Council said, was "fiscal drag"—a federal tax system that not only generated more revenues as economic activities increased, but also generated them more rapidly than government expenditures increased. This built-in fiscal imbalance acted as a brake on economic expansion and caused a gap between potential gross national product at full employment and attainable GNP. The way to bring the unemployment rate back down to the level of 1948 and 1957 was to adopt fiscal policies that would close that gap between potential and actual GNP. Reference to 1948 and 1957 implies unemployment at a rate of approximately 4 percent, which no doubt seems incredibly high for a "full employment" rate to the citizens of Great Britain and Western Europe. Nevertheless, the Council of Economic Advisers explicitly specified the 4 percent rate as the "interim full employment target" for the United States.[2]

After strenuous internal debate, the administration position came to be that the preferred form of fiscal stimulus was tax reduction rather than increased government expenditure. There were some relatively minor reductions in business taxes in 1962. Then the "centerpiece" of the administration's economic policy in 1963 and 1964 became a $14 billion reduction in personal and business income taxes. This measure was passed early in 1964, and then in 1965 there were substantial reductions in a variety of excise taxes. Thereafter, even after large-scale intervention in the Vietnam conflict had started to swell the expenditure side of the federal budget, prominent figures in the administration publicly discussed the size, nature, and timing of still more tax cuts. Thus, "fiscal stimulus" and "tax cuts" came to be almost synonymous in the administration lexicon, although there were occasional nods in the direction of "vast unmet needs" in the public sector.

Let us now examine the theoretical basis for the Council's position. I must emphasize that not all of the rationale was fully developed in 1961, or even in 1962 or 1963. Some of the rationalizations came after the policy decisions and the actions. Neither was there complete unanimity concerning this policy within the administration. Nevertheless, in the interest of clarity and relative brevity, I must treat the theory as an integrated whole instead of tracing its gradual evolution; and I must

---

[2] The Council's position was stated in a presentation to the Joint Economic Committee of the U.S. Congress in 1961, and was elaborated in subsequent annual *Economic Reports*, especially those for 1962, 1963 and 1964.

ignore the qualifications and dissents on particular points which were recorded by some economists who supported most aspects of the Council's position.

When the Kennedy administration took office in 1961, there was abundant evidence of structural changes in the American economy since World War II. As already noted, some of the evidence had been extensively discussed in congressional hearings and scholarly articles seeking the causes of creeping prosperity unemployment in the United States, and I shall examine it further in an ensuing section. How did the New Economics deal with these developments? Less by direct confrontation of the pertinent data than by the elaboration of doctrine.[3] Let us consider as an example a description of the labor market endorsed by one of the leading expositors of the New Economics.[4]

> *It is the proper function of a market to allocate resources, and in this respect the labor market does not function differently from any others. If the available resources are of high quality, the market will adjust to the use of high quality resources; if the quality is low, methods will be developed to use such resources.... In a slack labor market employers must have some means of selecting among numerous applicants, and it is not surprising that educational attainment is often used as a convenient yardstick, regardless of its direct relevance to the requirements of the job.*
>
> *We have found it useful to view the labor market as a gigantic "shapeup" with members of the labor force queued in order of their relative attractiveness to employers.... The total number employed and unemployed depends primarily on the general state of economic activity. The employed tend to be those near the beginning and the unemployed those near the end of the line. Only as demand rises will*

---

[3] The Council did rely heavily on one econometric study which purported to "test" the available data for evidence of a rise in structural unemployment with negative results. The principal author of this study was Edward D. Kalachek, who had begun it as a doctoral dissertation at Massachusetts Institute of Technology [6]. I have elaborated elsewhere the view that this study was remarkably defective. Its most lamentable defect was that it "tested" a version of the "structural hypothesis" that was not justified either by anything ever written or spoken on the subject up to that time, or by any reasonable interpretation of the data cited in previous discussions on the subject. Thus, his study was an exercise in irrelevancy. Unfortunately, Kalachek's formulation was subsequently taken—without any effort at independent verification—as the only valid statement of the "structural hypothesis" by a cluster of econometricians, who produced a substantial body of literature which possibly equals the irrelevancy of the original Kalachek study.

[4] The quoted passage is from [16]. The most prominent economist on the Commission on Technology, Automation, and Economic Progress was Robert M. Solow of the Massachusetts Institute of Technology, a principal staff member of the Council of Economic Advisers during the early 1960s and subsequently a principal consultant to the Council.

> employers reach further down the line in their search for employees. ... And because workers of low educational attainment are the least desirable to employers, nonwhite and older workers are concentrated at the rear of the line, not only because of their lower educational attainment, but also because of direct discrimination.

The argument may be stated somewhat more fully as follows: Workers who are displaced in agriculture or manufacturing will be guided by the labor market to new lines of employment, provided only that aggregate demand is maintained at a sufficiently high level by means of governmental fiscal policy. It does not matter if a large proportion of the displaced workers are poorly educated and lack skills. The market will see to it that employers redesign jobs and provide extensive training in order to make use of this low-quality labor, given an adequate level of aggregate demand. If large numbers of the less desirable workers are in fact unemployed, this simply proves that there is an insufficiency of aggregate demand. If this insufficiency is remedied, the most disadvantaged workers will benefit the most. Employers will be induced to make the necessary adaptations to hire them, and consequently their unemployment rates will drop much farther and much faster than the overall rate does.

It has long been conventional in economic theorizing to assume that labor is homogeneous. The New Economics moves a step beyond this assumption; it concedes some degree of heterogeneity in the labor force, but it asserts that the labor market will automatically compensate or adjust for the differences in quality of labor. In short, the New Economics asserts that the labor market is a powerful automatic homogenizer of labor. There is an implied recognition of some imperfection, in that time-lags in the homogenization process are admitted. It is specifically asserted, however, over and over again in the pronouncements of the New Economics that the level of structural unemployment had remained constant in the United States throughout the postwar years despite the major structural changes cited above.

The doctrine that I have just summarized indicates a strong faith in the efficiency of the labor market. This faith is really one aspect of a broader faith in a market-controlled economy. Walter W. Heller, the first Kennedy-appointed chairman of the Council of Economic Advisers, recently published the following observations on the subject:

> It is often said that the study of economics makes people conservative. In the microeconomic sense, it undoubtedly does. It is hard to study the modern economics of relative prices, resource allocation, and distribution without developing a healthy respect for the market mechanism on three major scores: first, for what Robert Dorfman calls its "cybernetics," for the incredible capacity of the price system to receive and generate information and respond to it; second, for its technical effi-

ciency and hard-headedness as a guide to resources and a goad to effort and risk-taking; and third, for its contribution to political democracy by keeping economic decisions free and decentralized [4, p. 8].

Let us simply note, without elaboration, that both the specific faith in the efficiency of labor markets and the more general faith in the efficiency of a market-controlled economy stand in considerable contrast to the conclusions of specialists in the behavior of large corporations and empirical investigators of labor markets; one of the latter, for example, has written that "labor markets are less adequate than any other type of factor or product market in the economy."[5]

The faith of the New Economics in the beneficent operation of markets leads to one of its strong but little-noticed characteristics: a private-sector bias. Note that in the foregoing passage Heller seems to be claiming for himself, with some pride, the label of "conservative." In United States political terminology, that label usually denotes one who—among other things—prefers less rather than more government participation in economic life. (Of course, Heller would label himself a "conservative" only with regard to microeconomics.) The progression of ideas is obvious. Increased government spending means an increase in politically based decisions concerning resource allocation; tax-cutting, as an alternative method of demand stimulation, means more market-based decisions, because the additional spending will be done by millions of individual consumers; therefore, tax-cutting is preferable. Thus, we have a more sophisticated version of the earlier, more primitive conservatism which in the United States has contributed to squalor, decay, and inadequacy in the public sector despite burgeoning affluence in the private sector—and which has largely ignored the failures of the market economy in such vital areas as low-cost housing.

Let me summarize this section by saying that the New Economics goes beyond Keynes in three major respects:

1 By asserting that the labor market automatically holds structural unemployment to some low, constant level, the New Economics takes a major step toward converting the short-run cyclical analysis of Keynes himself into a long-run analysis. Demand stimulation through fiscal policy becomes the key to long-run, balanced growth, rather than merely the remedy for cyclical fluctuations.

---

[5] See [13, p. 375]. On the more general issue, see the recent three-cornered debate among Robert M. Solow, John Kenneth Galbraith, and Robin Marris in [12]. The reader should not infer that I would automatically prefer government spending to private spending; my position merely is that this choice should not be made on the basis of simplistic assumptions of questionable validity. Neither do I argue that the labor market is incapable of performing any economic function; I argue only that the idealized model described in the quotation in the text bears a faint and imperfect resemblance to reality.

2   By emphasizing tax-cutting as the preferred form of demand stimulation, the New Economics encourages the more rapid growth of the private sector than the public sector; it encourages private consumption rather than public investment. Keynes did not have this private-sector bias.

3   The New Economics assigns a low priority to the development of social programs to remedy the structural displacement of workers. The need for such programs is conceded; but the teaching is that major emphasis on them should be deferred until the time when all possibilities for demand stimulation have been exhausted. Recent experience strongly suggests, however, that when that time is reached, the highest priority must then be assigned to fiscal restraint in order to curb price inflation. Keynes did not assign these priorities.[6]

II.

There has been considerable confusion concerning what the "structural hypothesis" is. A part of this confusion results from the fact that one prominent Congressman at times seemed to take the position that the unemployment problem of the early 1960s was wholly structural; another part results from the misremembering of who said exactly what during those years; and perhaps the largest part results from the gross misrepresentation of the "structural hypothesis" by some economists whose purpose was to discredit this view.[7] Perhaps also an innate desire for symmetry predisposed many people to assume—incorrectly—that the "structuralist" view was the exact opposite of the "aggregate demand" view. A structuralist is correctly defined as a Keynesian who believes that changes in the structure of the economy can have an independent effect on the levels of employment and unemployment. More precisely, the United States structuralists of the early 1960s recognized that a part of this country's problem of a rising level of prosperity unemployment was properly attributable to a chronic weakness of aggregate demand, and that fiscal policy could remedy that weakness; but they also argued that structural changes since World War II were another important cause of this secular rise in the unemployment rate, and they concluded that *both* fiscal policy and other "structural" kinds of remedies would be required to achieve full employment.

There is abundant evidence that quite extensive structural changes

[6] My attention has been called to a series of articles by Keynes which appeared in the *Times* of London on January 12, 13, and 14, 1937, in which Keynes argued that since recovery was then well under way, attention should be shifted to a variety of structural problems. "We are in more need today of a rightly distributed demand than of a greater aggregate demand . . . ," he remarked. The unemployment rate in Great Britain was still above 10 percent at the time.

[7] See footnote 3 above.

had occurred in the United States economy from the end of World War II up to the early 1960s. The crucial question was whether these structural changes had increased labor market imbalance, or whether instead the labor market had automatically induced adjustments on the part of workers and employers that offset the effects of these structural changes. Before addressing this crucial question, it will be worthwhile to review quite briefly four main aspects of structural change in the postwar United States economy.[8]

The first aspect was a revolution in agricultural technology, especially after 1947. This development raised the rate of agricultural productivity improvement far above prewar levels. Since the demand for agricultural products continued to grow at a much slower rate than output per man hour increased, employment in agriculture turned sharply downward and continued to decline throughout the 1950s and into the 1960s. Heavy displacement in this sector pushed millions of low-skilled, poorly educated workers into urban labor markets, where they intensified the competition for low-skilled jobs.

The second aspect was a fundamental change in the composition of employment in manufacturing. The total showed no trend either upward or downward after it receded from the high levels achieved during the Korean war (1950-1953). However, throughout the period after World War II, white-collar workers were replacing blue-collar workers on manufacturing payrolls. White-collar workers were 16.4 percent of total manufacturing employment in 1947 and 26 percent of the total in 1961. In my judgment, much of this substitution can be properly attributed to automation.

During the same years, employment in what we classify as service-producing industries (government, trade, finance, transportation, public utilities, and miscellaneous services) had continued a strong upward trend, while total employment in the goods-producing sector drifted downward after the end of the Korean war in 1953. The most rapidly growing service-producing industries were those with the largest proportions of highly trained workers: education and health care. And the service-producing industries generally were less prepared to provide on-the-job training than the goods-producing industries.

Finally, geographical employment patterns changed. Employment growth in the large cities of the north central and northeast regions—the traditional centers of heavy manufacturing activity—slowed or stopped. Employment grew more rapidly in the suburbs and in the southern and western regions of the country. These shifts operated to the detriment

---

[8] I have discussed these structural changes at much greater length in a paper prepared in 1964 [9].

of residents of central cities and workers with low mobility, particularly the old, the less-educated, and the less-skilled.

I argued in 1963 that the combined effect of such structural changes in the postwar United States economy had been to "twist" the demand for labor: to push up the demand for highly skilled, highly educated workers while pushing down the demand for low-skilled, poorly educated workers. Demographic forces had been concurrently changing the structure of labor supply. By and large, the new additions to the labor force were better-educated and sometimes better-trained than the older workers who were disappearing from the labor force through death and retirement. But there was evidence that these two basic types of structural change were out of phase—that the changes in the structure of demand were outrunning the changes in the supply of labor. One piece of evidence on this point is presented in Table 8-1.[9]

TABLE 8-1 *Unemployment Rates by Years of School Completed, Men, 18 and Older, March 1950 and March 1962 (U.S.A.)*

YEARS OF SCHOOLING	UNEMPLOYMENT RATES 1950	UNEMPLOYMENT RATES 1962
0–4	8.6	10.4
5–7	8.3	8.5
8	6.6	7.5
9–11	6.9	7.8
12	4.6	4.8
13–15	4.1	4.0
16 and over	2.2	1.4
All groups	6.2	6.0

As these figures show, in 1950 and 1962 overall unemployment rates for men were virtually identical; but the rates for the less-educated had risen substantially, while those for the better-educated groups had de-

---

[9] Sources of data and adjustments for comparability are set forth in [8]. I have emphasized unemployment rates by educational level in my analysis because, in my judgment, the occupational and industrial classification systems on which United States statistics rest result in a high degree of heterogeneity in those classifications. There appears to be a much better correlation between educational attainment and skill level than between occupation (as broadly defined in labor force statistics) and skill level.

clined. Hence, there was an increase in labor market imbalance.[10] Additional evidence of the growth of labor market imbalance during the 1950s and early 1960s is found in the disproportionate rise in unemployment rates for Negroes, teen-agers, and—most especially—teen-age Negroes.

On the basis of these findings, and additional findings regarding employment trends by education level from 1950 to 1962, I concluded in 1963 that demand stimulation would not be likely to contribute greatly to a reduction in unemployment rates among the less-educated. Demand stimulation would be likely to increase employment among the better educated at a considerably greater rate than among the less-educated, at least to the point at which labor supply bottlenecks were encountered; and then, I thought, price inflation would be a more likely outcome than massive redesign of jobs by employers in order to utilize the less-educated workers on jobs that were better performed by the more-educated. This reasoning led to the further conclusion that only a part of the problem of excessive prosperity unemployment would be remedied by a correction of the "fiscal drag" that the New Economics presented as the sole villain. I argued that demand stimulation was one essential part of the remedy, but that this by itself would not be enough. Another essential remedy, in my view, was some major programs of social intervention in the labor market—in the form of large-scale retraining, relocation of workers, direct employment by government, early retirement, and encouragement of higher rates of school attendance.

III.

There is now a widespread belief among economists in the United States—and perhaps elsewhere as well—that the course of events has passed a conclusive verdict on the structural versus aggregate demand controversy. The rationale is simple. When the massive tax cut of 1964 was passed, the national unemployment rate stood at 5.5 percent. In 1967, the annual average was 3.8 percent. Q.E.D.! This is how Walter Heller puts the matter:

> *Employment developments in 1965–1966 rendered a clear-cut verdict on the structural-unemployment thesis: the alleged hard core of unemploy-*

---

[10] Actually, the imbalance is understated by the unemployment rates. There had been a general decline in labor force participation rates among the less-educated men during this period, including even those in the central working ages, 25–55, resulting in a substantial amount of hidden unemployment; participation rates among the better-educated men were generally higher in 1962 than in 1950.

My findings on these matters are generally supported by a recent study which compared unemployment and participation rates for 1950 and 1960, utilizing unadjusted data from the 1950 and 1960 censuses [5].

ment lies not at 5 or 6 percent, but even deeper than 4 percent—how deep still remains to be ascertained [4, p. 64].

Heller's successor as chairman of the Council of Economic Advisers, Gardner Ackley, concurs in the following language:

It is as clear today as it can possibly be that, in the situation of 1961, the inadequate demand camp was right and the structuralists were wrong [1].

And the British economist, Michael Stewart, concludes his discussion of changes in United States unemployment rates from 1964 to 1967 with the following observation:

It is striking evidence for the view that high unemployment in America in recent years has not been the result of structural maladjustments nearly so much as of a shortage of effective demand [15, p. 242].

A multitude of similar examples could be cited.

It is surprising, and distressing as well, to find so many economists relying so heavily on this kind of simplistic, *post hoc ergo propter hoc* analysis. The tacit—and unexamined—assumption is that nothing other than stimulation of aggregate demand through fiscal policy had any significant effect on unemployment. No extensive analysis is required to reveal the fallaciousness of this assumption. The fact is that programs that can fairly be called "structural" in nature (or in their effects) have had a substantial impact on the unemployment rate.

In early 1964, the only significant manpower program was a new and still modest retraining effort under the Manpower Development and Training Act. In 1965, however, a number of programs that involved what was essentially "work relief" were undertaken by the federal government. Eligibility for these programs was essentially based on two considerations: financial need, and inability to find employment in the conventional labor market. Concurrently, the definition of "employment" used in the national labor market statistics was modified to count enrollees in these programs as "employed," although in the historical statistics (that is, those relating to the 1930s) the enrollees in work relief programs are still reported as "unemployed." But I am not quarrelling with the change in definition. The point is that starting in 1965 rising enrollment in these programs had a substantial effect on the national unemployment rate. A staff member of the U.S. Bureau of Labor Statistics has estimated, on the basis of rather conservative assumptions, that by 1967 four of these federal programs were responsible for a reduction of 0.4 percent in the unemployment rate [2].

There was another set of changes in the official definition of "unemployment" in January 1967. We need not consider the nature of the changes here; the point pertinent to this discussion is that, according to a statement of the Commissioner of Labor Statistics, the net effect of these changes was a reduction of approximately 0.2 percent in the national unemployment rate.

Starting in the latter part of 1965, there was a major expansion in the armed forces of the United States as a result of military escalation in Vietnam. This expansion amounted to more than 700,000 men by early 1967, and men in the armed forces are not counted as part of the "civilian labor force," which is the basis for all of our unemployment statistics. Virtually all the 700,000 men would have been in the civilian labor force if they had not joined the armed forces. The principal alternative at this age is college enrollment; since draft deferment was almost automatic for full-time enrollees, all who were able to travel that road did so. Indeed, the combination of increased draft calls and the educational deferment policy brought a sharp rise in the number of full-time male students of college age in the fall of 1965. The rise was about 185,000 larger than would have been expected on the basis of population growth in this age group. Thus by 1967 about 885,000 young men had been affected, directly or indirectly, by the Vietnam military buildup. On the fairly conservative assumption that for each two men withdrawn from the civilian labor force under these circumstances one new entrant is attracted into it, we can conclude that net shrinkage of the civilian labor force by the military draft and its side effects reduced the unemployment rate by about 0.5 percent below what it otherwise would have been.

There were other structural programs and structural effects that clearly had significant impacts on the unemployment rate, although it is difficult to measure them. These include extensive liberalization of early retirement provisions under both public and private pension plans, which induced a shrinkage of the labor force at the upper end of the age scale; the enlargement of federal retraining programs, under which some 400,000 workers completed courses between 1962 and 1967 (most of the workers were unemployed before retraining and most were employed after); and the enlargement and liberalization of college loan, scholarship and fellowship programs, which further reduced labor force growth at the lower working ages. Finally, attention should be called to the effect of increased war production on the structure of employment. The U.S. Department of Labor has estimated that the increase in expenditure for war goods from mid-1965 to mid-1967 created roughly one million new jobs in war plants; nearly 60 percent of these jobs were filled by blue-collar workers, although only 40 percent of total employment in 1965 was composed of blue-collar workers. The rise in war expenditures disproportionately benefited durable goods manufacturing, and especially blue-collar workers in that sector; obviously tax-cutting would not have had the same structural effect.[11]

Although the structural developments just described must have had a substantial effect on the unemployment rate, I shall not make a numerical estimate of it. Instead, I say to those who may be inclined to discount the figures given earlier that the effects of these developments which I have not quantified would surely exceed any reasonable discount. In other words, it is an understatement to say that all kinds of structural programs and related structural effects accounted for 1.1 percentage points of the drop in the national unemployment rate from 1964 to 1967 (that is, 0.4 due to work relief programs, 0.5 due to direct and indirect effects of armed forces expansion, and 0.2 to the 1967 change in definition). What this implies is that, in the absence of these programs, the unemployment rate would have declined no more than to about 4.9 percent. Or, to state the same thing a little differently, if economic expansion due to fiscal policy had by itself been capable of reducing the unemployment rate to 4 percent (as predicted by the Council of Economic Advisers), then these structural programs and structural effects would have achieved a further reduction at least to 2.9 percent.

In some respects, the behavior of specific unemployment rates for the most disadvantaged groups provides a more valid basis than does the national unemployment rate for judging the extent to which labor market imbalance has been remedied since 1964. However, to an even greater degree than with the national rate, it is essential to remember that the rates for disadvantaged groups have been differentially affected by the structural programs. It is even more misleading to assume that changes in these specific rates have been caused exclusively by "economic growth" than was the case with the national rate. It would be a very difficult and in some respects an impossible task to separate out the effects of structural programs and demand expansion on each of these detailed unemployment rates. The basic point can be illustrated, however, by one program and one group. The Neighborhood Youth Corps (NYC) is one of the work relief programs referred to above. It enrolls only young people aged 16 to 21. As already noted, enrollees are now counted as "employed," although the enrollees in a closely similar program in the 1930s were and are counted as "unemployed." The necessary data are available to recalculate the teenage Negro unemployment rate on the basis of the old definitions and thus to get a rough approximation of what this unemployment rate would be if there were no Neighborhood Youth Corps. The officially reported unemployment rate for this

---

[11] The Department of Labor estimates are reported in two articles [11] [14].

group in most recent quarters has been between 22 and 25 percent (the highest rate in the official statistics for any separately identified group). Adding teenage Negro NYC enrollees to those now counted as unemployed raises their rate by nearly 50 percent—that is, to about 33 to 37 percent. Clearly, demand expansion did nothing to reduce the unemployment rate for this most disadvantaged group; and a structural program with a large impact on this group merely averted a sharp rise in its unemployment.

Keeping in mind the fact that we are measuring the effect of a combination of forces, we can compare relative unemployment rates before the great tax cut of 1964 with the rates some substantial period of time after. I have made such a comparison, using data for the first quarter of 1964 and the fourth quarter of 1966. The latter quarter was picked because by then enough time had elapsed to show the full effect of tax-cutting, and because in immediately ensuing quarters there was a pause in economic expansion. (However, use of later quarters would not greatly change the relationships shown below.) The comparison is as follows:[12]

UNEMPLOYMENT RATE FOR	FIRST QUARTER 1964	FOURTH QUARTER 1966	PERCENTAGE CHANGE 1964–66
All groups	5.5	3.8	−31
All whites	4.9	3.3	−33
All nonwhites	9.8	7.5	−23
Teen-age whites	13.6	10.0	−26
Teen-age nonwhites	22.7	23.5	+ 3

During this period, the group that had the lowest unemployment rate to start with (all whites) had the largest relative drop, and the group that was the most severely disadvantaged in 1964 (teen-age nonwhites) had not a decrease but an even higher rate in 1966. Thus, the combination of demand expansion and structural effects that was operating during this period did not prevent an increase in labor-market imbalance. In the 1964 quarter, the highest rate was about four and a half times the lowest rate; in the 1966 quarter, the highest was about seven times the lowest. Contrary to the teaching of the New Economics, economic expansion (even when supplemented by structural programs) did not confer its greatest relative benefits on the most disadvantaged.

Another series of figures, with another basis of classification, gives us a much fuller picture of the forces at work in the labor market in the

---

[12] Data from [3, pp. 114, 116]. The unemployment rates are all seasonally adjusted.

mid-1960s. The first set of the series shows unemployment rates for men by level of education. These rates are shown in Table 8-2.[13]

TABLE 8-2 *Unemployment Rates by Years of School Completed, Men 18 and Older, March 1962 and March 1967 (U.S.A.)*

YEARS OF SCHOOL COMPLETED	UNEMPLOYMENT RATE 1962	UNEMPLOYMENT RATE 1967	PERCENTAGE REDUCTION 1962–67
All groups	6.0	3.1	48
0–4	10.4	5.7	45
5–7	8.5	4.7	45
8	7.5	4.0	47
9–11	7.8	4.6	41
12	4.8	2.5	48
13–15	4.0	2.2	45
16 or more	1.4	0.7	50

The first impression from these figures is that the relative reductions in unemployment rates were more similar than different, and that the growth of labor-market imbalance was considerably slowed, although not completely stopped. But let us go beyond these figures to see what we can learn about the forces that reduced the rates. Table 8-3 in this series reveals a quite different kind of situation. For analytical purposes, we can divide the male labor force into two parts; the median educational attainment of male workers is 12.2 years, so that those with less than twelve years of schooling are approximately the lower half and those with twelve years or more are approximately the upper half of the labor force. Table 8-3 tells us that unemployment rates fell in the lower half despite very large *reductions* in employment. (The group with 9–11 years of school is an apparent exception; but it is quite likely that most if not all of the increase in employment shown for that group was attributable to the Neighborhood Youth Corps.) How could unemployment rates fall when employment was also falling? Because the labor force at these educational levels was shrinking more rapidly than employment was declining. Part of the labor-force shrinkage was due to deaths and to retirements at the "normal" age of 65; another part was due to an acceleration in the rate of early retirements at ages 55 to 65. But a major part was due to declining labor-force participation rates even in

[13] Tables 8–2 and 8–3 are taken from my article [10]. The data are from U.S. Department of Labor reports.

TABLE 8-3 *Employment by Years of School Completed, Men 18 and Older, March 1962 and March 1967 (U.S.A.)*

YEARS OF SCHOOL COMPLETED	NUMBER EMPLOYED (THOUSANDS) 1962	1967	CHANGE 1962–1967 THOUSANDS	PERCENT
All groups	42,332	45,132	+2,800	+ 6.6
0–4	2,171	1,616	− 555	−25.6
5–7	4,130	3,508	− 622	−15.1
8	5,895	5,254	− 641	−10.9
9–11	8,137	8,349	+ 212	+ 2.6
12	12,308	14,946	+2,638	+21.4
13–15	4,498	5,349	+ 851	+18.9
16 or more	5,193	6,110	+ 917	+17.7

the central working ages, 25 to 55. Hence, a substantial part of the decrease in the officially reported unemployment rates resulted simply from an increase in hidden unemployment at the lower educational levels.[14] Let me restate the point for the sake of emphasis: A detailed analysis of male participation rates by age and educational attainment in the lower half of the labor force reveals that in virtually every category the participation rate was substantially lower in 1967 than in 1962. At this level of the labor force, job mortality exceeded human mortality by a considerable margin, and the unemployment rate fell only because many of those who lost jobs simply dropped out of the labor-force count. In the light of these facts, it is completely clear that the lower reported unemployment rates for the less-educated cannot be attributed to "economic expansion." And these facts make it much easier to reconcile falling unemployment rates and rising relief rolls, a conjunction which has hitherto puzzled some American analysts.

When we consider the upper half of the labor force, we see quickly that we have moved into a different kind of world. Roughly 95 percent of the gross increase in jobs for men during this period went to this better-educated group. The increase in employment exceeded the rate of population growth at this level, and participation rates increased sig-

[14] In the U.S. labor force statistics, a man who is not employed but who is able and willing to work is not counted as unemployed unless he has engaged in an active search for work within the past 30 days. Thus, for example, a laid-off coal miner who has discovered that there are no jobs available in his community and who has therefore not made a recent effort to find a job is counted as "not in the labor force." In my terminology, he is among the "hidden unemployed" if he is nevertheless still willing and able to work.

nificantly for virtually all age groups among the better-educated.[15] Thus, five years of record-breaking economic expansion, plus new programs to combat structural unemployment, have not remedied the twisting of the labor market and the resulting imbalance which the New Economics had attributed to an insufficiency of aggregate demand.

IV.

If all the foregoing shed light only on who was right and who was wrong in a controversy of five years ago, it would hardly be worth the bother. But the matters discussed have an obvious and immediate bearing on future policy choices. As we have seen, leading spokesmen for the New Economics have quite emphatically and quite erroneously concluded that the experience of the past five years demonstrates that the stimulation of aggregate demand *by itself* is capable of driving the United States unemployment rate well below 4 percent. The implied policy conclusion is that the prime and sufficient remedy for an unemployment rate at or above 4 percent is demand stimulation, presumably by means of tax cuts; and another implied conclusion is that, in case of a future rise in unemployment, further development of programs aimed specifically at structural unemployment should await the restoration of some rate substantially below 4 percent.

The fuller analysis of labor-market developments during the past five years that has been undertaken in this chapter reveals that demand stimulation alone would not have reduced the unemployment rate much below 5 percent and that the rate fell below 4 percent only because structural programs and structural effects contributed substantially to the reduction. The fuller analysis also reveals a significant impact on official unemployment rates from a little-noticed type of adjustment: an accelerated rate of labor-force withdrawal even in the central working years

---

[15] The only significant exceptions are among the youngest, whose civilian labor-force participation rates were affected by the military draft, and the oldest (55 and over), whose rates were affected by liberalized early retirement provisions. But even among the older workers, the declines in participation rates were much smaller at the higher levels of education than at the lower levels. There have been suggestions that employment of the better-educated men has increased simply because their numbers have increased. Such suggestions ignore the large average earnings differentials as between men at different educational levels. For example, the average annual earnings of the college-educated man in the United States are about three and a half times the average earnings of the man with less than eight years of education. Such "price" differentials have tended to widen (both relatively and absolutely) in recent years. One of the basic fallacies of the "queuing" model of the labor market (cited above) is the implicit assumption that all workers are available at the same price. If workers queued up in the order of attractiveness of their price tags to the employer, obviously the best-educated would be at the far end of the line.

among less-educated males. Hence, considering only the changes in reported unemployment rates leads to an exaggerated notion of the progress made in recent years toward full utilization of human resources.

In the post-Vietnam years, some of the structural effects that have contributed to lower unemployment rates in the United States are likely to be reversed. Reduction in the size of the armed forces to the pre-Vietnam level will accelerate the growth of the civilian labor force, and cutbacks in war production will have an especially heavy impact on the demand for blue-collar workers, especially in durable goods manufacturing. Even if the pressure of aggregate demand is maintained at its present level, a substantial rise in unemployment rates—especially among the young, the less-skilled, and the less-educated—is a strong likelihood, unless intensified competition for lower-level jobs induces a further acceleration in rates of labor-force withdrawal in the lower strata of the labor market. The proper remedy for such post-Vietnam unemployment will be more adequate programs to offset the specific effects of structural change rather than concentration on the stimulation of aggregate demand.

The heart of the disagreement between the structuralists and the exponents of the New Economics has lain in their fundamentally different estimates of the ability of the labor market to offset the effects of structural change on the demand for various grades of labor. The view of the New Economics that the labor market is an efficient, automatic homogenizer of labor rested initially on a priori reasoning, and has been supported more recently by simplistic analysis resting on the *post hoc ergo propter hoc* fallacy. The structuralist view has rested on case studies and other empirical investigations which have shown that the labor market is "less adequate than any other type of factor or product market in the economy." The structuralists have contended that the labor market lacked sufficient power by itself to induce the employer adjustments that would offset the adverse effects of structural change on job opportunities for the less-skilled and less-educated. I conclude that an adequate analysis of the pertinent data bearing on the performance of the labor market in the past five years provides solid support for the structuralist view.

REFERENCES

1 ACKLEY, GARDNER. Address at Southern Illinois University, October 26, 1966. (Mimeographed.)
2 COHEN, MALCOLM S. "The Direct Effects of Federal Manpower Programs in Reducing Unemployment," *Journal of Human Resources*, Fall 1969.
3 *Employment and Earnings and Monthly Report on the Labor Force*, U.S. Department of Labor, January 1967.

4. HELLER, WALTER W. *New Dimensions of Political Economy* (Cambridge, Mass.: Harvard University Press, 1966).
5. JOHNSTON, DENIS F. "Education and the Labor Force," *Monthly Labor Review*, September 1968, pp. 1–11.
6. KALACHEK, EDWARD D. *Higher Unemployment Rates, 1957–60: Structural Transformation or Inadequate Demand*, Joint Economic Committee (87th Cong., 1st Sess., 1961).
7. KEYNES, JOHN MAYNARD. *The General Theory of Employment, Interest and Money* (New York: Harcourt, Brace, 1936).
8. KILLINGSWORTH, CHARLES C. Statement in *Hearings before the Subcommittee on Employment and Manpower*, U.S. Senate (88th Cong., 1st Sess., 1963) Part 5, pp. 1482–1483.
9. ———. "Structural Unemployment in the United States," in Jack Stieber (ed.), *Employment Problems of Automation and Advanced Technology* (London: Macmillan, 1966).
10. ———. "The Continuing Labor Market Twist," *Monthly Labor Review*, September 1968, pp. 12–17.
11. OLIVER, R. P. "The Employment Effect of Defense Expenditures," *Monthly Labor Review*, September 1967.
12. *The Public Interest*, Fall 1967, pp. 100–119; Spring 1968, pp. 37–52.
13. REYNOLDS, LLOYD G. *Labor Economics and Labor Relations*, 4th ed. (Englewood Cliffs, N. J.: Prentice-Hall, 1964).
14. RUTZICK, M. A. "Worker Skills in Current Defense Employment," *Monthly Labor Review*, September 1967.
15. STEWART, MICHAEL. *Keynes and After* (Harmondsworth: Penguin, 1967).
16. *Technology and the American Economy*, Report of the National Commission on Technology, Automation, and Economic Progress (1966).

9
INDUSTRIAL ORGANIZATION

Richard E. Caves [*]
E. Bryant Phillips [**]

BETWEEN the Davids and the Goliaths on the scale of American private enterprise lie an incredibly diverse 4.75 million individual business units. They absorb the savings and labor services of the American populace. They ingest the nation's raw materials. They produce the stream of goods and services which we count as the gross national product.

In studying the behavior and performance of the economic system, economists concern themselves with many features of business units. For it is through the actions of these millions of individual firms that many of the general goals of the economy are gained or lost. Do they make the most efficient use of the nation's scarce factors of production? Do they produce the "best" combination of guns, butter, shoeshines, and other goods and services desired by ultimate users? Do they contribute, within their ability, toward achieving a desirable rate of economic growth? Do they plan their activities in a way that helps stabilize employment?

Studying the behavior of all the individual business units in the nation together amounts to nothing less than studying the whole economy. Studying them one by one, we promptly lose sight of the forest for the trees. The subject of "industrial organization" was conceived in an effort to split the difference between these two extremes.

[*] Harvard University.
[**] University of Southern California.

Individual business units come in contact with one another in *markets*. A market includes a group of buyers and sellers of a particular product engaged in settling the terms of sale of that product. The sellers participating in a product market are called collectively the *industry* producing the product. Our concern here is how the organization of these sellers affects the performance of the market and thus the nation's economic welfare. Therefore, we use the term "industrial organization."

Industrial organization, the investigation of real-life industries, is actually a form of applied microtheory. In using microtheory to study the actual behavior of business in the community, we cannot avoid asking whether the assumption of profit maximization which underlies the theory will furnish us with reliable predictions about business decisions.[1]

Actually, corporate managements have many goals. Perhaps they are more interested in making their firm big than in making it profitable. The fact that short-run profitability might deny certain opportunities for long-run growth suggests that survival and profitability and growth must all be long-run objectives. Thus, despite the great differences between the "entrepreneur" of economic theory and the large business unit of modern life, they do bear a family resemblance.

Market Structure Market structure, including some attention to the number, size, distribution, and market concentration of firms within an industry, becomes an important segment of any study of industrial organization. Economic theory provides a set of categories or market models that offer valuable guidance, but they fail to go the whole distance. A "monopoly" implies a single seller, and "pure competition" a very large number of sellers of a standardized commodity within the relevant markets. "Monopolistic competition," like pure competition, depends on a large number of sellers occupying the market, even though each of them has some touches of individuality. "Oligopoly," usually defined as a few sellers occupying the market, covers everything else.

We need a measurement tool to take account of both the number and the size distribution of firms in a market, one simple enough so that the result is easy to interpret. The most widely used device is the *concentration ratio*. To compute a concentration ratio, one ranks the firms in the industry. (Size is usually measured in terms of either sales or employees.) Then, starting from the top of the list, one adds up the percentages for the largest four, the largest eight, and sometimes the largest twenty firms in an industry. The concentration ratio for a monopoly would, of course, be 100 percent; the ratio for the largest four firms in a competitive industry would have to be very small, perhaps 5 or 10 percent. The ratio for an oligopoly would lie between these extremes.

---

[1] For more complete coverage on this point, see [4].

Table 9-1 gives concentration ratios for selected American industries in 1958. It also gives some idea of how industry boundaries are set according to the statistics collected by the federal government.

TABLE 9-1 *Concentration Ratios in Selected American Industries, 1958*

INDUSTRY	TOTAL NUMBER OF COMPANIES	PERCENTAGE OF VALUE OF SHIPMENTS ACCOUNTED FOR BY 4 LARGEST	8 LARGEST	20 LARGEST
Aircraft propellers	17	97	99	100
Soap and glycerin	231	90	94	97
Salt	27	81	90	99
Matches	18	64	88	100
Distilled liquor	88	60	77	94
Work shirts	43	52	68	88
Plastic materials	273	40	56	79
Flour and meal	703	38	51	68
Radios and related products	1,797	27	38	52
Cotton broad-woven goods	321	25	40	59
Commercial printing	13,023	10	16	25
Fur goods	1,651	5	8	14

SOURCE: [11, table 1-1].

A major problem of *industry boundaries* exists—boundaries between products, boundaries in space, boundaries in time. Simply counting the heads of buyers and sellers participating in a product market does not solve all the problems associated with labeling its sellers as a separate industry. Economic theory tells us that all participants in a market should be highly sensitive to changes in the terms of transactions offered by the other participants. And they should *not* be sensitive to such moves by outsiders located in other markets. The industries that we identify for discussion in the real world ought to satisfy this requirement.

For instance, as aluminum has grown more important among the key basic metals used in the modern economy, it has found itself in close rivalry with steel and other metals for more and more uses. Should the industry boundary be drawn around the sellers of aluminum or around the sellers of "basic metals"? That is the problem of industry boundaries. Drawing the boundaries too widely lumps together producers who are somewhat insensitive to one another's actions. Drawing them too narrowly places in separate industries firms that are actually sensitive to one another's actions.

Another major problem of industry boundaries arises for products sold in regional markets. Consider the example of beer, a product consisting—let us face it—mostly of water. Its transportation costs are thus high relative to the sale value of the product. In the United States a number of brands are advertised and sold nationally, but in every area they compete against a different group of "local brands," which typically sell at a lower price and often hold a large share of the local market. Should we consider breweries a national industry or a group of interrelated regional industries?

Our information on seller concentration pertains only to national markets; it does not detect local or regional concentration. Among industries with regional markets, even the unconcentrated industries may sell locally under conditions of oligopoly.

Another important qualification for interpreting concentration ratios is the role of foreign trade. A single seller monopolizing the entire domestic market is a very different thing from a single domestic producer holding half of domestic sales in competition with imports. Concentration ratios, however, are calculated on the basis of sales by domestic producers only, and so the statistics show the same concentration in both cases.

Much of the discussion of industry types in this chapter draws upon the concept of concentration ratios. We shall often find it easier to talk about "more concentrated" or "less concentrated" industries than about the separate types of industries described in economic theory, such as purely competitive or oligopolistic ones. This does not mean that we are dropping these theoretical models. We shall use the theories of monopoly and oligopoly to derive predictions about how "highly concentrated" industries are likely to behave. We shall use the theories of monopolistic competition and pure competition to tell us what to expect from "unconcentrated" industries. Switching over to describing industries by their concentration, however, has two major advantages: (1) we can readily measure concentration in the actual industries around us; and (2) concentration is a "continuous variable," reminding us that actual industries do not fall into a few neat categories but range continuously in concentration from top to bottom.

What about concentration in industries other than manufacturing? Published statistics largely fail us in this area, but the general patterns show through clearly. Public utilities and transportation, which in the United States are regulated by various agencies of federal and state government, mostly operate under conditions of local monopoly or very high seller concentration. The local telephone company or electric utility holds a monopoly of its service in almost all cases—for good reason.

Many industries that produce primary raw materials, on the other hand, are fairly unconcentrated. Agriculture is the classic example of the purely competitive industry. Not only are there over 2 million commercial farms in the country, but each individual crop or product is grown on a relatively large number of them.

Market structure is important because it determines the behavior of firms in the industry, and that behavior in turn determines the quality of the industry's performance. Explaining the quality of performance—the industry's contribution to attaining major economic goals—is our ultimate objective. Industrial organization helps us understand what makes for good or bad performance. It also assists public-policy formation by indicating ways to make the economy perform better.

Highly concentrated industries are likely to perform poorly because they allocate resources inefficiently—employing too few factors of production and channeling too many into less concentrated industries. The other elements of market structure—product differentiation, barriers to entry, growth rate of market demand, price elasticity of market demand, and ratio of fixed to variable costs in the short run—share this power to influence performance.

If we can uncover reliable links between elements of structure and elements of performance, we can with relative ease and confidence predict the performance of any industry in which we are interested. Even more important, the elements of market structure can be changed in some cases as a result of public policy. If we can spot some feature of market structure which regularly causes poor market performance, we may find the key to designing policies that change the environment and raise the level of performance.

The next trait of market structure which we need to consider goes by the name of *product differentiation*. As Professor Chamberlin defined it in his classic volume [6, p. 56]:

A general class of product is differentiated if any significant basis exists for distinguishing the goods (or services) of one seller from those of another. Such a basis may be real or fancied, so long as it is of any importance whatever to buyers, and leads to a preference for one variety of the product over another. Where such differentiation exists, even though it be slight, buyers will be paired with sellers, not by chance and at random (as under pure competition), but according to their preferences.

A seller, in fact, can jointly manipulate three variables: "(1) . . . his price, (2) the nature of his product, and (3) his advertising outlays" [6, p. 71].* Growers of many kinds of fruits find that it does not pay to advertise the product of their own orchards under a brand name, but they often band together and advertise their crop cooperatively. They may be able to swing consumers' preferences away from grapefruit to lemons, but one lemon continues to look about like another, no matter what anybody says.

Barriers to entry constitute another major segment of the firm's economic environment. Just as concentration reflects the number of actual market rivals of a firm, so the condition of entry tells the story about potential rivals. To see the importance of the condition of entry, imagine a good produced by a monopolist who has no actual rivals, but knows that raising his price above the level that yields just normal profits will draw numerous rivals into competition with him. To preserve a quiet life, he may choose to set a "competitive" price, earning no excess profits but attracting no rivals. We can think of an industry's barriers to entry as measured, in principle, by the *highest price that will just fail to tempt new firms into the industry.*

Barriers may be due to (1) the need to produce very large amounts of the product in order to achieve efficiency (scale economy barriers); (2) the existence of patents, commercial secrets (Coca-Cola formula), control over a limited supply of some especially significant input (high-grade copper ore), or the high cost of capital to a new firm; or (3) product differentiation, as when an established brand name gives an existing firm advantages that a potential entrant can overcome only by much larger advertising and sales-promotion expenses.

Market Conduct   *Market conduct* consists of a firm's policies toward its product market and toward moves made by its rivals in that market. A market functions to determine the price of a product and the quantity that people choose to buy. It also sets the quality of the product, its style or range of styles offered, and the type and amount of advertising and other lures used by firms to attract customers. Somehow, the firms must set their own offers and policies in the market and react to those

---

* Editors' note: For an extended discussion of product differentiation and product variation by Professor Chamberlin, see [5].

of their rivals until a consistent result prevails across the entire market. These actions and reactions constitute market conduct.

Consider an industry that matches the textbook model of pure competition. In terms of the elements of market structure, it would exhibit very low concentration, insignificant barriers to entry, and no product differentiation. In this environment the individual firm has no significant freedom of choice. The market sets the price for the product, and a single firm cannot meaningfully ask a different one. The absence of product differentiation means that the firm has no choice to make about its product—to make it blue or green, with fins or without. No problems arise over advertising. The firm, by assumption, cannot create product differentiation in its favor, and has nothing to gain individually by advertising. Pure competition, moreover, permits a firm no choice in deciding how efficient it will be! If its many rivals keep their costs as low as possible, it can only do likewise or else be forced out of business as a result of subnormal profits.

The pure monopolist is almost as limited in playing an independent hand. If he maximizes his profits, then one particular combination of price and output will prove optimal for him. The "quality level" of his product—the range of sizes and colors in which it is offered, as well as the level of his advertising budget, can all be set by some plan so as to maximize profits.

The only choice open to the monopolist, really, is whether or not to be a profit-maximizer. Unlike the firm in pure competition, he does not have to. He can settle instead for some lesser level of profit which seems "reasonable." He can turn to other goals, such as increasing the size of the firm or his own prestige in the community. He can simply take it easy and not put in the hard work necessary to stay optimally efficient.

Pricing policies in an oligopolistic market consist normally of individual firms setting their own "list prices." They adjust these prices in response to changing market conditions or to changes introduced by their rivals. When the product is undifferentiated, this process of adjustment and response goes on very quickly and sensitively.

The trouble with discussing how oligopolistic firms reach their internal decisions on setting and changing prices is that economists know rather little about it. As with any organizational decision, businesses follow certain "rules of thumb" to reduce the decision to manageable proportions. They may set a certain normal rate of return on their investment as a target, or add a standard mark-up to their costs to determine the price.[2] Some economists have declared that the use of these rules of thumb proves that large corporations do not seek to maximize their

---

[2] For a description of pricing policies followed by some major U.S. corporations, see [9].

profits, because the rules obviously will not pick the profit-maximizing price every time. But most people would not draw such a sweeping conclusion. A rule of thumb is, after all, only a practical tool for approximating some ideal objective. The "normal" profit or mark-up sought might well be the most a firm thinks it can earn without attracting entry.

The other major question about the pricing policies of oligopolists, besides the question of what profit goal they seek, is how they estimate the responses of their rivals. For instance, an oligopolist may consider raising his price. If the price prevailing in his market is too low to maximize profits, and if all his rivals also raise their prices, then his profits will increase. Conversely, if one oligopolist lowers his price without his rivals' also lowering theirs, he has a good chance to increase his market share and thus his profits. What to do depends very much on how his rivals are expected to react.

Oligopolists coordinate their prices by (1) agreements among themselves, (2) price leadership assumed by one of the firms, or (3) tacit collusion, in which firms take one another's responses into account without betraying any external signs. Take the case of an industry dominated by a few firms, and with substantial product differentiation. The differentiation removes some of the pressure for uniform prices. Now, suppose that each seller knows that the others will generally behave predictably in changing the product they offer to the public. Suppose, also, that each seller knows roughly how each of his rivals calculates his price and changes it in response to changing cost and demand conditions. With this much information, it becomes possible for the industry to extract much of the monopoly profits potentially open to it without explicit collusion.[3]

In addition to the competitive practices discussed up to this point, there is a whole range of possible coercive tactics, such as (1) using predatory price-cutting (price wars) for taming, weakening, or eliminating existing business rivals, and (2) raising the barriers to entry to curtail the supply of potential rivals.

Public Policy toward Business Economists can state clearly enough their reasons for thinking that some reform or regulation might improve the performance of the economy. They oppose monopoly situations because such situations signal an inappropriate use of society's scarce productive resources; monopoly profits stem from restricting the flow of resources into the monopolized sector. Unfortunately, public policy, which is the result of many voices and many minds, living and dead, carries no such rationale for what it seeks to accomplish. Nonetheless, most major

---

[3] For an interesting discussion of product differentiation, see [2, appendix D]. See also [7] and [1].

policies directed toward competition and monopoly in the United States make some sense in terms of economic analysis. We can describe in terms of the categories of market structure and market conduct what United States policies seek to prevent or to change in the United States economy. And we can infer thereby what type of change they seek to promote in market performance.

We can describe economic policies "to prevent monopoly and promote competition," on the one hand, and "to prevent competition and promote monopoly," on the other. The nation is most famous for, and proud of, policies falling in the first class.

It will help to distinguish carefully between policies that aim at the structure of industries and those that aim at their conduct. A policy requiring the dissolution of firms that hold too large a share of their markets seeks to change market structure in a "more competitive" direction. Likewise, a policy of preventing mergers that would result in a high level of seller concentration affects market structure, but in a preventive rather than a curative manner. On the other hand, a law forbidding agreements among firms to fix prices rules out one form of price coordination between rival sellers, and thus affects market conduct.

For four-fifths of a century the United States has had antitrust laws—the Sherman and the Clayton Acts. These acts—variously interpreted, amended, and enforced—have sought to compel competition, prevent designated business practices, and forbid certain mergers and other types of combinations. As amended and interpreted, they have delved increasingly into the intricacies of competitive practices. The Sherman Antitrust Act (1890) makes monopolistic restraints of trade illegal. The scope of the act was subsequently narrowed to "unreasonable" restraints of trade. The Clayton Antitrust Act (1914) blocks *tying arrangements,* whereby a seller gives the buyer access to one line of the seller's goods only if the buyer takes others as well; it forbids *exclusive-dealing arrangements,* whereby a seller gives the buyer access to his line of goods only if the buyer agrees to take no goods from any of the seller's rivals; and it prohibits mergers that substantially lessen competition or tend to create a monopoly.

Many recent antitrust decisions have turned upon the size and market power of firms in a merger that had already taken place. In Los Angeles, for example, Von's supermarket grocery chain was denied the right to absorb the Shopping Bag chain because the merged unit would control nearly 8 percent of the grocery business in the Los Angeles market. Though no abuse of marketing power was charged, the Justices announced that this percentage would constitute too great a concentration in the face of a declining number of small stores. Critics pointed out that never before had so low a percentage of concentration been condemned; also, they reminded their listeners that it was the current marketing evolution, not a supermarket chain, that had spelled the doom of "Pop and Mom" and other small stores. In fact, several knowledgeable antitrust experts in and out of government were rising to the defense of large firms generally, because they tend to be more efficient. In the course of the debate, Professor John Kenneth Galbraith declared that firms which were already large were indeed efficient and that they were relatively immune from antitrust prosecution. It was the merger attempt of two middle-sized firms to increase their size and market power which was subject to prosecution, he said [8].

Upon occasion, a government will choose actually to restrict competition between business firms. Local governments license firms, thus restricting their numbers and their entry. Crop restrictions are common in agriculture, where overproduction and unstable prices are prevalent. Patents give inventors a limited monopoly. Retail sales below cost are restricted in most states by so-called fair-practice acts. Advertising and promotional allowances and discounts for volume and for other reasons must pass the Federal Trade Commission's "equitable formula" rule, lest they be overthrown as unfair to small firms under the terms of the Robinson-Patman Act.

Market Performance When we ask how the economy's performance can better the lot of its citizens, we can agree that four economic goals, or performance traits, hold special importance. (1) Our economy should be *efficient*, employing its scarce factors of production so that they yield us the greatest possible real income. (2) Our economy should be *fully employed*, because we waste factors of production even more by leaving them idle than by using them inefficiently, not to mention the personal hardships associated with unemployment; but it should not achieve this goal through unreasonable inflation of the general price level. (3) Our economy should be *progressive*; that is, it should add to its stock of factors of production, raise the quality and variety of goods which it makes available, and improve the techniques with which it organizes factors of production, all at reasonable rates of progress. (4) Our economy should be *equitable*, distributing its real output among its members to provide for their essential needs and reasonable expectations as well as to reward their productive efforts.

We define *market performance* as the appraisal of the economic results of an industry's market behavior compared to the best possible contribution it could make to achieving these goals.

Notice that when we speak of good or bad market performance, we are not passing a flat judgment on the American private enterprise system. In providing us with the world's highest standard of living, the system obviously works well in comparison with those of other countries. Our questions here concern the actual, as measured against the potential, market performance of individual industries. Can we find gaps in the performance? Can we locate reasons for these gaps and suggest ways to eliminate them?

We might ask whether a world of competitive industries or a world of monopolies, low entry barriers or high, would contribute more to maintaining a high and stable level of employment. So far as we know now, it does not seem to make much difference.

On close inspection, the connection between industrial concentration and the distribution of income turns out to be not very close. Some people, however, give a different twist to the goal of equitable distribution in our economy. They feel that ours would be a better society if all businesses were small, if the maximum number of citizens were independent proprietors rather than employees serving the economic interest of an employer. They would oppose monopoly, even if all of the giant industries were competitive enough to give the best possible market performance.

Turning to the goal of a satisfactory rate of economic progress, we find general agreement that the level of seller concentration does have some influence, but there are strident disputes over the direction of that influence. The argument that rapid technical advance requires some degree of monopoly stems originally from the writings of Joseph Schumpeter. To bring about massive innovations, Schumpeter felt that firms had to be protected by some degree of monopoly—to have some room for maneuver [10]. Other economists point out, though, that one of the strongest incentives to innovate is to gain an advantage over determined market rivals, and that this force induces businessmen to try innovations which the monopolist would never bother with.

The Schumpeter hypothesis poses a troubling prospect—must we sacrifice efficiency to get progress, or vice versa? There is no definitive answer. Larger firms are more likely to engage in research and development than smaller ones, and industrial research is heavily concentrated in a few industries consisting to a great extent of large firms with moderate to high levels of concentration. This, however, does not necessarily mean that the most important innovations come from the laboratories of large firms.

When we reach the goal of efficiency in the economy, the study of industrial organization comes into its own. The foremost aspect of efficiency is how resources are allocated among the various types of goods and services produced in the economy. The test comes in the satisfaction that resources produce—as measured by the returns they earn when used in various ways. If capital earns more in producing apples than oranges, clearly too much capital is engaged in producing oranges. If some were to be transferred out of orange groves and into apple orchards, the worth to consumers of the extra apples would exceed the value of the forgone oranges. Thus, showing what conditions will produce an even level of profit rates from industry to industry, reflecting an optimal distribution of resources, is the main challenge to a study of industrial organization.

The notion of "normal profits" as a sign of proper resource allocation lies at the heart of our analysis. The equity capital that entrepreneurs supply to firms in different industries does the job of balancing business costs and revenues. If entrepreneurs make wrong guesses about the use of resources, their costs tend to run ahead of revenues. They must dip into their equity to make up the difference, and they earn a negative rate of return. On the other hand, if they find highly productive uses for scarce economic resources, then their revenues run far ahead of costs and they earn high rates of return.

A quick glance at the data convinces us that industries earn very different rates of profit. The U.S. Treasury compiles figures on the net profits of corporations after taxes, from which we can figure the return on the owners' investment in some broad groups of industries. In fiscal year 1961, corporations making motor vehicles and equipment earned 12.3 percent, but producers of textile-mill products only 4.8 percent. The chemicals and allied products group earned 10.0 percent, manufacturers of furniture and fixtures only 3.3 percent. Banks made 8.0 percent, while hotels lost 1.8 percent.

This variety of profit rates among large industry groups suggests that resource allocation is not all it might be. Furthermore, the evidence points to certain traits of market structure as the source of excessive rates of profit. Industrial concentration and high barriers tend to produce high profit rates—giving firms a chance to garner potential monopoly profits without fear of entry.

Profit rates deal with market performance in allocating resources *between* industries, testing whether some industries employ too few factors through monopolistic restriction. Other aspects of market performance concern the allocation of resources *within* industries. For instance, most industries seem to contain plants that are too small to exhaust all economies of scale. Industries with large amounts of inefficiently small capacity seem to be those in which product differentiation holds sway.

The influence upon an industry's efficiency of expenditures for sales promotion and product changes should be noted. For some industries, such as cement, meat-packing, and farm machinery, less than 1 percent of revenues go to advertising. For typewriters and automobiles the number creeps up to a range of 2 to 4 percent. The cigarette, liquor, and fountain-pen industries spend 5 or 6 percent of sales revenue persuading us to buy the product, and the soap industry soft-soaps us to the tune of about 10 percent of sales revenue [3].

Once again, we can easily spot the link between market structure and this aspect of market performance. Sellers without any product differentiation have little to gain from advertising, which aims more at selling steel companies than selling steel. By contrast, where product differentiation exists, each rival must advertise to keep some buyers in a frame of mind to prefer his product to others.

Various industries have been suspected of making their products less durable than would have been possible. The annual model changes of the consumers' durable-goods industries have been widely attacked as using up resources in retooling costs and the like without improving the "real" utility of the product to the user.

Everybody wants to keep the two major landmarks in the antitrust scene—the Sherman and Clayton Acts. Indeed, their basic soundness is confirmed by the fact that a number of other industrialized countries have swung away from an acceptance of cartels and monopoly toward adopting portions of United States antitrust policy to spur competition in their economies.

But these industrialized nations have not taken over our antitrust policies lock, stock, and barrel, and here at home arguments still occur over the wisdom of particular provisions. Our limited knowledge of what makes market performance good or bad contains some lessons for public policy. Two views exist over the main point of contention: section 2 of the Sherman Act. Some would push it farther toward outlawing situations of high seller concentration—the "market power" test. Others would largely drop the element of market structure and examine performance, especially progressiveness—the "rule of reason" school. Our evidence indicates that the market-power test would be more likely to improve economic performance.

Suppose, now that *you* had the opportunity to rewrite America's laws relating to competition and monopoly, with the goal of promoting the best attainable market performance. What would you do? Does the market performance of American industry, constituted as it is now, rate a mark of excellent or a mark of acceptable? If most firms and industries are making a profit, by what other standards should they be judged? Would you try to reorder the structure of many of the country's industries? Would you seek to rechannel market conduct so that the economists' theories of pricing and competition would replace the businessman's "rule of thumb" pricing and his emphasis upon product differentiation and promotional practices? Would you redesign or redirect the government's policies toward business? What changes, if any, *would* you make?

REFERENCES

1. ABBOTT, LAWRENCE. *Quality and Competition* (New York: Columbia University Press, 1955).
2. BAIN, JOE S. *Barriers to New Competition: Their Character and Consequences in Manufacturing Industries* (Cambridge, Mass.: Harvard University Press, 1956).
3. ———. *Industrial Organization* (New York: Wiley, 1959).
4. CAVES, RICHARD E. *American Industry: Structure, Conduct, and Performance*, 2d ed. (Englewood Cliffs, N. J.: Prentice-Hall, 1967).
5. CHAMBERLIN, EDWARD H. "The Product as an Economic Variable," *Quarterly Journal of Economics*, 67:1 (1953).
6. ———. *The Theory of Monopolistic Competition*, 8th ed. (Cambridge, Mass.: Harvard University Press, 1956).
7. DONELLY, P. J., and R. H. HOLTON. "A Note on Product Differentiation and Entertainment Expense Allowances in the United States," *Journal of Industrial Economics*, 10 (March 1962), pp. 134–138.
8. GALBRAITH, JOHN K. *The New Industrial State* (Boston: Houghton Mifflin, 1967).
9. KAPLAN, A. D. H., J. B. DIRLAM, and R. F. LANZILLOTTI. *Pricing in Big Business: A Case Approach* (Washington, D. C.: Brookings, 1958).
10. SCHUMPETER, JOSEPH A. *Capitalism, Socialism, and Democracy*, 3d ed. (New York: Harper, 1950).
11. U.S. CONGRESS, SENATE JUDICIARY COMMITTEE. *Concentration Ratios in Manufacturing Industry, 1958* (1962).

10

ECONOMIC ANALYSIS OF THE PUBLIC SECTOR

Arthur Smithies[*]

I.

THE Planning–Programming–Budgeting System (PPBS) is a current enthusiasm in the federal government. Literally hundreds of civil servants are attempting to learn what it is all about and are having some difficulty in doing so—partly because of the complexity of the subject, but largely because of a lack of training in elementary economics. PPBS is essentially an extension of the economics of choice to public decisionmaking [4]. Economists are entering and beginning to dominate this field not only because of the relevance of economics, but because other disciplines, such as political science or public administration, have not addressed themselves to the task.

Every economist, however, should temper his ideas of what is feasible by the work of political economists like Aaron Wildavsky [8], who reminds us that changes in the budgetary process are likely to alter the balance of political forces and are therefore apt to meet with strong opposition. Wildavsky makes the important point that traditional methods work remarkably smoothly, while the PPBS is likely to involve costly and clamorous debate over the relative merits of alternatives. His advice is not to tamper with something that is working reasonably well—advice that does not appeal to economists.

The basic article of faith of the economist is that explicit choice among alternative courses of action

[*] Harvard University.

leads to more rational, and therefore better, decisions than those reached by other available methods. The reason for this faith stems from the prevalence of scarcity in a modern society. Scarcity in this sense does not mean absolute scarcity, such as insufficient food to keep a population alive; it means wants that run ahead of means of satisfying them. Whether these wants are "spurious" or "meritorious," "artificial" or "natural," everyone is faced with a budget constraint, the force of which does not appear to diminish as individuals or countries grow richer.

There is no evidence that we are moving toward the "full complement of riches" contemplated by Adam Smith or the benign stationary state of satiety of John Stuart Mill. To use another phrase of Adam Smith, the demand for "equipage," both civilian and military, is unlimited. Moreover, Keynesian economics has taught governments how to avoid even temporary surfeits of resources. It is no easier to get a 10 percent increase in factors of production in the United States than in Europe or Japan; hence, there is need for allocation in the public as well as the private sector. The current interest in PPBS reflects this fact.

I stress the point that economists believe in the virtue of explicit choice among alternatives. I am an economist and entertain this belief, but I feel uneasy about it. Many of the creative acts of history—by poets, scientists, statesmen—have resulted from the pursuit of goals without regard to consequences rather than from the cold calculation of costs and benefits. One of the attractive characteristics of the United States is its willingness to undertake great enterprises with enthusiasm. Much of the richness—and much of the turbulence—of our society would disappear if the enthusiasts were overwhelmed by the calculators.

But the need for allocation remains. At the present time, the United States is the arena for a competitive struggle among claimants for foreign undertakings, claimants for social welfare, and taxpayers. At the highest political levels, difficult marginal choices involving small fractions of total national resources have to be made—choices that may greatly affect the course of history. The question is whether choices can be made more effectively by processes that fully inform decisionmakers concerning the costs and consequences of their acts, or by processes that are essentially haphazard.

I think of PPBS not as a method of reaching definitive conclusions, but as one of organizing discussion and marshalling evidence in a way that leads to an effective advocacy procedure.[1] The situation is analogous to a legal trial. One cannot tell, by the application of any objective criterion,

---

[1] See the testimony of Alain C. Enthoven before the Jackson Committee [7, particularly p. 73]. Despite such assertions by the main architects of PPBS, the opinion persists that analysis can be a substitute for, rather than simply an aid to, judgment and intuition.

whether a jury has reached the right decision. One has confidence, however, that if the rules of evidence are followed and both sides are well represented, the decision is more likely to be good than bad. This does not imply that jurors become mere mechanisms. It implies that they act as human beings with their emotions tempered by good information.

Many economists will not share my point of view, and they will be partly right. There is a growing and highly erudite body of literature which attempts to provide definite criteria concerning what governments should or should not do. I shall refer briefly to cost-benefit analysis and the theory of public goods.

Cost-benefit analysis[2] is frequently identified with PPBS. It is, in fact, part of PPBS, but far from the whole of it. What it attempts to do is to measure and compare, in terms of money, the discounted streams of future benefits and future costs associated with a proposed project. If the ratio of benefits to costs is "satisfactory," the project should be undertaken. ("Satisfactory" in this connection means, among other things, superior to any public or private alternative.) Or if the government itself is subject to a budget constraint for public investment, projects should be ranked in the order of their cost-benefit ratios. By cost-benefit analysis, the government attempts to assess its investments in the same way as a private investor makes his decisions.

There is, however, an important difference between the environments in which public and private decisions are made. A government agency has an incentive to estimate favorable ratios for its own projects. It must compete for funds with other agencies, and its estimates are rarely subject to market tests. It is difficult to assess the returns to a project—say, an irrigation or highway job—once it has been completed. And government agencies cannot go bankrupt. Private investors have been known to exaggerate their claims in appealing to stockholders; nevertheless, they are generally subject to market sanctions that encourage them to err on the side of caution.

For government projects, high cost-benefit ratios can be grounds for rejecting projects. But low ratios do not necessarily mean project acceptance. It is only human for estimators to be optimistic—however professionally competent they may be.

Another difficulty is that in most public undertakings some of the expected benefits are not economic and not measurable in money. Water projects are intended to produce regional and sectoral as well as national benefits. The cost of training a high school dropout is to be measured not only against the income he will earn, but also against the social benefits of making him a productive member of society. In other areas, such

---

[2] For an admirable and exhaustive survey of the literature on the subject, see [5].

as defense, preservation of natural beauty, and preservation of wildlife, the expected benefits are applicable either not at all or only to a minor extent.[3]

In short, economic benefits are but one component of the total consequences of a government program. Even if they were measurable with a high degree of precision, cost-benefit analysis cannot replace the need for judgment by the decisionmaker.

Another way in which economists have sought to provide objective criteria is through the theory of public goods. Since Wicksell, it has been recognized that the private market fails to provide goods which are collectively consumed and from which no one can be excluded (lighthouses are a classic example). While everyone wants the good, everyone has an incentive to let someone else pay for it. Consequently, government action is required to compel consumers to "reveal their preferences." Economists, with a high degree of ingenuity, but less success, have set themselves the task of devising voting procedures to supply public goods in sufficient quantities.

The theory of public goods is convincing in demonstrating cases of market failure, but it is far from satisfactory in providing criteria for the limits and extent of government action. For it rests on the assumption of fixed consumers' tastes and holds that the function of government is to give effect to these fixed tastes.

The private economy is, of course, actively engaged in changing individual tastes; and I maintain that the government is similarly engaged, whether or not it ought to be. It is ridiculous to say that the uninformed consumer has a taste for national defense which should provide a guide to government action. It is the task of national leaders to evolve a defense policy and persuade the public to accept it. Similarly, conservationists attempt to awaken the public to the beauties of wildlife and the wilderness. Public health attempts (with little success) to alter peoples' taste for cigarettes.

Democracy, as Schumpeter maintains, does not attempt to interpret and give effect to the predetermined will of the people. It is not government by Gallup poll, even though Gallup polls may make it move in that direction. Rather, democratic leaders attempt to win the approval of the electorate for what they have done, or what they propose to do—including changing tastes. I may well vote for someone who undertakes to make me dislike smoking, in preference to a politician who promises cheaper cigarettes.

Richard Musgrave [3] distinguishes between "social wants," which should be subject to consumer sovereignty, and "merit wants," such as

---

[3] For an excellent discussion of this point, see [1, p. 208].

defense, which should be dealt with on some other basis. To social wants, the theory of public goods applies, but Musgrave does not provide criteria for the satisfaction of merit wants. And what of the lighthouse? Seafaring individuals may be deeply conscious of the disasters of shipwreck. But one can readily agree that it is a proper function of government to create in the minds of landlocked individuals a desire to avoid shipwrecks. Examples can be multiplied to show that the distinction between merit and social wants cannot be made operational. And, anyway, many important decisions relate to merit wants.

I conclude, therefore, that even if individual preferences could be ascertained and aggregated into a social preference function, or even if voting procedures could be devised that would induce individuals to reveal their preferences, we still would lack adequate criteria for government action. The objectives of policy cannot be provided by economists or social scientists. They must be determined in the political arena. But the political process can be illuminated and improved by the application of economic principles.

National goals must in a significant sense be feasible. In the first place, the country must be able to afford them. Their attainment must not involve some intolerable cost in another direction. For example, a guaranteed income of $5,000 a year for the population of the United States would not be feasible in the light of the taxation that would have to be imposed on earned incomes. A goal of $100 a year is a different matter. Going to the moon by 1970 has been demonstrated by Apollo 11 to be a feasible goal, but to go to Mars at the same time would not be, even if there were no technical obstacles. Probably, such a goal would involve an intolerable drain on the scientific resources of the country. Even though each goal is feasible in this sense, it does not follow that all feasible goals can be attained simultaneously. The program adopted by the government must involve compromises among its various goals. In the second place, goals must be technically feasible. It does not make sense to set goals for the conquest of space or cancer unless the means can be created for attaining them. On the other hand, the advance of science and technology produces goals and objectives not hitherto contemplated.

As in the private economy, there is continual interaction between public ends and means—new ends stimulate the creation of new means, and vice versa. It follows that goals or objectives cannot be taken as given, as they are in the economics textbooks. *Determining goals and deciding on the methods for attaining them are part of the same process.*

That is the major point I have to make. Most economic theory and operations analysis starts with the assumption of a given preference function or objective function and seeks an optimum situation under it. For the most important decisions, this umbrella is not provided. Within a broad context, the objective function itself must be articulated and refined as part of the decisionmaking process.

II.

PPBS had its origin in the Department of Defense; in 1965, President Johnson decided to extend the system to the whole government. In a memorandum of August 25, 1965, to agency heads, he stated that:

Once the new system is in operation ... it will enable us to:

1 Identify our national goals with precision and on a continuing basis

2 Choose among those goals the ones that are most urgent

3 Search for alternative means of reaching those goals most effectively at the least cost

4 Inform ourselves not merely on next year's costs, but on the second, and third, and subsequent year's costs of our programs

5 Measure the performance of our programs to insure a dollar's worth of service for each dollar spent.[4]

I shall make some brief comments on each of these matters.

IDENTIFICATION OF GOALS The goals of a government agency depend partly on legislation, legislative histories, and Presidential announcements. It is, however, the business of the agency to propose new goals. New goals come about as a result of research into social needs, an increasing public awareness of social problems, and the acquisition of fresh capabilities, such as the ability to cure cancer or polio. Whether imposed from above or recommended by the agencies themselves or by private bodies, goals become established through the political process.

Some goals can be established with precision. Going to the moon by 1970, reducing hard-core unemployment to 5 percent, constructing so many units of low-income housing per year are examples. Other goals cannot be precisely defined. Beautification of highways, promotion of general scientific advance, assistance to underdeveloped countries are examples. In these instances, it is a matter of the more, the better. The extent to which they are pursued depends on the opportunity costs involved.

Even if goals are identified with precision, that fact does not mean that they should thereby take priority over goals that must be more generally described. It may be preferable to stretch out the moon program rather than delay the destruction of billboards. And even if all goals can be

---

[4] Reprinted in [7, pp. 12–13].

defined with precision, they may not all be attainable simultaneously. The problem of policy, in that event, would be to reach a satisfactory compromise among the degrees of fulfillment of the various goals.[5]

URGENCY OF GOALS   The statement that the goals chosen should be the most urgent ones could have been more happily expressed, at least from an economist's point of view. It seems to imply that the most urgent goals should be selected intact, and the less urgent ones abandoned.

What is needed is a compromise position among goals in accordance with their relative urgencies. The system should yield the rates at which the pursuit of various goals can be traded off. Can the general objectives of an agency be furthered by transferring $1 million from program X to program Y? In what way should an increase in the resources available to an agency be distributed among its various programs? The establishment of such trade-offs is the essence of our advocacy procedure.

REACHING GOALS MOST EFFECTIVELY AT THE LEAST COST   The Presidential syntax seems somewhat complicated at this point, but the statement seems to apply to cases where a goal is definitely fixed; the problem then becomes one of cost minimization. In many, if not most, practical situations, the problem poses itself the other way around. Given the need for action in an area, the decisionmakers ask themselves how given sums can most effectively be spent. By considering alternative ways of spending varying sums, they can arrive at a series of optimal budgets. Hence, the term "cost-effectiveness." The actual size of the agency's budget will depend on competition with other agencies and with the taxpayer.

There is an essential difference between minimizing the cost of attaining a given objective and maximizing the results of a given expenditure. In the latter case, objectives or preferences are not necessarily fixed. *The process involves the discovery or revision of the preference function itself.* Old objectives may be discarded or downgraded and new ones introduced. This is what the President presumably means by identification of goals "on a continuing basis."

THE TIME DIMENSION   In most cases, government programs involve commitments of resources over a considerable period. Time is needed to get a program under way, and benefits are realized over an extended period beyond that. Typically, a new program involves a research and

---

[5] In this connection, Theil's concept of a quadratic objective function is useful and suggestive. It makes "welfare" depend on a weighted sum of the deviations of actual from desired levels of the goal variable. This approach implies that all goals are defined with precision but that none of them is actually attained [6].

development phase; an investment phase, during which physical facilities are constructed and manpower trained; and finally, an operating phase, during which benefits are yielded. Consequently, a long view over an uncertain future is required.

Incidentally, the Presidential memorandum does not acknowledge the fundamental question of uncertainty. In the face of uncertainty, one's best course is usually to preserve sufficient flexibility and adaptability to permit programs to be revised in the light of an unfolding future.

On the other hand, the requirements of short-run stabilization policy, as well as tradition, require that budgeting be conducted on a short-run—usually a one- or two-year—basis. One of the major unsolved problems in PPBS is how to reconcile the need for short-run adjustment with the equally important need for effective medium- and long-range programming.

REVIEW OF PERFORMANCE Here the President emphasizes a matter that the government does not normally find congenial. It does not accord with American tradition to spend much time praising or bewailing the past. In the federal government—at least in the legislative and executive branches—reviews, assessments, and audits have never claimed the attention of the best available talent. Something, of course, is lost by this inattention. The same mistakes tend to be repeated and the same inefficiencies perpetuated. Efforts to review the past systematically with a view to illuminating a course of future action are not misplaced.

The phrase about insuring "a dollar's worth of service for each dollar spent" can be misleading. It supports the widespread misconception that benefits should be measured in dollars. It can lead to illegitimate extensions of the cost-benefit technique, or to a bias in favor of benefits that appear to be measurable in dollars. One example of dollar-estimating gone wrong is the practice in the federal government of assuming that recreation projects yield $1.50 worth of pleasure per head per day.

Many of the official justifications of the space program rest on the productivity and technological spillover into the private economy. This spillover is a relevant by-product, but in no sense the main product. If promoting technology on earth were the only issue, there surely would be more cost-effective ways of promoting it than going to the moon. And even if there were no spillover, going to the moon might still be considered to be worth the cost.

My own view of going to the moon is that it is like climbing Mount Everest. The activity is exciting and ennobling, but the end product is zero. I subscribe to Marshall's view that "each new step upward is to be regarded as the development of new activities giving rise to new wants, rather than new wants giving rise to new activities" [2, p. 89]. If this point of view is disconcerting to those addicted to benefit measurement, so much the worse for their procedures.

These comments are made by way of elucidation rather than criticism. Everything could be made easier if the President could address his Cabinet in terms of the elementary economics of choice. But everything may then appear beguilingly simple. When one thinks of the extraordinary complexity of the government, one throws up one's hands in despair. Nevertheless, I cling to the belief that explicit rational decisionmaking has an important role to play in the federal government.

REFERENCES

1. MAASS, ARTHUR. "Benefit-Cost Analysis: Its Relevance to Public Investment Decisions," *Quarterly Journal of Economics*, 80:2 (May 1966), pp. 208–226.
2. MARSHALL, ALFRED. *Principles of Economics*, 8th ed. (London: Macmillan, 1953).
3. MUSGRAVE, RICHARD A. *The Theory of Public Finance: A Study in Public Economy* (New York: McGraw-Hill, 1959).
4. NOVICK, DAVID (ed.). *Program Budgeting: Program Analysis and the Federal Budget* (Cambridge, Mass.: Harvard University Press, 1965).
5. PREST, ALAN R., and RALPH TURVEY. "Cost-Benefit Analysis: A Survey," *Economic Journal*, 75 (December 1965), pp. 683–735.
6. THEIL, HENRI. *Optimal Decision Rules for Government and Industry* (Amsterdam: North-Holland, 1964).
7. U.S. CONGRESS, SENATE COMMITTEE ON GOVERNMENT OPERATIONS. *Planning—Programming—Budgeting* (1967), part I, pp. 1–63; part II, pp. 64–160.
8. WILDAVSKY, AARON B. *The Politics of the Budgetary Process* (Boston: Little, Brown, 1964).

11

ECONOMIC REASONING AND NATIONAL DEFENSE

Thomas C. Schelling*
Malcolm Palmatier**

ECONOMISTS have been closely associated with problems of defense for more than two decades. World War II brought with it taxation and debt management, price and wage controls, allocation of manpower and scarce materials, controls on investment and construction, large-scale contracting and renegotiation, readjustment benefits for veterans, import and export controls, and a host of other issues that kept large numbers of economists preoccupied, inside government and out. Many of these issues reappeared, on a smaller scale, with the Korean war. And currently, during the conflict in Vietnam, a point of concern to economists is the economic impact of our present defense effort— questions of how much the nation can afford, whether a peaceful settlement would have economic repercussions, how severely the stationing of troops overseas aggravates our balance-of-payments difficulties, and so forth.

Other problems of defense are less obviously "economic." Scarce resources have to be allocated between the European and the Far Eastern theaters; between immediate military production and investment in future capacity; between our own military forces, military aid for allies, and economic aid to permit allies to increase their own military strength. Scarce resources have to be allocated between maintaining

* Harvard University.
** The RAND Corporation.

current inventories of tested but obsolescing bombers and procuring sophisticated missiles for the future, between weapon systems that are ready for production now ("off the shelf") and those that can be available sooner or cheaper or better in the future *if* we invest more in their development now. We also have to allocate real income indirectly among the members of the population by deciding what age groups and sex will be subject to the draft, and what intellectual talents, levels of training, and degrees of physical fitness will qualify citizens for service. (Selective service is seldom recognized as "economic," because the "income" gained or lost by undergoing the servitude, risk, family disruption, or physical and emotional discomforts of military service is not commonly marketable, although different draftees may have different "opportunity costs." Comparison with the Civil War, when one could avoid military service by hiring his own replacement, reminds us that it is an economic policy decision to treat the matter as though it did not involve economics.)

We are not going to discuss the kind of economic problem that might be called the "impact of defense on the economy." We are not going to discuss inflation, price controls, foreign trade controls, or the relation of economic stability, strength, or growth to military strength. Such matters are familiar enough to economists and can be analyzed by conventional techniques.

Economics in Military Decisions What we shall discuss is the economics of military planning, military decisionmaking, military investment, allocation of military resources, and selection of military objectives. The point of view is that of the military planner and operator on the one hand, and that of the political decisionmaker on the other—a person concerned with how much to pay for how much security against what dangers, how to distribute the burdens, and how to design the bureaucratic structure within which the military services are to operate. With respect to military decisions, we shall look at the economic reasoning involved in making *conscious choices* and at the problem of designing military institutions that will increase the likelihood of making right decisions.

Values and Criteria It is important to keep in mind that, while the military services "produce" something of value, they suffer from two restraints not usually present in an ordinary business firm. One is that they may not get to test the correctness of their most important decisions until that unique occasion when it is too late to learn by experience. The other is that there is no "market test," analogous to an external price system, that can eliminate inefficiencies, provide incentives for cost savings and productivity increases, reward successes, and permit incremental policy adjustments of the kind that a manufacturer of cars or cake mixes can take advantage of. Moreover, the military services have no way of sensing whether the appropriate "consumer sovereignty" is being served. If Ford produces its own tires, it can look around to see whether its tire manufacturing is competitive and can elect to purchase its tires if it is not. Corporate directors can weigh sales, prices, share of the market, and profits before making a policy adjustment. The military services, like many government services, lack these advantages.

Economics as the Science of Economizing   What we are really talking about is not so much "economics" as "economizing." It is the role of economic reasoning in military decisionmaking, in the design of military institutions, and in political choices among military strategies. A large part of economics is concerned with the science of economizing. In fact, even the "social science" component of economics—the study of business behavior, consumer behavior, the behavior of labor, and so forth—is based on a theoretical analysis of how a businessman, a consumer, or a potential employee "should" react to the costs and values that confront him, in the interest of maximizing profits or welfare or real income. It is this economizing part of economics—the science of allocating versatile but scarce resources among competing objectives—that in the sixties found new applications in business consulting, operations research, and "applied welfare economics" such as water-resource or highway development or the design of a faculty salary structure.

Economics is also concerned with incentives. Designing military procedures and institutions so that decentralized decisions made by far-flung base commanders, procurement authorities, weapon designers, or logistics specialists will be "correct" ones, under some kind of "invisible hand," is a genuine problem in economic organization.

Finally, we should remember that game theory itself is, at least in the monumental book that brought it into fashion (Von Neumann and Morgenstern's *Theory of Games and Economic Behavior*), closely allied—or believed to be closely allied—with economics. There is more than a semantic connection between price war and real war, and more than a superficial likeness between a threat to retaliate with nuclear weapons and a threat to retaliate by calling a labor strike [10]. Economic reasoning then has much to contribute to national security.

An Example: The Design of an Airplane   Let us look at some typical military choices to see in what sense they can be construed as "economic." Consider first the traditional problem of designing a bomber airplane. We like it to be cheap, fast, maneuverable, and reliable; capable of flying at very high or very low altitudes; not too visible to optical, radar, or infrared sensory devices; predictable in its performance; not too fatiguing to the crew; not too demanding in its requirements for basing, maintenance, or spare parts; available in a short time; modifiable as new developments become available; and, finally, capable of carrying a large "payload." Similarly, we know what we like as consumers: good food, good schools, a warm house, good health, pleasant working conditions, leisure, economic security, independence, and a thousand other things. Our economic problem is that we can have more of some of these only if we take less of others. We can have more money if we work harder; we can send our children to better schools if we take a job somewhere else; we can have a bigger house if we consume less liquor or cheaper food. Airplane design is also an economic problem. An airplane can carry a bigger payload or fly higher if it carries less fuel and takes a reduction in operating range; it can carry more bombs if it carries less electronic equipment; it can be more reliable if it has less fancy gadgetry; it can be less reliable, and still acceptable, at the cost of more maintenance personnel and a larger supply of spare parts; it can be bought in larger quantities if it is cheaper; and it can be procured sooner if less advanced models are specified. Everything in an airplane comes at some *opportunity cost*.

In economic terminology, there is a "transformation" curve among two or more commodities, the commodities being characteristics of the airplane. More generally, we are dealing with a "production function," relating a variety of costly inputs—raw materials, investible funds, personnel, real estate, and fuel—to a multiproduct production process.

We also have a *valuation* problem. We cannot just draw the transformation curve corresponding to a given budget, and pick the point on it—the particular blend of range, speed, payload, and maneuverability—that maximizes the achievement of a certain goal (maximizes "profits"). No market exists where we can sell range and speed at going prices (or against downward-sloping demand curves) and maximize profits like a businessman. We have to find some way of combining these characteristics of an airplane into a *value system*, or a set of criteria. We must draw up "indifference curves" among speed, range, payload, and so forth. We are not altogether different from Robinson Crusoe, who balanced his consumer preferences against his production possibilities in reaching a decision on what to produce and consume.

Even a typical military-design problem of this sort can thus be cast into the familiar language of economics: the economics of production, consumption, valuation, optimization, and choice. In fact, this is the way the problem has to be construed if one is to do a good job with it. It is not enough to say that we want the fastest possible airplane, as long as it will carry at least 25,000 pounds of payload and fly at least 50,000 feet high; that is like saying that we want the prettiest possible house that has nine rooms, a modern kitchen, and a good heating system.

Typically, no *one* of these characteristics is so dominant that we can subordinate the others and simplify our choice to the point where it no longer looks like economics. We *do* have to balance payload against speed, speed against range, sophistication against reliability, and so on.

You may say that all this is true but trivial. Anybody can see that it is a simple economic problem—proving only that military officers, like businessmen, have always been practicing economics without being aware of it. Such an argument would underrate the achievement of economics. These problems are not so "obviously" economical in their structure that there is nothing further to be gained by putting them explicitly, in terms familiar to someone who has had training in economics. Furthermore, viewing these choices as essentially economic problems makes for a more straightforward and less strained analytical approach; it provides a logical framework and a set of familiar concepts, even a terminology that should not be underrated. It is not an altogether trivial accomplishment to cast the problem in economic terms.

An Example at a Higher Level: "Offense" and "Defense" But let us go up one level. Consider defending the United States population in time of war. One way is to dig holes that we can get into when the warheads arrive. Another is to intercept the missiles in flight or confuse them so that they miss their targets. A third is to destroy them in the launching silos. A fourth (more relevant to World War II than to a likely future war) is to strike the enemy factories that make the weapons he sends against us. And of course we can do a mixture of these things. Alternatively, we can just sit still and suffer the losses he can inflict, if these losses are less than the costs of taking action.

Some of these possible actions we might call "offensive," some "defensive." Some we might call "active," some "passive." Some we might call "military action," some "civil defense." In World War II the question arose whether it was better to defend convoys against submarines, to go after the submarines on the open sea, to get them in their pens, to bomb the shipyards where they were being built, to build more ships of our own and produce more goods to offset losses due to submarines, or to fight the war in a way that required transporting less material overseas. These are essentially economic choices, in the sense that they are alternative ways (substitutes) of accomplishing much the same objectives. With limited resources one can do a little of all of them, or more of some and less of others; but they all compete with each other for limited resources. Similarly, one can keep warm by insulating his house better, installing a more efficient heating system, buying more fuel, wearing warmer clothes, moving into a smaller house with the same heating system, or relocating in a warmer climate. He can also just get used to feeling colder if he had rather stick to his present house and location and spend his money on commodities other than fuel and insulation.

Does this suggest that offense and defense, or civil defense and military action, are really the same thing? Clearly, yes. Offense versus defense, streetcars versus automobiles versus living in town, more fuel versus more insulation versus warmer clothes—all are largely economic alternatives.

Values and Criteria Again We have to recognize, however, that these are usually not alternative ways of achieving a *single* objective. Catching enemy missiles in their launchers or intercepting them on arrival, defending against submarines or just building more ships, wearing warmer clothes or living in a smaller house—these are, in a very general sense, alternative ways of winning the war, defending the population, or keeping warm. But the "product mix" is different with different choices. We have to think about how we value shortening the war versus taking more casualties, easing the damage to ourselves versus easing the damage to our allies, or perhaps improving the most likely outcome of the war versus improving the worst likely outcome of the war.

We are not simply maximizing profits, or maximizing anything in a single dimension. We need our indifference curve again; we need our explicit valuation scheme. We have not only production economics but consumer economics. We need *criteria* for choosing among varying product mixes where each may meet a little more of one objective and little less of another, both being objectives that concern us enough to require an explicit balance. In the jargon, we must "optimize," not "maximize." We have to reach a proper balance, where the marginal gain in switching to an alternative mix is less than the marginal loss, taking all of the objectives into account.

Relevance of the Economist It is peculiar to the training of an economist that he is continually aware of the need to optimize rather than just to maximize, of the need to weigh explicitly the value of more progress toward one objective at the expense of progress toward another. By training, he is suspicious of any analysis that singles out one conspicuous variable, some "dominant" feature, on which all attention is to be focused, and which is to be maximized by putting arbitrary limits on the other variables. It is also characteristic of an economist that he is aware of substitution possibilities, that he views alternative mixes of inputs as different ways of achieving much the same thing, and that he is suspicious of arbitrary judgments about which product characteristics are the "right" ones. An economist is dubious of any measure of efficiency that is a simple ratio of one output to one cost, or of any attempt to arrive at the "best" design of a weapon or program without considering the costs that go into it. He recognizes that, while a Cadillac may be better than a jeep, it is not necessarily better than two jeeps (depending on the purpose) and it may cost as much as two jeeps; so that any choice between a better item and a worse is likely to be also a choice between fewer and more.

He may, of course, have bad judgment. He may exaggerate substitution possibilities, or pretend that continuous variation of the product mix is possible when it is not; he may make a nuisance of himself by insisting that in principle one has to take all factors into account, when in fact many of them really do not matter. Nevertheless, the economist's way of construing these problems is an important one—perhaps not the only way, but one that has a great deal to contribute. And it does not seem to come naturally to businessmen or military officers. Customarily, designs have been specified, resources allocated, and product mixes decided on without explicit regard to relative costs; traditionally, costs have been considered inappropriate at the level of deciding, say, on the organization and equipment for an armored division, or on the allocation of funds between offensive and defensive forces. This situation improved in the sixties with the application, by Secretary of Defense McNamara, of explicit methods of weighing costs of projected weapon systems against benefits. In 1965, President Johnson directed that analytical methods developed in the Department of Defense—including "program," or output-focused, budgeting—be adopted by all federal departments.[1]

The Science of Strategy   Let us turn to some problems that go beyond "operations research." Take the subject of strategy—traditionally the science of conducting a war. But today's strategy is concerned less with how to conduct a war that has already begun than with using *potential* military force in the conduct of foreign affairs. "Deterrence" is a strategic concept, but not a purely military one. Certain military might is necessary to deter aggression; but deterrence is concerned essentially with manipulating or working on or influencing a potential enemy's preferences, intentions, and understandings. Deterrence depends not only on what one can do in a purely military sense, but also on how one can display one's ability in ways that will convince an enemy that one not only *could* do it but *would* do it. It achieves conviction (or "credibility") through knowledge of how the enemy makes his decisions, what his values are, what his information is, and how he evaluates costs and risks and gains. And it is concerned with promises as well as threats. To deter,

[1] For an excellent discussion of the role of economics in military planning ("operations research"), see Charles J. Hitch [4]. Hitch was Defense Comptroller under McNamara. For more recent references, see [3, 5, 11, 12, 13].

one has to convince a potential enemy not only that he would be punished if he misbehaved, but also that he would not be punished if he behaved. One has to appear threatening, but only with respect to certain contingencies.

Or consider limited war. Limited war is essentially a bargaining process in which violence and the threat of violence are used, in which one tries to coerce or deter an enemy and cause him not to pursue all the actions of which he is currently militarily capable. Or consider arms control. Arms control is concerned with making arrangements between parties that dislike and distrust each other, in their mutual interest.

The theoretical side of this subject is really game theory—or would have been if game theory had made progress in these directions. In truth, this field does not belong to anybody. It is not part of traditional military science; more than military skills are needed to produce successful combinations of threats and promises in dealing with enemies, allies, and neutrals. It could be called political science, but it is closer to economics. Duopoly, bilateral monopoly, collective bargaining, antitrust enforcement, partnership agreements, price wars and truces, market-sharing arrangements, and even ordinary commercial bargaining contain elements of strategy that are not wholly dissimilar to international military strategy. Perhaps if we had paid more attention to the economics of blackmail and extortion, of racketeering, of burglary and crime deterrence, and if we had treated the more violent side of industrial relations as a central part of economics, we would be better prepared for handling these problems.

But even in conventional economics there are analogies for problems of military strategy. When one looks at discipline in a cartel arrangement or an international commodity agreement, or at the tacit (and sometimes explicit) agreements that limit competition to nonprice behavior, or at the understandings among automobile companies about restraining the introduction of new accessories, one sees something analogous to surprise attack and arms control. The key feature of most of these arrangements is that everybody has some interest in jointly abstaining from certain kinds of conflict or competition, but everybody is subject to a powerful temptation, in the event that somebody breaks the agreement, to get in first; and everybody suspects that everybody else is contemplating precisely that. The first company to introduce a new fuel-saving carburetor gains a one-year advantage over its rivals. The first company to break a coffee agreement and dump its surplus on the market gains a once-for-all advantage. The partner who absconds with the funds and the country that launches a preventive attack may wish there had been an absolutely foolproof system of contract enforcement so that they could have continued to enjoy the benefits of mutual restraint, but they may be unable to find an institutional arrangement that would tie everybody's hands so securely that nobody would bolt or fear anybody else's bolting.

This is a fascinating subject, one to which economists have contributed as much, perhaps, as anybody else; one that does not yet belong wholly to any faction, certainly not to the military services; one that could use some theoretical development. It is also, we might add, one in which there is an interested audience. Thus, for example, lawyers drawing up contracts, parents dealing with children, price leaders dealing with small companies, unions dealing with management, and the United States dealing with the Soviet Union are all coping with the elusive problem of deterrence, of coercing an opponent or a partner by working on his expectations of how one will react.

An Example of Adaptive Adjustments: The "Arms Race" A good example is the phenomenon known as the "arms race." What most people seem to have in mind, in speaking of this phenomenon, is a situation in which two (or more) adversaries or competitors are so motivated, in building their military establishments, that a main determinant of their decisions is the level of armaments that the other has built or is building. Each side is concerned about its arms position vis-à-vis the other's. But for each side, arms are expensive. Each tries, subject to budgetary constraints, to achieve a level of armament that bears some "normal" or "safe" or "desirable" relation to the other side's. The arms race is thus a dynamic process of adjustment, in which each side reacts to what the other is doing [1, 8, 14].

Notice the analogy to, say, duopoly behavior or "duopolistic competition," in which each of two competitors with differentiated products attempts to set his prices or levels of output with a view to the other's prices or levels of output. In such a price war, each competitor seeks a price low enough, but not too low, relative to the other's; but it is costly for both to lower their prices together. In an arms race, each wants his armaments to be high enough, but not too high (because they cost so much) relative to the other's; but if they both raise their armaments together, the result is costly.

This analogy is perhaps not close enough to deserve much emphasis, but there is at least a similarity in the analytical techniques that the two processes call for, in the concepts they may draw on, and in the investigative talents that may be needed. One is economic and the other is military; but while the contents of the two problems are dissimilar, the structures and the processes are not. The problems are species of the same genus. Other examples might include the political platforms of two candidates competing for election, two cars competing to be first in an intersection, or two students competing for highest honors on their theses—examples that in their contents would seem to fall within political science, traffic management, or gamesmanship, but that analytically fall in the category of *interdependent decisions.*

Social Choice Let us turn to another area where economic reasoning is essential: civil defense. Protection against radioactive fallout could make a difference in casualties in the event of war. For our present purpose, we shall not worry about how great a difference protection would make, or what it would cost. (This depends on how the war is conducted, who starts it, how it is ended, and who the enemies are.) Consider the question of whether civil defense makes sense; and if so, how much defense is needed, what kind, and for what parts of the population.

Here is a problem of social choice, not wholly different from that of allocating tax resources into police protection, better schools, slum clearance, or public health. There *is* an important difference, though, in that we are dealing with points far out on the extremes of our value scales, far beyond the normal region in which we make choices. These are life-and-death questions, of the kind that the ordinary consumer rarely makes, or at least is rarely conscious of making. We make it when the doctor tells us that our eyesight may be restored by an operation that has some probability of being fatal; we make it, in a sense, in that fateful economic choice about what profession to enter, or whether to tie ourselves down with children and the expenses that go with them.

In a way, civil defense is a simple problem. We estimate what the casualties would be in a war with, and without, prior civil-defense arrangements. We attach some kind of "utility" or valuation to the difference it makes, multiply that by the probability of war, and compare it with the utility we give up by spending money on civil defense. In principle, this is an ordinary economic decision; but it is an extraordinarily hard decision to make. Notice that we have to find some way of estimating the likelihood of war. (We must even estimate the relative likelihoods of different kinds of wars.) And we must find some way, deep in our souls, of deciding what it is really worth to be alive in a hostile environment rather than dead, or to be alive with our children rather than leave them as orphans, or to have other Americans alive with us (or without us). This is a real test of whether our economic decision models are at all realistic in assuming that consumers know how to value—in the sense of imputing utility to—the alternative outcomes or commodity mixes with which they are confronted, particularly when great uncertainty attaches to the outcome. Is there really a "rational" way of deciding how much better it is to be alive and in great pain rather than dead, alive and lame rather than dead, alive at the Brazilian rather than the Chinese level of income, or alive to meet family responsibilities rather than dead in the event that some of the children live? Can people really cope with the problem of deciding whether the likelihood of general war is 75 percent, 25 percent, 5 percent, 1 percent, or less? And can people collectively use this knowledge and these feelings in reaching a political decision for the nation?

Some people reply to these questions by saying that they would rather be dead if war occurs and that they would not degrade themselves by thinking about how to preserve the possibility of a worse fate than death. They probably evade the issue. It is not clear that they really would rather be dead when the time comes; nor does it appear that many of them have taken ordinary precautions to die painlessly. Furthermore, people who have faced great pain and privation, like, say, the Pilgrims who landed off our coast a few hundred years ago, have typically not preferred quiet suicide; their choice does not seem to be entirely explained by an irrational inability to make an end of things.

A better explanation is that we do not often, either as economists or consumers or voters, make choices so far out on the extreme end of our value scale. When we do, we find it so painful that, somewhat irrationally, we refuse to face the choice (and thus make a choice by default).

Here is an engrossing field of study for an economist, a study of consumer choice where the alternatives are very distant from each other along the value scale, and where the uncertainties are of a more elusive kind. Whether one studies how people and political bodies actually make (or refuse to make) these choices, or how they ought to make them, it is a challenging study intellectually and one of the greatest social importance.

Take another case, peacetime fallout from testing nuclear devices in the atmosphere. (Such testing is banned by treaty, but nonsignatory nations like France and Communist China continue to detonate devices in the atmosphere.) There is some controversy about the facts of peacetime fallout, but it is small compared with the controversy over how we should attach a value to the damage it may cause. Should we look at millions of deaths or disabilities and express shock at how large the absolute number is, or look at them in proportion to the world's population (and the cumulative total of future generations, through some stretch of time) and remark on how minute it is? Do we say that 10,000 cases of leukemia in children are an appalling tragedy, or that they are a small number compared with deaths by malaria? How do we value inflictions on future generations compared with inflictions on ourselves?

More is needed here, of course, than a materialist economic calculation. But evaluations of this sort do contain an important, even an essential, element of economic reasoning. It is relevant, for example, to ask what it would cost to save lives and reduce suffering in an amount statistically equivalent to the human damage that would be done by peacetime fallout. At any given time, ways exist to save lives and reduce suffering; we know them and can estimate their effectiveness. We can install traffic lights, improve public health, provide better medical service, improve diets, provide better storm warning, educate people, produce safer cars, and do a variety of things that will reduce accidental death, death by disease, infant mortality, and the like. We can presumably even analyze these ways of saving lives in terms of their geographical distribution, age and sex distribution, distribution among the strong and the weak, among the rich and the poor. Do we not arrive at some measure here of the possible significance of policies or circumstances that cause pain, death, or disability?

This may not be a good measure, or the only measure, but it is at least a bench mark. We can use it to translate what may appear to be incommensurable into something measurable, familiar, and directly pertinent to our experience and our policy decisions. We may discover in the process that we have been applying wrong valuations to decisions about accident prevention and public health. We may find that, with a sufficiently wide margin for error, we can attach lower and upper limits to the valuation we ought to put on potentially tragic circumstances.

We may also find fresh insights into problems that economists have perhaps given too little attention to. There is an interesting difference between the way people respond to a slight statistical increase in the number of deaths expected during the next twelve months and the way they respond to the imminent death of a particular person. Let the newspapers announce that a little girl will die unless she can undergo a $40,000 operation, and nickels and dimes will pour in. Let it be said that improvements in hospital facilities throughout the state of Massachusetts, costing approximately $40,000, would probably save the life of one little girl in the course of the next twelve months, and no movement for immediate tax increases will take place.

In other words, the value system that we are describing may be a subtle and complex one, with components that at first glance appear irrational. But it is so central to the process of social valuation that an economist would be fooling himself and everybody else by leaving it out of his analysis. One advantage of making frontal attacks on problems of war and peace, death and destruction, pain and servitude, and the discriminatory distribution of death among the population is that we are forced to measure seemingly intangible and incommensurable valuations.

The Design of Military Institutions   A final topic for this brief discussion is the design of institutions and procedures for the military establishment which make for efficiency in the allocation of resources, the creation of military systems, and the choice of strategies. We shall look at four areas of study.

Decentralized Decisionmaking The first is designing procedures so that efficient decentralized decisions can be made. As we mentioned earlier, the military establishment—though it is as rich in resources as the entire economies of some countries—is for the most part to be thought of as a "firm" rather than a "competitive economy." It is a single institution with a chain of command and a planning process of a centralized and hierarchical sort, not a set of atomistic units acting independently and competitively. A wing of B–52s, a squadron of submarines, or an infantry division is not an independent unit competing for business, serving objectives of its own. It is subordinate to the whole organization; it consciously fits into the scheme of things and has its basic objectives laid down from above. But an organization consisting of millions of people and scores of billions of dollars a year can no more be planned in meticulous detail than can a whole economy. There must be some set of procedures or incentives or regulations which permits decisions to be made from day to day and from year to year.

Somebody has to decide whether to discard a worn-out piece of equipment or to repair it, whether a little more target practice is worth the expenditure of ammunition or the opportunity cost of some other kind of training, whether spare parts for missiles or aircraft should be prepositioned or airlifted on demand, whether to add antiaircraft equipment to the deck of a ship, making use of space and weight and maintenance personnel that might have been assigned to some other kind of equipment. Somebody has to decide, under the military assistance program, whether to buy new equipment for an ally, give him reconditioned equipment and replace it with new equipment for the United States forces, or give him equipment out of surplus stocks of obsolescent equipment. Someone has to decide whether to work his highly specialized personnel as hard as they can be made to, in the interest of maximum current effectiveness, or to make life a little pleasanter for them so that they will not resign at the end of their enlistment period, taking with them the expensive skills that the military service has invested in.

These problems are not so very different from those that occur within an ordinary business firm. But it comes naturally to a business firm to think in terms of costs; and most of the things that a firm deals with can, one way or another, be cost-estimated. Experience in recent years has shown that decisionmakers in a defense establishment are traditionally reluctant to think of themselves as engaged in a cost-reducing, profit-maximizing business.

A knowledge of costs is, of course, necessary to someone who is disposed to reduce them. When the matter at hand involves saving gallons of fuel, or spare parts in a catalog, or civilian typists, it may not be difficult to value the savings involved. But when the matter involves using privates to repair buildings on an army base, using skilled personnel for unskilled jobs, increasing this year's combat-readiness at the expense of antisubmarine defenses, special arrangements may be necessary to permit a correct economical judgment. Thus, one of the problems in designing an efficient military establishment, over and above creating cost-consciousness on the part of those who dispose of costly resources, is to provide the criteria and information they need to make intelligent decisions.

Another is to give them an incentive. The commander of an air base certainly does not lack incentive; his incentive is mainly directed toward the condition and effectiveness of the base he commands, the combat effectiveness of equipment and crews, the morale and discipline, and the other "positive" values that he promotes. He may be vaguely conscious of the taxpayer, because of the various "watchdogs" that the taxpayer sets against him. He may feel some sense of obligation to, or affinity with, other commands in the same service; nevertheless, if he can acquire some scarce commodity that might have gone to some other air base, he is apt to feel proud rather than guilty. Strong motivation to duty requires an attitude of exaggerated preoccupation with one's own command. A base commander who knows that he is being allowed to consume resources that cost the service more than they are worth to him may be reluctant, perhaps pardonably, to give them up voluntarily. Every agency of the government, and every department of a university, knows that if it reports through budgetary channels that it is currently being allowed to spend money on low-priority items, it will not be told, "Thank you, spend the money better," it will be told, "Thank you, we'll cut your budget accordingly." One proper reason for incentives is to make it possible for someone who can save resources to use them (or part of them) in meeting his own goals.

Across-the-Board Prices Another area for study is the setting of across-the-board prices, costs, and specifications. A good example is military pay. Other things being equal, it might be efficient to let local commanders bid for the specialized personnel they need, setting whatever wage differentials for military and civilian employees were needed for an economical mix. Other things, of course, are usually *not* equal; it would probably be intolerable in overall personnel policy if the wage differential between corporals and privates, or between mechanics and radar operators, were to differ from base to base. But there must be a wage policy, and some thought must be given to wage differentials. It is remarkable how little attention has been shown by economists to wage policies and employee relations within the military services. Yet in what other parts of the economy would an industry of comparable size be as likely to require economic reasoning as there, where rules of thumb, union action, and competitive market forces are weak or irrelevant enough to leave a wide range for conscious decisions?

Planning and Budgeting A third area is in the planning and budgetary process. As remarked earlier, the choice and design of weapon systems require attention both to money costs and to opportunity costs; a "best" piece of equipment or method of operation cannot be determined without regard to costs and alternatives. The same is true at the highest level of budgetary allocation, whether it be the allocation of resources between the Strategic Air Command and the Aerospace Defense Command, or between the Air Force and the Navy. Efficient choices and decisions must be made—usually in the course of a budget cycle—in the defense establishment and its expenditure of resources.

Contact with the Civilian Market Finally, there is the important area of contact between the military services and civilian industry. More than half of the defense budget goes to procure equipment or materials, or to hire services. The defense establishment is essentially a huge, but not necessarily potent, monopsonist, facing industries that range from fairly competitive to extremely oligopolistic. The military services, furthermore, are in the business of consciously generating their own future demands, in contrast to the ordinary consumer, who rarely negotiates consciously with a manufacturer about the kinds of products he would like to see available several years from now. Uncertainty is shared by the buyer and the seller (not altogether unlike the problem of a consumer who contracts with an architect or contractor for the construction of a house). The contractual relationships between the military services and their suppliers constitute an important field of study—particularly because they raise the question of where the line should be drawn between private industry and the military services. Ours is not an "arsenal" concept; defense industry is not nationalized. Weapons are built, for the most part, by private business firms. (The Navy has some shipyards, but the Air Force owns no missile factories.) Even much of the training of military personnel is done by private business on contract.

Strategic Thinking on Contract A great deal of strategic thinking is now done for the military services on contract. This is not a matter of conscious policy, but rather reflects the fact that strategic thinking and the design of weapons are closely interrelated processes; the firm that builds a missile or a propulsion system with some new characteristics is likely to do a great deal of the thinking about how those qualities relate to strategic objectives and contingencies. New strategic ideas are likely to be developed by a manufacturer who has a new product and is thinking about how to justify it or sell it to a military service. Furthermore, private business can hire people outside the bureaucratic personnel system and keep them as full-time specialists on strategic problems, while the military services are committed to the notion that their officers should rotate in a wide variety of jobs and not become specialists. So it is natural, even if not a matter of conscious design, that strategic thinking as well as manufacturing should be contracted out to private industry rather than nationalized in shipyards and arsenals.

The Line between the Military and the Civilian Sector Here there arises the question of what the purpose of a military establishment is at all. Why are missile bases manned by Air Force officers rather than civilian technicians and engineers? The answer is clearly that there is something about military organization that transcends ordinary commercial relationships. Some commitments cannot be bought; they can be obtained only through emotional bonds and ties of the kind suggested by terms like "loyalty," "duty," and "honor." It is possible to make a strong case for the existence of military services outside ordinary civil service procedures, and to treat a missile crew as different from the employees of a post office. But it can be instructive to analyze precisely what the difference is.

And it can also be an important practical matter to think about where the line ought to be drawn, because the modern defense era is one in which tradition is by no means a sure guide. Just as in the design and manufacture of weapon systems, in the development of strategic thinking, and in the training of military personnel there is a shifting line between what is military and what is private, so there may also be a line between military service and civilian personnel in the operation of military equipment and the performance of military tasks. The line is subject to change, to uncertainty, and to new decisions; it deserves to be an important matter of policy.

The military services are not unique in this. The medical profession, the local fire department, university faculties, and many commercial and private organizations face similar problems on their own scales. (How does one keep a night watchman from resigning on the particular night that he hears a suspicious noise and faces danger for the first time?) Here is another case in which attention to military problems requires one to face extraordinary, nontraditional, somewhat unconventional problems of economics. In other parts of the economy they may, whatever their importance, be considered "peripheral" and thus evaded; in military economics they cannot. And a by-product of paying more attention to military economics may be that we discover, with force and clarity, interesting and important problems that we have heretofore overlooked.

REFERENCES

1. BOULDING, KENNETH E. *Conflict and Defense: A General Theory* (New York: Harper, 1962).
2. DEAGLE, EDWIN A., JR. "The Politics of Missile-making: A Dynamic Model," in *Public Policy*, XVI, Yearbook of the John Fitzgerald Kennedy School of Government.
3. ENKE, STEPHEN (ed.). *Defense Management* (Englewood Cliffs, N.J.: Prentice-Hall, 1967).
4. HITCH, CHARLES J. "Economics and Military Operations Research," *Review of Economics and Statistics*, 40:3 (August 1958), pp. 199–209.
5. ——— and ROLAND N. McKEAN. *The Economics of Defense in the Nuclear Age* (Cambridge, Mass: Harvard University Press, 1960).
6. HOAG, MALCOLM. "On Stability in Deterrent Races," *World Politics*, 13 (July 1961), pp. 502–527.
7. KAUFMANN, WILLIAM W. *The McNamara Strategy* (New York: Harper & Row, 1964).
8. McGUIRE, MARTIN C. *Secrecy and the Arms Race* (Cambridge, Mass.: Harvard University Press, 1965).
9. McKEAN, ROLAND (ed.). *Issues in Defense Economics* (New York: National Bureau of Economic Research and Columbia University Press, 1967).
10. NEUMANN, JOHN VON, and OSKAR MORGENSTERN. *Theory of Games and Economic Behavior* (Princeton, N.J.: Princeton University Press, 1944).
11. NOVICK, DAVID (ed.). *Program Budgeting: Program Analysis and the Federal Budget* (Cambridge, Mass.: Harvard University Press, 1965).
12. QUADE, EDWARD S. (ed.). *Analysis for Military Decisions* (New York: Rand McNally, 1964).
13. ——— and WAYNE I. BOUCHER (eds.). *Systems Analysis and Policy Planning: Applications in Defense* (New York: American Elsevier, 1968).
14. SCHELLING, THOMAS C. *The Strategy of Conflict* (Cambridge, Mass.: Harvard University Press, 1963).
15. ———. "War without Pain, and Other Models," *World Politics*, 15 (April 1963), pp. 465–487.

12

ECONOMICS OF HEALTH AND EDUCATION

Seymour E. Harris *
Estelle James **

DURING the past decade, economists have devoted increasing attention to "human capital"—investment in people, rather than machines. Expenditures for health and education constitute two much-discussed forms of human capital. Because of their many analytic similarities we examine them together in this chapter.[1]

To some readers, the "economics of health and education" may seem like a contradiction in terms; health and education are, or should be, basic human rights, outside the materialistic framework of our society. What can the discipline of economics say about such matters?

Health and education, like other goods and services, can only be provided if resources—land, labor, capital, and entrepreneurship—are allocated to them. If society's resources are limited relative to wants, these services involve an *opportunity cost*: more health and educational facilities necessarily mean less of something else. What are the relative advantages of these and other demands on our resources? In other words, what are the benefits and opportunity costs of expenditures on health and education? How much of our resources should we consequently devote to health and education? Is the current annual expenditure of $60 billion (almost 7

---

* University of California at San Diego, formerly of Harvard University.
** State University of New York at Stony Brook.
[1] Some of the issues discussed in this chapter are treated more fully in Seymour Harris's [5] and [6].

percent of the United States gross national product) on each optimal, and is this sum growing at an optimal rate? More specifically, what proportion should we assign to elementary schools versus colleges, to science versus the humanities, to hospital construction versus pollution control, to cancer research versus curing the common cold? These are all questions in applied microanalysis—natural targets for the economist's temperament, training, and tools—and as such they will be explored in the first two major sections of this chapter, on the benefits and costs of health and education.

Closely allied with our need to define optimal resource use is a second major concern: By what mechanism can we best achieve a desired allocation? What set of institutions and incentives will most effectively move resources to sectors where their value is greatest?

Conveniently, economic theory tells us that the "invisible hand" of the competitive market will automatically bring about efficient resource allocation—provided that certain underlying conditions are satisfied. These necessary conditions may not prevail, however, in health and education. Thus, it may be desirable to rely in part upon an alternative method of economic organization—government planning. Indeed, a complex system of shared public and private responsibility has evolved, one of the distinguishing features of this sector of our economy. What are the appropriate roles of the government and the free market in financing and producing education and health? Here, too, no obvious answer emerges; the economist thinks in terms of *choice among policy alternatives*, as we shall do in the third major section of the chapter.

A structural characteristic of the health and education services is the predominance of a special public-private hybrid, the nonprofit institution, which comprises almost all hospitals and schools outside the government sector. We shall be talking primarily about benefits and costs to the individual consumer and to society as a whole, and very little about the response of the non-profit-producing unit, although this is clearly an essential ingredient in public-policy formulation. A comprehensive theory of the behavior of these complex institutions has yet to be developed, one of the larger gaps in the human-capital literature.

In the course of our sojourn through controversial social issues, we shall frequently encounter conceptual and measurement problems, thereby illustrating simultaneously the potential contributions and the limitations of the economist's particular view of the world. We shall see how the economist can help provide answers to many important questions in the fields of health and education; how these answers are partial at best, misleading at worst; and how numerous crucial questions remain unanswered, awaiting future theoretical and empirical analysis.

BENEFITS OF HEALTH AND EDUCATION

How large a portion of our resources should we allocate to health and education? Broadly speaking, resources should be diverted to these sectors so long as the benefits there exceed the potential benefits of using the resources elsewhere—that is, so long as marginal (or additional) benefits exceed marginal opportunity cost. But what are these benefits and costs, and how do we measure them? This is the crux of the problem.

Many people might throw up their hands and claim that this is surely a noneconomic question. How can we assign a tangible value to the life of a man who has just been saved by a new antibiotic? How can we impute a monetary value to education, which preserves and expands the cultural life of an entire society?

True, the answers are not simple and clear-cut. But somehow, in the presence of scarce resources, allocational decisions *are* being made every day about these very issues. The economist prefers explicit to haphazard decision processes and criteria. He suggests systematic and sometimes ingenious methods of categorizing and quantifying these benefits and costs.

Consumption Benefits A person may simply "enjoy" better health and more education, deriving increased satisfaction from his present and future personal life. If society's welfare depends on the welfare of its individual constituents, the community as a whole also benefits from his additional consumption of education and health.

How can we quantify this consumption value of health and education? Ideally, by getting inside the purchaser's psyche. More practically, to find the marginal value of a product or service to a consumer, we merely look at how much he has paid for it—this is one of the surprisingly simple yet logically plausible implications of economic theory. He would not have purchased the item if it were not worth its price to him; on the other hand, he would have purchased additional units if it were worth more than its price. Relative prices therefore inform us of relative marginal values of different goods.

This holds for a given income distribution, of course. Change the income distribution (for example, to a more egalitarian one) and you also change the distribution of demand among—and hence the relative prices of—different goods. Accepting current prices as a meaningful index of social value, therefore, also implies accepting the existing distribution of income.

Relative prices, furthermore, depend upon total income and tastes. Over the long run, income will rise and tastes will change, so relative prices, too, may shift. When dealing with investment where the gestation period is long and the durability great, as in human capital, uncertain future values, rather than knowable current prices, are the essential planning inputs.

Additional complexities arise for many health and educational services. What is the consumption value of tenth grade at a public high school; of a music course at a university with flat annual tuition; of admission to Harvard, which rejects most applicants; or of a tonsillectomy or a new set of teeth, particularly to a fully insured medical patient? If these services are "lumpy" in nature, or if they are not sold on the market, or if consumption is compulsory, or if price rationing is not used to equate demand with supply, or if the individual is not required to pay the full fee, the standard theory, unqualified, does not apply and price is not a valid index of value. An objective measure of consumption value has yet to be found for many such services—a fact which, needless to say (but often forgotten), does not mean that its subjective existence or policy relevance should be ignored.

Investment Benefits A better educated or healthier person will probably also have higher lifetime earnings, and this is one of the benefits he is paying for. Expenditures on health and education may thus be partially regarded as an investment; they reduce current consumption of other goods and services but increase future income and consumption possibilities—hence the term, human capital. In 1965, for example, an average male elementary-school graduate earned $4,663, a high-school graduate $6,899, and one with four or more years of college $10,823 [4, p. 15]. Greater public awareness of this phenomenon is probably one reason for the rising demand for education in recent years.

These increased earnings count as a benefit not only to the private individual, but also to society as a whole. Why? The higher earnings presumably reflect higher productivity, increased output in real as well as monetary terms. Just as the price a consumer pays for a product tells us the marginal value of that product, so, in a competitive market, the price an employer pays for a worker tells us the marginal value of that worker—another helpful principle derived from economic theory. A profit-maximizing firm will expand its hiring if wages are less than the worth of the extra amount thereby produced; on the other hand, it will not hire a worker whose wages exceed his marginal output. Therefore, if we want to know how much an extra worker is worth to the employer and to the consumers who indirectly purchase his services—seemingly a difficult calculation—we need simply to look at his wages.

This immediately suggests how to measure, more tangibly than we could with psychic consumption benefits, the private and social investment value of an extra year's education: compare the lifetime earnings of population groups with and without that year of education. For example, the lifetime earnings of a typical high school graduate were computed to be $175,000 versus $281,000 for a college graduate, a difference of over $100,000 [7, p. 28]. Using a variation on this technique, one major study by Edward Denison estimated that education directly accounted for a 0.68 percent yearly increase in national income between 1929 and 1957; this was 23 percent of our total annual 2.93 percent growth rate and 42 percent of our annual 1.60 percent productivity advance [3, p. 73]. Similarly, to compute the value of disease-eradicating research, find the lifetime earnings of those who would otherwise have been debilitated by illness.

Several qualifications—and there are many in this chain of reasoning—may already have occurred to the thoughtful reader. First, in computing the earning and output gains from education, the two groups compared must obviously be equal in every other way—in ability, ambition, family connections, and so on. Otherwise we cannot attribute the income difference *solely* to education. In practice, these variables are highly intercorrelated, making it exceedingly difficult to separate out the effects of each.

Second, this method involves extrapolating from the past to the future, assuming that the previous wage structure, disease susceptibility, and other relevant conditions will continue to obtain. Actually, however, as we move further into the future, many conditions will change—including the demand for, supply of, and relative wages paid educated personnel and the prevalence of various diseases—often in unpredictable ways.

Third, a dollar of extra income or output accruing ten years from now simply does not have the same value to the individual or to society as an extra dollar today, which could be used productively in the interim. Thus, future revenues must be reduced in value in adding up lifetime earnings; $105 next year is counted as $100 currently when discounted at 5 percent. A certain amount of artistic discretion enters in here too, for the choice of an appropriate discount rate is significant and by no means obvious. When discounted at 3 percent, the present value of the returns to a college education is cut by two-thirds, from over $100,000 to only $34,000; at an 8 percent discount rate this figure drops precipitously to $5,000 [7, p. 28].

Observe, incidentally, what the discounting process does to the lifetime value of a baby, whose earning powers are years away, as compared with a teenager about to enter the labor force. Is this differentiation reasonable, or an unwarranted distortion? Similarly, observe the impact of our basic market wage criterion on the relative worth of a business executive and a blue-collar worker (which one should be chosen for a heart transplant?). And what about the economic value of a housewife's life? The legitimacy of the income-output benefits to health and education cannot be denied, but neither can we easily dismiss the interpretive ambiguities and policy biases they create.

External Benefits The two types of benefits considered so far have been shown to have value both for the individual and for society. This is significant, for it means that decisions made on the basis of private interests are consistent with the social good. Much economic theorizing has been carried on with this model in mind.

More realistically, private and social benefits do not always coincide. Because of employer ignorance or bureaucratic rules, a college graduate may be paid more than a high-school graduate who does (or could do, if given an opportunity) the job equally well; in this case, the private benefit from education—increased earnings—would not have the same social counterpart it had earlier—increased output. Casual observation suggests that this phenomenon of "job up-grading" has been growing in importance. Our concern here, however, is with the opposite type of situation—one where benefits accrue to society at large, but not to the individual consumer. These "externalities" are characteristic of the returns to human capital.

Education, for example, may make people better neighbors and citizens, so society makes attendance at primary school compulsory, even for those who prefer to remain illiterate. An exceptionally bright student may enhance (or detract from?) the education of his peers. Vaccination against smallpox not only protects the individual (whose chances of illness are slim anyhow), but also means that he will not become a carrier to those around him. Taxes reduce the additional income of a healthier person, but not the additional output he produces.

Potentially the most important—and controversial—external benefit of education concerns its impact on technological change. Increased education, it has been argued, will stimulate research and thereby raise productivity, a clear gain for society as a whole. The individual inventor, however, may not be fully compensated for his discoveries. Thus, his incentive to conduct research and prepare himself through higher education may be reduced below the socially optimal level. Denison's study, reported above, is widely cited to support this point of view. After estimating the contributions of labor (including educated labor) and physical capital to our economic progress, Denison found an average annual residual of 0.59 percentage points [3, p. 230]. He attributed this residual to increased knowledge, a term that has been translated into research and, indirectly, higher education. If the entire residual indeed stemmed ultimately from education, as some human-capital enthusiasts have implied, this would mean that education, directly or indirectly, contributed over 40 percent of total output growth and 80 percent of increased productivity from 1929 to 1957.

Is Denison's residual truly due to research? Is productive research truly stimulated by additional education or best carried on at educational institutions? And is the researcher, his results highly uncertain, paid less than the probable social value of his output? If—and only if—this chain of questions is answered in the affirmative, we have herein identified a major external benefit of education, and provided a powerful argument for government support.

COSTS OF HEALTH AND EDUCATION

So much for benefits; let us now look at the other side of the coin. To allocate resources optimally, benefits should be compared with opportunity costs. The expansion of a university, the construction of a hospital, the training of a physician—all require a diversion of land, labor, and capital from elsewhere. What is the value of goods and services given up to get more health and educational facilities?

Here again, economic theory contributes a gigantic simplification. As we have seen, in competitive markets resources are paid the value of their marginal output and can get this same remuneration from any one of numerous employers. Thus, the opportunity cost of a janitor in an elementary school is exactly equal to his wage; resource prices convey real as well as monetary information!

Problem solved? Not quite. As usual, closer examination reveals several inadequacies of the first approximation.

Joint Costs and Feedback Effects Educational and medical institutions engage in the joint production of many services. A university, for example, produces physics and philosophy majors, B.A.s and Ph.D.s, research and instruction. Should the government encourage it to expand its graduate program, as many institutions are now doing without careful forethought? To answer this question we must calculate the relevant benefits and costs, the latter presumably derived from previous experience with graduate work. But what percentage of total administrative expenses, library facilities, professorial time, and the like should be attributed to the graduate program, and how will these resource needs increase if graduate enrollment expands? To what extent will, for example, a better library also mean better research and improved undergraduate education? Will the better research then have a positive feedback on graduate training; will the graduate school reduce the costs and quality of the undergraduate program?

Similarly, a hospital repairs broken legs, treats victims of heart attacks, and delivers babies. How should joint costs be allocated among these diverse activities? Medical schools conduct research, run hospitals, and offer advanced courses and degrees; all their expenses should not be charged to the undergraduate medical student—but what is the correct division? So long as the "product mix" (the relative proportions of these different services) is variable—subject to manipulation by the institution or by government intervention—these questions cannot be ignored.

Imputations and Forgone Earnings If a resource is purchased on the market, it has a price which is often identical with its social opportunity cost. But some real costs do not involve market transactions, and hence do not possess an explicit price; for these an imputation must be made. For example, the social cost of schools and hospitals includes an imputation for the "free" police and fire protection they receive, a quantity that, like all imputations, is usually not known with certainty.

A cost that assumes particular importance in health and education is the time of the patient or student, probably the single most important input into the production process. This time is not purchased as part of the educational or medical package; its value must be imputed. The economist's basis for the imputation is forgone earnings—output lost by society and income lost by the individual while he is out of work.

The inclusion of forgone earnings may change the cost picture considerably. As an illustration, such earnings and therefore the real costs of plastic surgery are less for a child than for the family breadwinner; if hospital space must be rationed, should this be a consideration? To take another illustration, prices of medical services have seemingly risen much faster than those of other consumer goods, yet cures (for example, of pneumonia) that previously required several weeks' hospitalization and absence from work now require only a few days. An index of the overall cost of medical treatment per disease might be helpful; if an index were constructed, it probably would not have increased as rapidly as the price indexes for daily hospital service, physicians, and drugs.

More significant yet is income forgone during the process of education. Explicit annual costs per student are currently over $500 in public elementary and secondary education, and over $2,000 in higher education;[2] the disparity becomes greater still when we impute forgone earnings. At the college level, forgone earnings constitute approximately three-quarters of all private costs, helping to explain why many young people coming from low-income families cannot afford higher education, even at "free" commuter universities. In graduate school, the prohibitive size of these costs to the individual is probably a major reason

---

[2] Calculated from data in [4].

for the prevalence of fellowships and assistantships, which subsidize family subsistence as well as tuition.

External Costs   Most costs, like benefits, are charged both to the individual and to society at large. The firm, and indirectly the consumer, pays an explicit money cost; society gives up the amount that this resource would have produced elsewhere. Some private costs, however, have no social counterpart—as where custom or law requires the payment of a substantial wage to a worker who would otherwise have been unemployed. And some social costs have no private counterpart—as where the community provides free elementary education or polio immunization, philanthropists and foundations finance below-cost tuition in higher education, or insurance companies cover the cost of hospitalization. In these cases of external costs, prices to the consumer do not provide correct information about real costs, nor (in the absence of compensating external benefits) do they provide the incentive for private decisions to coincide with the social good.

MARKET FAILURE AND PUBLIC POLICY

Most goods in our economy are produced by private firms and consumed by individuals who are willing to pay the price. For some products, such as toothpaste and detergents, the predominance of the private sector is unchallenged. In others, such as defense, the failure of the market and the primacy of government are generally recognized. Health and education, however, fall into a mixed public-private sector—compulsory schooling and immunization programs coexisting with voluntary higher education and medical care, state hospitals and universities coexisting with proprietary and nonprofit institutions, and federal subsidies and loans coexisting with philanthropy and consumer financing.

Currently, 90 percent of total elementary-secondary educational expenditures are funded by the government in government-run schools; in higher education, 60 percent of all expenditures are publicly financed, much of this going to private as well as to state universities. For health care the government's share falls to 25 percent [4, p. 17; also 11, p. 69]. The relative roles of the market and government—of private and collective decisionmaking—vary from state to state and from period to period. The ultimate, "best" mix is controversial and as yet undetermined.

Why has the private market, by itself, apparently failed to achieve optimal results? And what is the appropriate government response—or response alternatives—for each defect? These questions provide us with a systematic framework for analyzing public policy toward health and education, as well as other sectors of the economy.

Externalities and Public Subsidy We have observed that certain benefits from health and education may accrue, not to the direct consumer, but to members of society as a whole. The private individual, who does not take externalities into account, may cease purchasing these services at a point where marginal social benefits still exceed marginal costs; that is, the community desires additional expenditures and resource flows into this sector. What remedy does the economist suggest?

Typically, we do not propose a single simple solution, but rather a choice among and combination of alternatives, each with its own range of economic and political side-effects. To illustrate with the case of higher education: The government can increase demand by offering scholarships to some or all college students, a policy followed, for example, by New York State. This consumer subsidy, which might be based on either ability or need, would counteract external benefits, set each student free to select his preferred institution, and leave production in the private (or nonprofit) sector—results which many regard as desirable. But suppose that the short-run supply of college openings is inelastic, so the private market is slow to react to the increased demand. Then potential new students might have no place to go, admissions standards and prices might rise, and the government would be thwarted in its attempt to attract additional resources into education. Alternatively, the government could intervene on the supply side, paying for new construction, higher professorial salaries, special courses, and all-purpose grants to expanding institutions—as such agencies as the National Science Foundation and Public Health Service do now. But which inputs, which programs, and which institutions should be subsidized, and how will subsidies influence their size, quality, and price? Finally, the government can increase and control supply by direct production of higher education, as we observe in the growth of state universities. This has customarily—but not necessarily—meant low tuition rates, and hence substantial student subsidies as well, for all those who meet college entrance requirements, regardless of family income. But what about the likelihood of political interference, the limited scope of consumer choice, and the seeming incongruity of subsidizing the wealthy under this system? Should the responsibility and corresponding power in the field of education be vested in federal, state, or local government?

Similarly, in the health field the government can subsidize consumers, as by granting tax deductions for large medical expenses; can subsidize producers, as by financing the construction of new hospital beds; or can go into the business of providing public health services directly, as in state and Veterans Administration hospitals.

In fact, all these methods are currently used, to varying degrees, for different programs. Government support, supplemented by foundation and philanthropic grants, has meant that tuition charges at most schools are well below cost; while external benefits in education probably exist, external costs do too. Because of medical insurance and government financing, the same is true in the health field. Are additional public subsidies needed and, if so, where can they best be used? In which programs are the uncompensated external benefits greatest? Hopefully we now have a better grasp of relevant concepts and questions with which to attack this issue. However, economists are still trying to develop the measuring techniques demanded by more precise analysis.

Uncertainty, Loans, and Insurance Let us suppose that a shrewd family correctly calculates the high private returns to investment in health and education, but it has not accumulated sufficient wealth to self-finance them. Borrow, we might advise, and repay the loan out of the higher earnings received later. Indeed, borrowing is used—and reasonably so— to pay for houses, automobiles, and other costly items that yield their services over relatively long periods of time. Why not add education and health costs to the list?

One reason for not doing so springs from the fact that for many years banks would simply not make loans for human capital as they would for physical capital. A house is more tangible collateral than a college degree, and a man about to undergo lung surgery is a particularly bad risk. In other words, the private market has not been providing a service that many individuals might have eagerly purchased.

More basic is the great uncertainty that pervades the health and educational sectors and often prevents optimal resource allocation. In higher education, for example, the average returns may be high, but individual variation in returns is also high. Thus, banks fear frequent defaults among their less successful student-borrowers, and households hesitate to assume the long-term fixed obligation inherent in a loan.

Insurance is often a logical, socially desirable response to uncertainty. The lender's risk could be virtually eliminated by an insurance program that charges banks a premium on successful educational loans and offsets their losses on defaults. Or risks could be pooled more directly through expansion of the federal student loan program, which now covers only a small fraction of total private expenditures on higher education.

The borrower's risk, however, would still remain, and many students, uncertain of their ability and future earning capacities, might be unwilling to take advantage of available loans. Can this problem be overcome? A number of imaginative schemes are under consideration, most of them based on the concept of a public fund for educational loans, with repayment obligations pegged to future incomes; those who earn more would pay more for their college education. Such a program, with liberal loan provisions and long-term payback periods, would vastly ease the financing burden and thereby broaden the availability of higher education to lower-income groups; but, so far, government efforts to implement this proposal have been negligible.

In the medical industry, as we have seen, loan finance is impractical because of the high likelihood of default; self-finance is infeasible because of uncertainty about the incidence of serious illness and its exceedingly high cost. Once again, insurance is the appropriate way both to finance and to remove uncertainty about medical expenses. The market has at least partially responded to this need, which helps explain the smaller government role in health than in education. In 1965, private health insurance paid 33 percent of total consumer expenditures on health care, including 71 percent of hospital costs [9, p. 148]. Psychiatric or dental care, on the other hand, is rarely covered.

Paradoxically, the removal of one type of market failure has created another; the private (monetary) cost of insured medical services now falls far below the social (resource) cost. Rather than underutilizing these services, insured consumers may in fact overutilize them, drastically raising the demand for medical facilities. Pressure on the limited number of physicians and hospital beds has been exacerbated, and prices have risen rapidly, worsening the financing and servicing difficulties for those not covered by insurance. Superficially, the solution appears to lie in increasing the supply of, and competition among, resources in the medical industry; yet, if unrestricted, the inflow of resources might well become socially excessive, in a context where much of the real cost is external to the individual consumer. We might ponder whether additional checks, such as price controls, are needed in this system, or whether they would merely create a whole new set of problems.

Efficiency versus Equity This discussion has focused on public policies designed to improve economic efficiency—in other words, on resource allocation to maximize total output. But as citizens we are also concerned with the equitable distribution of this output. In the opinion of many, equity should be at the core of decisionmaking about health and education.

Theoretically, direct income transfers are the best way to achieve a desirable welfare distribution. In practice, of course, this is not always feasible. Suppose, for example, that one's social ethic includes a more egalitarian current distribution and a greater equality of opportunity for future generations. Suppose further that many wealthy people are willing to contribute to those less fortunate if they retain partial control over expenditures, but will strongly resist contributing otherwise. Subsidized educational and health facilities for lower-income groups, if properly administered, may then become a politically expedient and harmonious way of achieving the equity goal—possibly a more compelling argument for government finance than all those presented above.

In some cases, the goals of efficiency and equity may conflict. Efficiency, for instance, might dictate a positive price on all post-elementary schooling; equity might call for a zero price. Efficiency might dictate college admissions based on proven ability; equity might call for special standards for minority groups. Efficiency might dictate giving preference in kidney transplants to a highly skilled chemist; equity might call for equal treatment for a blue-collar worker. The reasoning developed in this paper does not imply that efficiency always takes precedence over equity, particularly in our affluent society. In cases of conflict, however, we should recognize the real cost of our contemplated actions, and search among the alternatives for the cost-minimizing way to accomplish our equity goal.

REFERENCES

1. BECKER, GARY. *Human Capital* (New York: Columbia University Press, 1964).
2. BOWEN, WILLIAM. Industrial Relations Section, *Economic Aspects of Education* (Princeton, N.J.: Princeton University Press, 1964).
3. DENISON, EDWARD F. *The Sources of Economic Growth in the United States and the Alternatives before Us*, Supplementary Paper No. 13 (New York: Committee for Economic Development, 1962).
4. *Digest of Educational Statistics*, U.S. Office of Education (1967, 1969).
5. HARRIS, SEYMOUR E. *Higher Education: Resources and Finance* (New York: McGraw-Hill, 1962).
6. ———. *The Economics of American Medicine* (New York: Macmillan, 1964).
7. HOUTHAKKER, H. S. "Education and Income," *Review of Economics and Statistics*, 41 (1959), pp. 24–28.
8. *Journal of Political Economy*, 70:5 (October 1962), supplement, part 2.
9. *Medical Economics*, 45:5 (New Jersey: March 1968).
10. SCHULTZ, THEODORE. *The Economic Value of an Education* (New York: Columbia University Press, 1963).
11. *Statistical Abstract of the United States*, U.S. Department of Commerce (1967).

13

URBAN ECONOMICS: THE PROBLEM OF THE GHETTO

*Benjamin Chinitz**

THE city in recent years has become the focus of national concern. Most of the problems that deprive us of a sense of social well-being find their most acute expression in the city. Even the war in Vietnam is frequently measured in terms of the diversion of resources from the monumental task of improving the city.

Heading the list of United States urban problems is the racial crisis—the tension between black and white—which has recently burst into violence on city streets. Wound into this tension are many other major urban problems: poverty, unemployment, substandard housing, crime, delinquency, poor education, and the financial crisis in local government.

But not all of the city's problems are related to poverty or the social crisis. Traffic congestion, air pollution, and water pollution are examples of problems associated with affluence rather than poverty. Before the racial crisis captured the headlines, what people had in mind when they talked about the urban problem was the inability of a technologically progressive private economic system to adjust the environment to the requirements of urbanization.

The urban problem as we view it today is therefore a composite of concerns—some inherently urban, in the sense that they arise out of a pattern of settlement which we call urban, others incidentally urban, in the sense that they arise primarily

* Brown University.

173

out of an economic and social system which fails to deal equitably with all the people, a large number of whom reside in cities. Whatever vision of a perfect city we may have had in earlier years must now be modified to reflect these new priorities. There can no longer be a "city beautiful" which does not deal successfully with the racial problem and the related problem of poverty. Our notions of optimality and efficiency must now be tempered by a concern for equity and stability.

Urban Markets What is the role of economics in advancing our understanding of urban problems and the search for solutions? To begin with, there is the traditional domain of economics: the marketplace, where buyers and sellers interact to determine the allocation of resources. A number of markets play a large part in shaping urban problems.

The market for land is perhaps the most important and the most generically urban. The freedom of the individual in the use of city space is constrained by local ordinance, but this constraint hardly determines the pattern of land use. Instead, this pattern, like the pattern of production in the economy, responds to the classic pressures of supply and demand. Households and business enterprises own land and make free decisions on its disposition; they also go into the market to acquire land for particular uses. How individual units make such choices and how these choices interact represent a classic application of economic analysis.

In other words, it is the business of urban economics to explain and predict the location of people and jobs in urban areas: why some industries concentrate downtown and others prefer dispersed, suburban locations; why population increases faster in some sections of the metropolis than in others. In the hands of economists, this explanation is likely to focus on such "economic" variables as the cost of land, the technological characteristics of production, the income of households, and the relative accessibility of different locations. But it does not follow that economic analysis must be restricted to such variables. For example, the influence of discrimination is an important part of any analysis that purports to explain the concentration of Negroes in city ghettos. Similarly, the fact of zoning as an influence on land use must be taken into account. As long as it is reasonable to assume that the decision to acquire or dispose of land is heavily influenced by financial considerations, the role of economic analysis is paramount.

A second important market in the urban context is the housing market, or, more broadly, the market for buildings (structures). The use of urban land is reflected mainly in the structures on it. The problems generated by the pattern of land use are—with the exception of parks and highways—associated with the pattern of structures, whether for habitation or other uses. The determination of this pattern is mainly a market process in which households and enterprises, operating under certain legal constraints, make decisions to buy, sell, rent, lease, build, rehabilitate, tear down, or otherwise dispose of buildings or parts of buildings, largely in pursuit of their own self-interest. It is a process in which financial considerations—prices and costs, sales and profits—play a dominant role.

The application of economic analysis extends, however, beyond these inherently urban phenomena. Increasingly we have come to recognize that the urban labor market requires special attention beyond that accorded to labor markets in the mainstream of economics. For example, consider the well-known concept of structural unemployment, discussed in Chapter 8. Structural unemployment is unemployment that is explained, not by an overall weakness in the economy, but rather by the inability of the labor market to match supply and demand for particular elements of the labor force, such as unskilled persons. The ordinary or traditional analysis, which abstracts from space and location, is insensitive to such potentially important aspects of structural unemployment as the heavy flow of rural unskilled Negroes from the South to major cities in the North, where they are constrained in their choice of residential location while their potential employers rove freely through the metropolis in search of cheaper space and improved access. Here is structural unemployment in a new form, one inherently urban and not susceptible to analysis unless explicit account is taken of the spatial configuration of the labor market. In sum, the performance of land, housing, and labor markets is a major object of analysis in the field of urban economics.

Public Policies But economics has also invaded areas of resource allocation where markets do not provide the framework for decision and action. Public finance, for example, a traditional field of research for economists, is concerned with the behavior of governments in the allocation process. Until fairly recently, the major issues in this field were taxation and fiscal policy. Economic analysis was brought to bear on such questions as the impact of particular forms of taxation on private economic behavior, or of the overall level of expenditure on the stability and growth of the economy as a whole. With government programs proliferating and "consuming" a rapidly increasing fraction of total national resources, the attention of economists has been increasingly drawn to the expenditure side of public budgets. The attempt now is to provide normative, or policy-oriented, criteria to guide the allocation of resources by the public sector.

This new development in "public" economics, enhanced by traditional concern over taxation, finds its most important expression in the city.

Consider the problem of urban transportation. How much space should be devoted to transportation facilities? What kinds of capital investments should be made? What prices should be charged to the users? How should such facilities and services be financed? These are questions which public bodies—federal, state, and local governments—must answer in shaping their policies with respect to an activity that absorbs many resources and exerts a profound effect on the performance of our cities.

The economist, with his traditional tools, tries to be helpful by analyzing the behavior of consumers of transport services. But more is required. In the public sector there is no market on which to rely for a reasonable approximation to the efficient allocation of resources. Instead we must engage in "cost-benefit" analysis, an essentially normative exercise in which we try to construct a balance sheet for society of the gains and losses associated with alternative policies and programs.*

First, the consequences of public policy must be identified. This is a problem in prediction calling upon the traditional skills of the economist. For example, if we build a new freeway, how many people will use it and how will patronage vary with the tolls charged? How will the existence of the freeway affect the location of population and industry in the city?

But beyond these questions, which test the predictive capacity of urban economics, there are "evaluative" questions such as, what is the cost of a right-of-way for a freeway around the center of the city? The cost of acquiring and clearing the land may be a poor measure, because such land is usually acquired by condemnation, thus depriving us of a true market test. What about the cost of relocating the families and businesses displaced by the right-of-way? Is the additional smog generated by the additional automobile travel a cost to be reckoned in the balance? If the freeway encourages the dispersal of industry, reducing the accessibility of jobs of the poor family without a car, is this a cost to be included in our calculation? What about the cost of lives lost in automobile accidents?

Economists are quick to enter a disclaimer at this point—their credentials do not necessarily make them competent to measure and attach dollar values to all the consequences flowing from a given public action. The value of an additional life saved or lost is indeed a number which an economist has no authority to specify. But, for better or worse, the discipline of economics is able to provide a perspective and a focus for a critical appraisal—however value-laden—of alternative public policies in terms of their net contribution to social welfare.

Thus, we include cost-benefit analysis under the heading of urban economics, along with the more traditional discipline of public finance,

---

* See Chap. 10, "Economic Analysis of the Public Sector."

especially as it concerns the financing of local government in the urban area. What does economics have to say about the local property tax? Should we substitute broad federal grants to cities for the existing categorical grants, which provide funds for particular programs? How can economic analysis enlighten us on the wisdom of our urban-renewal policies? How does it contribute to our appraisal of alternative policies for dealing with the problem of unemployment in the black ghettos of our major cities?

Urban economics, then, is the study of market forces that critically shape the urban setting. It provides, in addition, a framework for analyzing public policy designed to improve the performance of the urban environment in meeting society's objectives.

Urban Ghettos The scope of urban economics and its potential relevance to public policy can be illustrated by the most depressing feature of the urban crisis, the black ghettos of the major cities. Several remedies have been suggested for one of the key problems of the ghettos: excessively high unemployment. One remedy calls for the expansion of job opportunities through measures that would induce employers to locate their facilities closer to the ghetto labor force. A variant of this policy calls for the encouragement of "black capitalism" as a means of enhancing employment opportunities for ghetto residents. A second remedy calls for the expansion of job opportunities through transport subsidies that would bring the ghetto labor force closer to job opportunities in outlying locations. These two approaches assume that the critical obstacle to higher employment is access. A third remedy calls for investment in education and training to raise the skill level of the ghetto workers and improve their qualifications for existing job opportunities. Finally, there is the direct assault on racial discrimination, which is presumed to be an important determinant of the unemployment rate in the ghetto.

How do we choose among these policies; or, more precisely, how do we identify the best mix of remedies, since there is obvious complementarity among them? The state of our knowledge is inadequate to provide unequivocal guidance. Furthermore, we should not expect to handle these questions adequately with economic analysis alone. Yet there is some definite progress to report.

1. The lay observer, especially if he is black, is convinced that the Negro is constrained by discrimination to live in the ghetto. Needless to say, there is plenty of ad hoc evidence to support this conviction. But the urban economist, to the displeasure of the impatient radical, accounts for the ghetto population in terms of patterns of residential location in urban areas. He finds, for example, that income, family size, and location of employment are powerful variables in explaining the residential patterns of whites. He is naturally led to ask, therefore, whether the observed distribution of the black population is not also explainable in these terms—in which case, he could be skeptical (at the risk of incurring the wrath of his radical friends) of the presumption of discrimination.

A decade ago it would have been impossible to deal with the null hypothesis (no discrimination) in these terms, because we literally had no adequately detailed data on individuals and families. But thanks to surveys conducted in a number of major metropolitan areas in recent years, such information is now available. These surveys were undertaken as part of large-scale studies designed to provide a better base for estimating the future transportation requirements of these areas, as an aid to planning. In the surveys literally hundreds of thousands of families, selected on a random basis, were interviewed and information was obtained on a long list of socioeconomic variables. These data are now grist for the urban economist's mill.

An analysis conducted at The RAND Corporation—a nonprofit research organization which has traditionally specialized in defense-oriented research but has recently turned to studying urgent domestic problems as well—employing data for Chicago and Detroit demonstrates rather conclusively that the ordinary determining variables do not account for the residential pattern of Negroes in large urban areas. The methodology is simple. Given estimates of the influence of socioeconomic variables, other than color, derived from data on the white population, an "expected" distribution of the black population is derived by taking account of the values of the relevant variables for the black population.

The dashed curve in Figure 13-1 shows the number of nonwhites residing in each residence ring. The rings are numbered 1, 2, 3, and so on, in relation to their proximity to downtown. The solid curve indicates the number of nonwhites who would be "expected" to be living in each residence ring if low-income nonwhites were distributed in the same manner as their white counterparts. The comparison indicates that as many as 40,000 nonwhites would move out of the three inner rings if discrimination did not exist.

The difference between the *actual* and the *expected* pattern, as exemplified in Figure 13-1, can reasonably be attributed to discrimination. The conclusion has a further significance:

> *Centrally employed nonwhites make short work trips (i.e., they live closer to their jobs) and probably shorter than they would freely choose if the housing market were not segregated (e.g., more would prefer to live in the suburbs).... Non-centrally employed nonwhites (i.e., those not working downtown), on the other hand, seem to travel relatively long distances to work.... In general, the evidence is that discrimination forces minority groups into a disproportionate amount of cross-*

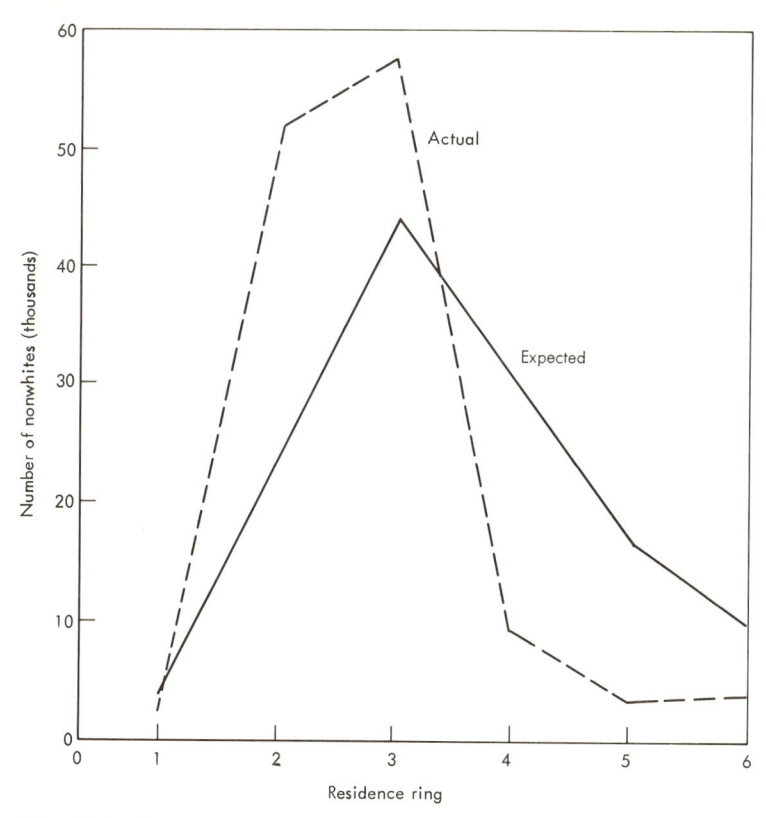

FIG. 13-1 Detroit nonwhites actually residing in each ring and the expected distribution in the absence of racial income differences and housing discrimination. (The expected distribution assumes that nonwhites have income levels and housing preferences similar to those of low-income whites and thus similar residential patterns.)

hauling and reverse commuting. Ghettos and their counterparts are usually near [central business districts]; accordingly, since more and more workplaces are located at the fringe of cities, more and more Negroes will be traveling to and from work in directions opposite to the main commuter streams unless housing discrimination is lessened [10, p. 166].

2. Already there is the suggestion that the ghetto imposes access difficulties on the Negro. But do we have more direct evidence? Can we "prove" that the Negro's chances of being unemployed are significantly greater because of the fact that he is constrained in his choice of residence? Further analysis of the same data throws light on this question.

Employing the multiple-regression technique,* John Kain derives an equation relating the proportion of jobs held by Negroes in a zone of the urban area (W) to the proportion of residents in the zone who are Negro (R) and to the distance from the nearest major ghetto (D). He finds a significant positive partial correlation between W and R, and a significant negative partial correlation between W and D. For the city of Chicago, these two variables account for 70 percent of the variation in W. Even when total employment is disaggregated by occupation and industry, the fundamental relationships are still observed in each occupation and industry. The suggested conclusion is therefore that the capacity of Negroes to participate in the job market depends in part on how close they live to the jobs.

To estimate the "loss" resulting from segregation, Kain makes a further calculation of what would happen to Negro employment if the Negro population was residentially distributed in a pattern consistent with its socioeconomic characteristics. He finds for Chicago that Negro employment would increase by more than 10 percent [7].

3. Any policy to increase employment opportunities in or near the ghetto must be based on an understanding of the forces affecting the location of industry within urban areas and a careful reading of trends. This subject has received considerable attention from urban economists because it has implications not only for the ghetto but also for the entire metropolitan area—its physical layout, its transportation systems, the fiscal capacities of its municipalities, and its public services.

A superficial reading of the facts and their causes goes something like this. New employment opportunities are growing much faster in the suburbs than in the central cities. Why? First, the automobile and the truck have in effect removed the fundamental advantages of the central city: proximity to rail terminals and harbors; proximity to large pools of labor; proximity to suppliers, customers, and competitors. Second, there is a scarcity of vacant land in the city for the expansion of old plants or the construction of new ones. Third, the population (partly in response to employment shifts) is growing much more rapidly in the suburbs. Fourth, the "public" climate is more favorable there—taxes are lower, services are better, and there is less racial strife and general insecurity.

This simple picture is not sufficiently detailed to offer a basis for policy. When Pan American builds a skyscraper next door to Grand Central Station in New York City, and United States Steel erects a 64-story office building in downtown Pittsburgh, the image of a declining central city and thriving suburbs is brought into question. Urban economists have therefore sought to decompose the overall picture, extending

---
* See Chap. 3, above.

its empirical foundations and refining the analysis. Even today, after approximately fifteen years of extensive research, an author has prefaced an essay with the following observation:

> But recommendations are being made with little hard information on the actual movement of jobs from city to suburbs—how large it has been, whether it is accelerating or decelerating, what industries are particularly responsible, and what the similarities or differences are among different cities. The present article represents an attempt to provide considerably firmer data on the suburbanization of employment than has heretofore been available [8, p. 2].

Another recent author begins his essay in a similar vein:

> The causes and consequences of suburbanization are—almost literally as well as figuratively—burning issues of our time.... But it is amazing how little we know about the subject.... Despite the thousands of pages...we have remarkably few hard facts or verified hypotheses [11, p. 1].

A major stumbling block in this field, as in so many other aspects of urban economics, has been the paucity of data. Reflecting the general neglect of urban problems at the national and state levels, government sources have only recently begun to respond to the urgent need for more detailed information on the location of employment within urban areas. The U.S. Bureau of the Census, the largest data-collecting agency in the world, provides considerably more data on *people* than on jobs, and does much more for *industries* than for areas. Nevertheless, basing his work entirely on this source, Raymond Vernon, who was then Director of the New York Metropolitan Region Study, was able in 1959 to construct a picture of intrametropolitan employment shifts over the period 1929–1954 for those categories of industry which are generally covered by the census: manufacturing, retail sales, wholesale sales, and selected services. While still highly aggregative in terms of both industry and area, Vernon's analysis takes us at least one step beyond the simple picture with which we began.

For each of the thirteen largest metropolitan areas, Vernon found that the central city's share of population and of retail, wholesale, and manufacturing employment had declined. However, the decline was generally steeper for all categories of employment than for population, suggesting that for this period the spread of jobs was the leading force in shaping metropolitan growth [20]. For the more recent period, the converse seems to be true.

In the New York Metropolitan Region Study, a profile of job location within the New York area was painstakingly constructed out of a great variety of sources, such as *County Business Patterns* (a source book based on social security files), special tabulations of reports filed with state and federal agencies by employers for unemployment-insurance and related purposes, and many ad hoc sources [6]. In recent years, the vast transportation studies alluded to earlier have yielded original data on the location of employment. A recent paper on the intrametropolitan location of industry cites Dun and Bradstreet as a principal source of data [18].

Now that we have more refined data on intrametropolitan employment shifts, what can we say that is relevant to policy? In a brief essay it is, of course, impossible to do justice to the vast literature that has accumulated on the subject. Our purpose here is only to provide illustrations. We started with a 1959 publication from the "primitive" period. Now let us look at more recent work.

Lewis' paper [8], from which we quoted above, focuses on a question of critical importance for the problem of ghetto unemployment: What accounts for the rate of growth of total employment in the central city? His technique is to isolate the influence of four factors: national growth, industry mix, regional shift, and suburbanization. His hypothesis is that the overall growth rate of a particular central city's employment in a given time period depends upon the rate of growth of national employment during that period, the industrial composition of the particular city between slow- and fast-growing industries (nationally), the growth rate of the surrounding metropolitan area, and finally the rate at which industry is suburbanizing in a given metropolitan area.

By skillful manipulation of available data, the author constructs estimates of total nonfarm employment for thirty categories of industry in fifteen cities for the years 1953, 1959, and 1965. Using an algebraic technique, he then proceeds to partition the rate of growth of total employment for a given central city, between two points in time, into the four categories cited earlier: national growth, industry mix, regional shift, and suburbanization. For example, in New York City total employment increased 5.9 percent between 1959 and 1965. This figure, when decomposed, consists of the following elements:

National growth	14.8%
Industry mix	2.3%
Regional shift	−7.2%
Suburbanization	−4.0%

The interpretation is as follows: If New York City had followed national growth patterns by industry, it would have experienced a growth rate of 17.1 percent because of its "favorable" industry mix. But the combination of adverse regional shifts and suburbanization depressed the growth rate to 5.9 percent.

For the fifteen cities as a group, Lewis offers the following findings:

(1) The central cities have lost jobs to the suburbs in all but one of the cities studied, and in virtually all industries, and this has consistently been a large negative factor in the downtown employment picture; (2) holding the cities constant, it is by all odds the national growth rate *[emphasis added] that explains most of the difference between higher and lower central city employment growth at different times; and (3) at a given time, it is the regional growth factor—i.e., whether the city is located in a fast or slow-growing region—that primarily accounts for whether employment growth in a particular city is high or low.... The industry-mix factor, which is a measure of a city's initial endowment of rapidly-growing industries, is the least important of the four factors measured [8, p. 13].*

What are the policy implications of this analysis? First, the maintenance of a high national growth rate is the most potent weapon for offsetting influences that tend to depress central-city employment. Quantitatively, these negative influences

exert a drag on central city employment of about 1¼ percent per annum.... Growth of real gross national product of 4 percent per year ... would entail an increase in employment nationally of about 1.6 percent a year, or, on past form, enough to produce a very slight increase in central city employment [8, pp. 20–21].

Second, and most important, the author is led by his analysis to question the accepted view that the kinds of jobs available in the central city are not well suited to the ghetto unemployed:

Manufacturing is certainly not unique in its requirements for relatively low-skilled workers; ... industries which have been growing most rapidly in the central cities are generally more intensive in their use of low-skilled (at least low-paid) employees than the industries which have been slower growing or contracting [8, p. 32].

The author goes on to express a strong preference for programs to train the unemployed over programs to attract industry to the city or programs to subsidize transportation to jobs in the suburbs.

4. Ten years ago the ghetto problem was not in the spotlight as it is today, and urban economists gave little explicit attention to it. "Black capitalism" did not even exist as a concept, let alone as an identifiable area of research. It is not surprising, therefore, that the idea has not received critical attention from economists. But the process has begun.

A recent paper by Mark Daniels defines the economic goals of black capitalism. They are:

> ...to effect community control over the local economic environment and...to redistribute business ownership in favor of the black community.... Black control...is expected to increase the level of real output in the community. Furthermore, it is expected that jobs will be created for local residents.... New black ownership...is expected to redistribute income in favor of labor in the black community [4, p. 3].

The author goes on to show that black capitalism could easily lead to a reduction in total employment. By making capital cheaper to the Negro entrepreneur, he will have an incentive to substitute capital for labor and only under specific assumptions will he end up with a larger labor force (income and substitution effects in standard economic theory). On the other hand, since the Negro employer will presumably not discriminate against blacks, there could be an increase in the employment of blacks in any case.

A similar conclusion emerges from Daniels' analysis of the redistributive effects of black capitalism:

> *There is no certainty* [that] ...*a simple transfer of real capital will increase labor income in the black community. Even if it does, it is likely on a priori grounds to be at the expense of labor in the white sector as well as present black owners of capital* [4, p. 15].

The real potential of black capitalism, therefore, must arise from *control* and not simply the cheapening of capital to Negro entrepreneurs. "For control effects to be manifest there must then be an effort of sufficient scale to involve the entire community..." [4, p. 19]. The author concludes, therefore, that a given amount of resources to encourage black entrepreneurs should be concentrated in a few communities rather than dispersed among many communities.

These examples of urban economic research suggest how the application of theoretical and empirical analysis may shed some light on complex and urgent social problems that find their locus in the urban environment. In contrast to the more traditional fields of economics, the uniquely new dimension here is *space*, a variable that is largely ignored in macro- and microeconomics but that lies at the heart of urban economic analysis. A second feature, which is not quite unique, is the intimate relationship among theory, data, and policy. The prospect of an even more fruitful relationship of this kind suggests an exciting future for urban economics.

REFERENCES

1 BREAK, GEORGE F. *Intergovernmental Fiscal Relations in the United States* (Washington, D. C.: Brookings, 1967).

2 CHINITZ, B. (ed.). *City and Suburb* (Englewood Cliffs, N.J.: Prentice-Hall, 1964).
3 ———. Scientific American, *Cities* (New York: Knopf, 1965).
4 DANIELS, MARK R. "A Policy Perspective on the Economics of Black Capitalism," draft paper submitted to Committee on Urban Economics, September 1969.
5 HAUSER, PHILIP M., and LEO F. SCHNORE (eds.). *The Study of Urbanization* (New York: Wiley, 1966).
6 HOOVER, EDGAR M., and RAYMOND VERNON. *Anatomy of a Metropolis* (Cambridge, Mass.: Harvard University Press, 1959).
7 KAIN, JOHN F. "Housing Segregation, Negro Employment, and Metropolitan Decentralization," *Quarterly Journal of Economics*, 82 (May 1968), pp. 175–197.
8 LEWIS, WILFRED. "Urban Growth and Suburbanization of Employment—Some New Data," draft paper submitted to *American Economic Review*, June 1969.
9 MARGOLIS, JULIUS (ed.). *The Public Economy of Urban Communities* (Baltimore: Johns Hopkins, 1965).
10 MEYER, JOHN, JOHN F. KAIN, and MARTIN WOHL. *The Urban Transportation Problem* (Cambridge, Mass.: Harvard University Press, 1965).
11 MILLS, EDWIN C. "Urban Density Functions," draft paper submitted to Committee on Urban Economics, September 1969.
12 OWEN, WILFRED. *The Metropolitan Transportation Problem* (Washington D. C.: Brookings, 1966).
13 PERLOFF, HARVEY S., and LOWDON WINGO, JR. (eds.). *Issues in Urban Economics* (Baltimore: Johns Hopkins, 1968).
14 *The Public Interest*, Special Issue, "Focus on New York," Number 16, Summer 1969.
15 *Report of the National Advisory Commission on Civil Disorders* (New York: Bantam, 1968).
16 ROTHENBERG, JEROME. *Economic Evaluation of Urban Renewal* (Washington, D. C.: Brookings, 1967).
17 SCHNORE, LEO F. (ed.). *Social Science and the City* (New York: Praeger, 1967).
18 STRUYK, RAYMOND J. "A Progress Report on a Study of Intra-metropolitan Location of Industry," draft paper submitted to Committee on Urban Economics, September 1969.
19 THOMPSON, WILBUR R. *A Preface to Urban Economics* (Baltimore: Johns Hopkins, 1965).
20 VERNON, RAYMOND. *The Changing Economic Function of the Central City*, Committee for Economic Development, 1959.

14

INTERNATIONAL ECONOMICS: THEORY AND POLICY

*Aurelius Morgner**

EXTENDING our study of economic relationships to the international scene introduces several complexities. At once we begin to detect national differences in resource distribution, labor productivity, and economic development. Even the currency used for exchange differs from country to country. Fortunately for the student, basic principles of international trade are well set forth in standard textbooks such as Samuelson [13] and McConnell [9].

Fortunately, too, one of the great economists of our time, Professor Gottfried Haberler of Harvard University, has provided us with a remarkable little book, *A Survey of International Trade Theory*.[1] In this work, Professor Haberler, who is also the author of a classic treatise on international trade, captures the essence of international trade in six terse chapters (analyzing the background of international trade theory, the classical theory of comparative costs and international values, the modern developments of pure theory, the terms of trade, the balance-of-payments mechanisms, and the theory of international trade policy). "The *Survey* [as the author states in his preface to the 1961 edition] is confined to a presentation of the theoretical skeleton, with a bare minimum of institutional details and no facts or figures. It is, furthermore, a summary in words, without the aid

---
* University of Southern California.
[1] The first edition of the *Survey* was published in 1955; a revised and enlarged edition appeared in 1961 [6].

of mathematics." The student is encouraged to look at this book. Nonetheless, a word of caution is in order: the *Survey* presupposes some acquaintance with the voluminous literature on international trade!

The present chapter has a more modest goal. It attempts to focus on a current issue of international trade—trade liberalization. During the 1930s, one could sadly observe that ". . . great progress has been made in the technique of Protection" [5, preface to the English edition]. In contrast, the international economist today is more fortunate. He can concentrate on various measures designed to remove our self-imposed shackles.

The Case for Freer Trade Great advantages are to be gained from freer international trade, as economists have pointed out since early in the last century in expounding the principle of comparative advantage. Free trade permits the most effective use of the world's resources. Some countries of the world have resources, particularly minerals or products of a certain climate, that other countries lack; the gain from such trade is obvious. But countries also differ in their possession of factors of production and in the special skills, developed over time, that enable them to produce goods more cheaply than their neighbors. Thus, a country such as Australia with an abundance of land and a relative shortage of labor can produce meat, a land-intensive product, cheaply. On the other hand, vegetables, a labor-intensive product, will be costly in Australia. Holland, a land-short but relatively labor-abundant country, will find the reverse to be true. Thus, an exchange of meat for vegetables between the two will be beneficial to both. However, if both have lived in isolation or if the meat-vegetable trade has hitherto been limited by protectionism, the proposed development of such trade will bring protests from the Australian vegetable growers and the Dutch meat producers.

Should the interests of the threatened parties be considered and trade barred? The answer of economists has usually been "no," unless it can be shown that tariff protection would be accompanied in time by increases in efficiency (the "infant industries" argument). For if vegetables grown in Australia cost 50 cents a pound, but vegetables imported from abroad only 30 cents, imported vegetables can be said to cost only 30 cents in meat exports, since this is how they are paid for. Thus, vegetables can be obtained indirectly by producing and exporting meat with only three-fifths of the sacrifice that would be involved if vegetables were produced directly.

As for the injury to the Australian vegetable growers, it must be noted that either they will stay in the industry and produce at 30 cents a pound, in which case their former price represented a gain by them at the expense of the consumer, or they will go into meat production. If at any price less than 50 cents for vegetables they make such a shift to meat production, this means that the 20 cents more formerly paid by consumers for vegetables was not even a gain to the vegetable producers. This is the important point. Protectionism at its best means simply a transfer of income from consumers to producers. Generally, however, to the extent that resources are mobile, the losses of consumers are greater than the gains of producers. So economists have argued that if an objective of national policy is the maximization of real income, protectionism is a mistake.

Development of the International Economy The international economy served the world well in the nineteenth century. It has done poorly by the world in the twentieth century. During parts of the nineteenth century, the world economy involved virtually the same economic arrangements as the domestic economy. Goods were free to move between countries, hampered only by modest tariff restrictions that often lagged behind the falling costs provided by revolutionized means of transportation. Not only did capital move freely between countries, but the mobility of labor was great, with nearly sixty million people migrating from the Eastern to the Western Hemisphere. While countries used currencies with different names, the gold standard automatically provided the world with what has since been unsuccessfully sought in our century through international agreements—stable exchange rates and complete convertibility.

Thus, the international economy of a century ago provided a magnificent mechanism for making most effective use of the world's resources and transmitting the great economic revolution occurring in the northern areas of the European continent to the farthest reaches of the world. But in time this mechanism faltered. While incorporation of the United States, the British dominions, and the southern part of South America into the world economy led to sustained internal economic development in these newly settled areas, the older cultural areas of the world (with the single exception of Japan) developed dual or enclave economies, where one section carried on the production of food or raw materials for export, while the other section, constituting most of the economy, failed to modernize and develop. In the twentieth century, the gap between developed and underdeveloped nations grew wider. Since the underdeveloped areas remained politically inarticulate, this widening effect passed almost without comment until their emergence as independent nations in the past two decades.

But the changing world economy has served even the developed countries less well. Toward the end of the nineteenth century, the United States and Germany became increasingly protectionistic. With the outbreak of World War I, the gold-standard mechanism in the belligerent countries was displaced by the needs of war finance, making stable exchange rates and general convertibility impossible. An attempt was made to reestablish the international gold standard in the aftermath of World War I, but protectionism and rising nationalism in the 1930s, and the unwillingness of countries with balance-of-payments deficits to submit to deflation in the face of their own internal unemployment problems, wrecked the international monetary and international trade systems.

Since World War II, the countries of the world have tried through international cooperation to promote freer trade, to facilitate the working of an international monetary system, to promote world economic development, and thus to construct a successful modern world economy. These efforts, however, have still not produced the wished-for success. Trade liberalization, for example, has been only partial, even among the developed nations. Furthermore, the Soviet bloc has remained relatively isolated from the West. Quotas and exchange controls (twentieth-century restraints on trade) as well as tariffs have yet to be removed. Trade liberalization has increasingly become a movement not toward worldwide markets but toward the establishment of regional common markets, which create problems for the "outsider" nations. In addition, the less-developed nations have come to feel that the workings of the international economy in the past inhibited rather than promoted their development. They now demand *new* international trade policies. Finally, the world has had to struggle with the inadequacies of the present international monetary system, discussed in Professor Triffin's chapter (Chapter 15), which does not appear to balance trade adequately and which casts the dollar in a central role that other countries are less and less willing to accept.

All these developments have greatly stimulated the thinking of economists with respect to the theory of international trade, the relationship between trade and economic development, and the theory of the balance of payments. Viewed as policies, these issues reflect conflicts among three groups. First, the United States, supported generally by the United Kingdom, wishes to liberalize trade upon a nondiscriminatory basis and to see common markets extended as a vehicle for general trade liberalization. Second, the European Common Market group led by France is concerned with the predominant role played by the United States in the international economic world and with the special status given the dollar as a reserve currency. Finally, the underdeveloped countries of the world feel that the international economic organizations developed after World War II do not serve their needs particularly well, and that the developed nations must drastically alter their trade policies if economic development of the underdeveloped world is to be accelerated.

In recent years, doubt has been cast by some economists upon the quantitative importance of gain to be realized through trade liberalization. Tariffs, it is argued, have been reduced considerably already, so that the benefit from further reductions is limited. Protection, however, is not merely a matter of what percentage of the product price is subject to the tariff. The true cost of protection is larger. For example, if a product is sold for $10 and the tariff is 20 percent, or $2, the protection afforded is solely to the domestic factors of production, which may cost only $5, the other $5 of the $10 selling price being the cost of imported materials. In this case, the protection offered by the tariff is equivalent to 40 percent, not 20 percent.

Furthermore, in judging welfare one must allow for the fact that more of the product will be consumed at the lower price resulting from liberalized trade conditions. In addition, the establishment of economically based, liberalized trade would presume the end not only of tariffs but also of quotas and domestically subsidized production, such as we observe in agriculture. Quotas and subsidies, even more than tariffs, involve a substantial misallocation of world resources. Beyond the gains of a once-for-all reallocation of resources to their most efficient use, there are also the gains from the on-going transmission and diffusion of growth made possible by high levels of trade. Thus, while trade liberalization may not bring spectacular increases in standards of living, the small figures usually cited understate the magnitude of possible gains.

Trade-liberalization Procedures   Today there are two avenues to trade liberalization. One is through the international organization with the odd name of GATT (General Agreement on Tariffs and Trade). The other is through the action of individual nations coming together to form multicountry organizations such as free-trade associations, customs unions, and common markets.[2] The first avenue definitely leads to a world of general liberalized trade relations; the second may arrive at this same end, but it could also lead to the world's being organized into major economic blocs.

GATT's principal function is to call conferences at which member nations can bargain for tariff reductions on a multilateral basis. It also provides a set of general principles for the conduct of trade. One of these principles is to end discrimination in international trade, the ultimate achievement being, of course, free trade. But GATT does not envision

---

[2] Under a free-trade association, member countries simply reduce tariffs with respect to one another, but maintain existing tariffs with respect to other nations. A customs union involves not only a lowering of tariffs by its members but also the adoption of a uniform tariff schedule by all the members. A common market is a customs union with the additional feature that the members agree to permit greater labor and capital mobility, and to consult on common economic policies.

such an eventual state of affairs. It seeks rather to see that no new preferences are introduced—with the important exception that free-trade areas, customs unions, and common markets may be formed. While these organizations obviously discriminate—the lower tariffs extended by the members to one another are not extended to outsiders—the presumption is that they represent movement toward freer trade. Another GATT principle is to protect existing industries exclusively by means of tariffs. Import quotas may be used only by countries suffering from balance-of-payments problems or willing to impose quotas on their own domestic production. Since many countries have agricultural-support-price policies based on the limitation of domestic production, this latter provision unfortunately sanctions the extensive use of quotas in agriculture.

Two economic objections may be made to GATT policies as a means of liberalizing trade. First, while the principle of nondiscrimination may appeal to one's sense of justice, economists have come to doubt that such a policy, involving levying equal tariffs against all nations, has anything to recommend it over a policy of discrimination. Discriminatory tariff reductions, that is, might allocate world resources more efficiently than nondiscriminatory tariff reductions. Second, it is to a nation's advantage to reduce tariffs even if other countries do not. Certainly, it is to the nation's further advantage that others *also* reduce theirs, but it is not a sacrifice to grant tariff reductions unilaterally. The process of reducing tariffs through bargaining, moreover, produces a paradoxical situation where the mechanism only works so long as it does not achieve its objective; for once a nation has ended its tariffs it has nothing to bargain with! For this reason, countries must bargain hard over their own reductions in order to save something for bargaining in the future.

The United States in 1967 completed the "Kennedy round" of tariff reductions after having negotiated through GATT since 1962 under the powers extended to the President by the Trade Expansion Act of that year. While reductions in industrial tariffs were obtained, the settlement did not reverse the Common Market's movement toward a highly protectionistic agriculture.

Free-trade associations, customs unions, and common markets present an alternative means for liberalizing trade. On a static level, such organizations improve the allocation of resources and expand trade among their members according to the traditional free-trade arguments of economic theory. But such organizations also have trade-diverting effects. For if nations A and B have lowered tariffs against each other but have maintained them against nation C, they may find that certain goods imported by them from C may now be obtained cheaper from their partner, although C is really the lower-cost producer of the goods. A and B thus produce things for each other that could be obtained at lower cost from

C, and so are losers, as also is C. However, A and B have the gains of trade creation to offset at least a part of the losses of trade diversion, whereas C has only a loss. The customs union would be ideal if A and B were capable of producing each other's products but neither was capable of producing the products sold by C. The more alike—that is, the more competitive—the countries in the customs union, the more opportunity for them to complement each other by specializing, and the greater the gains to both.

The gains derived from a customs union will also be greater if a high level of tariffs existed between the members before the union, giving more scope for trade creation. Obviously, too, gains will be greater, the lower the new common tariff agreed on by the union in relation to the rest of the world, since this will minimize trade diversion. Similarly, the larger the customs union, the less significant the trade diversion. If everyone belonged to the customs union, however, there would be no trade diversion at all—only trade creation—and no customs union!

In recent years economists have come to realize that another important aspect of a customs union has been overlooked. Trade creation between nations A and B involves on the part of each not only more specialization in production, but also, by changing relative prices, expansion of the consumption of goods originally bought from each other, as well as of goods formerly bought from nation C but now bought from each other. The formation of a customs union, then, can have positive and negative production and consumption effects. The trade diversion from C caused by both effects worsens the terms of trade against C. This adds a further loss for C, but reduces the loss due to trade diversion borne by A and B.

It has become apparent that nations A and B may realize further dynamic gains from a customs union. In addition to the static reallocation gains mentioned above, enlarged markets may bring about substantial economies in production. Firms used to operating in limited markets may achieve internal economies through concentration and expansion of output in enlarged markets. External economies may be realized through intensified competition and possible acceleration of technological change. Also, the uncertainties of international-trade policies may be reduced by customs unions, which are conceived of as having a permanent life. Thus, while there can be no absolute assurance that countries will gain by the formation of a customs union, many static and dynamic factors favor nations that form one.

There remains the problem of how customs unions affect the rest of the world. By trade diversion, the rest of the world loses. Once nations A and B expand production to satisfy needs formerly met from the rest of the world C, the appeal of further reciprocal tariff reduction between the customs union and the rest of the world is reduced, since the customs union leads to a misallocation of resources, whose correction would involve difficult readjustments by local industries that have expanded. It can be argued that the increased prosperity of the customs union would cause its imports from the rest of the world to rise; but general trade liberalization would *also* have brought prosperity to the customs union and to the rest of the world.

Thus, customs unions may represent a difficult path to general trade liberalization. To date, none has been founded for its trade-creating effects. Rather, customs unions have been proposed on such grounds as the desire to strengthen Western Europe as a political force, to unite people of the same language, culture, and religion, or to enable poor people to work cooperatively on the theory that in buying goods (even at high cost) from one another their economic development will somehow be promoted. Instead of clearing the way for greater trade liberalization, the increase in the number of customs unions may reorganize the world economically into self-contained trading blocs according to political considerations. If this comes about, it will mean that a world that is basically poor will have lost the opportunity to use its economic resources more effectively.

Trade Liberalization as Viewed by the Less-developed Countries While the developed countries are moving haltingly toward trade liberalization through GATT negotiations and customs unions, the less-developed countries put general trade liberalization increasingly into question. The selective liberalization of customs unions has stronger appeal for them than GATT, which has been called the "rich countries' club." GATT appears to the underdeveloped countries to involve two unfortunate principles. First, the principle that *all trade liberalization is good*. The less-developed nations cannot accept this principle, since they feel that protectionism is necessary to their development. However, GATT's articles of agreement are such that less-developed countries can, within its framework, protect their developing industries; thus, it cannot be charged with having been a barrier to the control of trade in these countries' developmental interests. Second, the principle of *bargaining and nondiscrimination*. The less-developed nations, while believing that they should not be discriminated *against*, feel that they should be given preference in trade relations with developed nations. Furthermore, they feel that they are not in a position, being poor and weak, to engage in bargaining. As they see matters, a reciprocal movement toward freer trade will trap underdeveloped countries in the production of food and raw materials and check the industrialization that they desire.

The less-developed countries, however, do benefit from GATT, even when they are not parties to an agreement. GATT regulations require that tariff reductions made by bargaining be extended to imports from all nations. Thus, if developed nations negotiate a reduction of tariffs, underdeveloped nations can then export to the developed nations at the new lower tariff rates, even though they did not participate in the negotiations and made no concessions. Such benefits, however, have inherent limitations for less-developed nations, since developed nations are likely to negotiate tariff reductions on industrial goods that less-developed nations are in no position to produce.

In recent years customs unions have drawn increasing attention from less-developed nations as a means for speeding economic developmnet. Often the markets of such countries are so small that important internal and external economies might be realized through the expanded market provided by a customs union. However, when trade creation and trade diversion are considered, the outlook appears less promising. Underdeveloped countries generally have little trade with one another, but large amounts with developed countries. Thus, the possibilities for trade diversion, with the losses it involves, may be substantial. When less-developed countries have similar manufacturing industries under protection, possibilities exist for trade creation and improved resource allocation. But the members of such customs unions generally dislike reducing the size of existing industries. It is usually on the question of tariff reductions for such industries that the customs unions of less-developed countries have foundered.

The continued interest of less-developed countries in the formation of customs unions is but one of many manifestations of a feeling that their trade relations with developed countries have served them badly.[3] Underdeveloped countries tend to believe, as we have noted, that the workings of the international economy have trapped them in the role of producers of food and raw materials for developed countries. Many underdeveloped countries of the world are highly specialized, with a few export commodities accounting for most of their foreign-exchange earnings. These main export items—typically food and raw materials—tend to fluctuate widely in price over short periods of time, causing similar foreign-exchange-earnings fluctuations and making it extremely difficult to carry out developmental plans. Less-developed countries often charge that agricultural and raw-materials prices are subject to continual deterioration over time in relation to industrial prices. The validity of this charge, as well as the analytical explanation offered, is generally contested by academic economists. In any case, the present foreign trade picture of most underdeveloped countries is a discouraging one—if we except the oil-rich underdeveloped countries.

---

[3] The position of the less-developed nations toward international trade is well expressed in [12].

Trade Policies for the Less-developed Countries To improve their position in the international economy as well as their own economic development, less-developed countries currently support three major policy proposals: stabilization of export prices through international agreements, development of import-substitute industries, and expansion of the volume of exports purchased by developed countries from less-developed countries.

The objective of commodity price stabilization through the actions of international agreements could be to reduce price fluctuations around the long-term trend, as determined by normal market forces. An international organization would buy in periods of falling prices and sell in periods of rising prices, thus smoothing out fluctuations in price. It was this simple objective that first led the United States government in the 1920s to become involved with the stabilization of American agricultural prices. But what if the trend of prices is downward, as was the case in the United States in the 1930s? The smoothing of such a movement would be of little consolation to producers. Thus, price-stabilization plans with this objective are likely to give way to plans whose objective is to obtain for producers a price above that of the long-term trend, as has occurred in United States agricultural policy.

Fundamentally, underdeveloped nations seek an improvement in their income. We observe from the United States agricultural program that a transfer of income from one group to another gains political respectability when it is brought about by raising a price affecting the recipient group's income. The same arguments advanced by economists in the United States for allowing farm prices to be set by market forces and *then* paying farmers direct bonuses to assure them appropriate incomes can be applied also to international price-stabilization agreements. Such agreements, like the United States farm program, involve great waste through the distortion of production and consumption by artificially high prices. Either surpluses arise, with the attendant problems of disposal, or production controls are imposed to maintain prices. Such programs can only work, of course, if the demand for the commodity is inelastic. Moreover, the whole scheme is self-defeating in the long run if the high stabilized price eventually forces the use of substitutes. In all, it would seem to be more desirable to make direct transfers from rich to poor nations than to seek the same objective by manipulating prices, whereby the resultant loss to developed countries may be greater than the gain to underdeveloped countries.

Import substitution may appear to be a more promising policy. In this case, the new domestic industries whose output is designed to replace imports should produce immediately at costs as low as those of the foreign producers; otherwise, they should be treated as "infant industries" that can, in time, produce at such cost levels. Caution must be used. Almost any industry with a product whose demand is sufficiently sizable to justify a minimal output can be established in an underdeveloped country *if* it is given sufficient protection. Such industries may be viewed as evidence of economic development, to be shown to visitors with pride; but if they involve the use of a greater quantity of resources than would be needed to produce exports by which to obtain the same product in trade, then even the most modern of factories, representing the technical efficiency of the most advanced nations, will nevertheless reduce the real income of the nation.

Export expansion offers low-income countries greater possibilities. Certainly, if they are to advance, they must expand their exports to meet the foreign-exchange needs of economic development, in the absence of massive grants and loans from developed nations. Increasingly, the recognition of this problem is causing underdeveloped nations to turn away from autarkic ideas of economic development (stressing national self-sufficiency), with their aura of escape from international trade problems, to a realization that somehow exports must be expanded. There may be little scope for much expansion of the traditional exports of food and raw materials, in view of inelastic demand and supply conditions for such products. In the interests of development, the less-developed countries are particularly motivated to encourage the local production of semi-manufactured and manufactured goods; but even with tariff protection the local market for such items may be so small that producers cannot achieve an efficient level of production.

Such considerations have led less-developed countries to propose that developed countries give them tariff preferences, contrary to the GATT idea of nondiscrimination. Thus, the tariffs of developed countries would in fact protect not only the domestic producers of developed countries but also the foreign producers of underdeveloped countries. The rationale for this proposal is that the less-developed countries could then mount larger production efforts than would otherwise be possible locally, and they could thereby achieve economies of scale. But unless such economies were realized, the world's allocation of resources would be worsened, for high-cost production in less-developed countries would replace low-cost production in developed countries.

In conclusion, developed countries can make a straightforward contribution to the development of the less-developed parts of the world (1) by liberalizing trade, particularly in agriculture, mining, and light manufacturing, such as textiles and clothing; and (2) by maintaining continuous high levels of employment and growth. Continuous high levels of employment in the developed nations would reduce fluctuations in the prices of raw materials and foodstuffs, which are so important to the underdeveloped world. High rates of growth in the developed world would produce rising costs at home as natural resources are used up. This would cause the developed nations to try to offset such increases by developing imports. Also, growth with ever-rising real wages in the developed countries would make the use of low-wage labor in the underdeveloped countries increasingly attractive. While such measures would not close the gap between the developed and the underdeveloped nations, they would create a better integrated world economy, one that would make more effective use of the world's resources for all of its citizens.

REFERENCES

1. BROWN, ALAN A., and EGON NEUBERGER (eds.). *International Trade and Central Planning* (Berkeley: University of California Press, 1968).
2. CAVES, RICHARD E. *Trade and Economic Structure* (Cambridge, Mass.: Harvard University Press, 1960).
3. CHENERY, HOLLIS B. "Comparative Advantage and Development Policy," *American Economic Review*, 51:1 (March 1961), pp. 18–51.
4. CORDEN, W. M. *Recent Developments in the Theory of International Trade*, Special Papers in International Economics, No. 7 (Princeton, N.J.: Princeton University, International Finance Section, 1965).
5. HABERLER, GOTTFRIED. *The Theory of International Trade*, English translation (London: William Hodge, 1936).
6. ———. *A Survey of International Trade Theory*, Revised and Enlarged Edition, Special Papers in International Economics, No. 1 (Princeton, N.J.: Princeton University, International Finance Section, 1961).
7. JOHNSON, HARRY G. "Optimal Trade Intervention in the Presence of Domestic Distortions," in R. E. Caves, H. G. Johnson, and P. B. Kenen, *Trade Growth and the Balance of Payments* (Chicago: Rand McNally, 1965).
8. LIPSEY, R. G. "The Theory of Customs Unions: A General Survey," *Economic Journal*, 70:279 (September 1960), pp. 496–513.
9. McCONNELL, CAMPBELL R. *Economics: Principles, Problems, and Policies*, 4th ed. (New York: McGraw-Hill, 1969).
10. MEIER, GERALD M. *International Trade and Development* (New York: Harper & Row, 1963).
11. MYRDAL, GUNNAR. *An International Economy: Problems and Prospects* (New York: Harper, 1956).
12. PREBISCH, RAUL. "Toward a New Trade Policy for Development," *Report by the Secretary General of the United Nations*, Conference on Trade and Development (New York: United Nations, 1964).
13. SAMUELSON, PAUL A. *Economics: An Introductory Analysis*, 8th ed. (New York: McGraw-Hill, 1970).
14. VINER, JACOB. *The Customs Union Issue* (New York: Carnegie Endowment, 1950).

15

INTERNATIONAL ECONOMICS: MONETARY REFORM[*]

Robert Triffin[**]

Is our international monetary system heading toward a sudden collapse as in 1931, or toward the fundamental reforms needed to cure its most glaring and universally recognized shortcomings? Or will it continue to drift precariously from crisis to crisis, each one dealt with by belated rescue operations and the spread of restrictions and currency devaluations? Judging from past history, official statements or even good intentions are unlikely to provide reliable answers to these questions, for they are more often designed to reassure than to enlighten. The Governor of the Bank of England, Sir Leslie O'Brien, candidly confessed to a Cambridge audience recently: "I am rapidly qualifying as an instructor on how to exude confidence without positively lying." Another reason is that major changes in the international monetary system have rarely been the result of conscious planning. They have most often been the by-products of broad historical forces or accidents, defying contemporary forecasts and official intentions.

I.

Official negotiations on international monetary reform were launched in 1963 with a confident agreement

---

[*] This chapter represents a revised and updated version of an article appearing in *Foreign Affairs*, April 1969, pp. 477–492. It was adapted with permission of the Council on Foreign Relations, Inc.; the copyright is held by the Council.
[**] Yale University.

"that the underlying structure of the present monetary system—based on fixed exchange rates and the established price of gold—has proven its value as the foundation for present and future arrangements."[1]

The snail's pace of these negotiations, however, and the recurrent and snowballing gold and foreign-exchange crises of recent years have spread mounting doubts regarding these two pillars of the gold-exchange standard. The disbanding of the famed Gold Pool and the introduction of the so-called two-tier gold market in March 1968 were not the planned and deliberate outcome of the negotiations in process, but rather the defeat of fourteen years of efforts to preserve the $35 price in the private as well as in the official market. The optimists—like myself—still hope against hope that these decisions will prove the first, and constructive, steps toward a gradual elimination of gold as the ultimate and obviously absurd regulator of international reserve creation and destruction. The speculators will choose to view it, however, as the harbinger of a further defeat of official policies and of an eventual and substantial increase in official, as well as private, gold prices. Few, if any, observers give much credence to the third interpretation professedly favored by the officials—namely, that the two-tier gold market is a lasting step toward the consolidation of the $35-an-ounce gold-exchange standard of yesteryear.

The second pillar of the Group-of-Ten policies—that is, the fixity of exchange rates—is equally assailed today, not only by academics, but even by congressional leaders and responsible officials, here and abroad. Various forms of exchange-rate flexibility[2] are seriously discussed and advocated as the only realistic cure for the recurrent foreign-exchange crises involving the major currencies of the Western world, and particularly for the persistent deficits of the United Kingdom and the United States, which both countries have repeatedly promised but failed to correct.

In brief, official intentions and pronouncements appear in retrospect a most unreliable guide to the recent evolution of the international monetary system, and are therefore widely mistrusted as a basis for confidence in its future stability. Far better clues and safer predictions can be derived, in my opinion, from analysis of a broader historical perspective

---

[1] Statement issued on October 2, 1963, by the Secretary of the Treasury of the United States on behalf of the "Group of Ten" members of the Fund.

[2] The so-called "band proposal" would enlarge the margin between official buying and selling rates, leaving market rates free to fluctuate around a stable middle rate, or par value. The "crawling peg" proposal would allow the par value of a currency to depreciate or appreciate in accordance with market forces, but by no more than 2 or 3 percent per year. The "crawling band" proponents would merge these two proposals, by allowing an enlarged band around a "crawling" par value. Others would retain the facade of stable rates, but favor special tax and subsidy provisions tantamount to exchange-rate flexibility for merchandise imports and exports.

and the persistent trends which emerge so clearly from it concerning the direction of changes in our national and international monetary institutions.

II.

The first lesson that history teaches us is that these institutions have always been carried forward by an irrepressible evolutionary process, the strength of which was repeatedly misunderstood, underestimated, or even totally overlooked by contemporary observers, academic as well as official. Even today, many people evoke with nostalgia the nineteenth-century gold standard, and remain blissfully unaware of the fact that silver far outpaced gold in importance until the latter half or third of that century, and that paper money—currency and bank deposits—had largely superseded both gold and silver moneys well before the outbreak of World War I.[3] Whatever stability can be ascribed to the monetary system of those days should not be credited to its automatic regulation by haphazard gold and/or silver supplies, but to the gradual euthanasia of these two "commodity-moneys" and their increasing replacement by man-made "credit-moneys." (Indeed, the near-monopoly of gold and silver money throughout the previous centuries had been accompanied by a gradual and uneven debasement of the coinage, reducing the pound sterling and the franc, for instance, to roughly one-fourth and one-tenth, respectively, of their thirteenth-century gold content.)

A second lesson derives from the first. In every national monetary system the world over, the broad direction of this evolutionary process has been from commodity-money to credit-money. At first the creation of this credit-money was left to the discretion and wisdom of multiple banking firms, but later it was gradually brought under the centralized supervision of national monetary authorities (treasuries and central banks).

As distinct from the former commodity-moneys, however, the new national credit-moneys commanded general acceptability only within the national borders of each country; they were not accepted, or at least retained, in payment by the residents of other countries. The settlement of international transactions required, therefore, the exchangeability of national currencies. This responsibility was gradually concentrated in the national central banks, and, to settle net imbalances in international transactions, it was necessary for each of them to accumulate *international reserves* acceptable to other central banks.

The evolution of these international reserves parallels closely, although

---

[3] In 1913 currency and deposits already accounted for about 85 percent of world money stocks, gold for only 10 percent, and silver for 5 percent.

with a considerable lag, that of the national monetary systems. Commodity-reserves are being gradually displaced by credit-reserves in the international monetary system, just as commodity-moneys were previously superseded by credit-money in the national monetary systems. A parallel evolution can be noted with respect to centralization of responsibility. Commodity-reserves—in the form of gold—accounted for about 91 percent of world monetary reserves on the eve of World War II, but for only 51 percent as of the end of 1968. Decentralized credit-reserves—in the form of foreign exchange, overwhelmingly dollars and pounds sterling—rose over the same period from 9 to 41 percent of the world reserves, and centralized credit-reserves—in the form of claims on the International Monetary Fund—rose from 0 to 8 percent.

This gradual shift from uncontrolled commodity-moneys and reserves to man-made credit-moneys and reserves, and later on to a conscious orientation toward the latter by national governments and international institutions, is likely to provide the best clue to future trends. This is the more true, as such a shift can be viewed in a broader perspective of the evolutionary process: the persistent endeavors of man to control his physical environment rather than be controlled by it. One may hardly accept the view that these efforts could, or should, be frustrated forever as far as the international monetary system is concerned, and that reserve creation should be abandoned indefinitely to the irrelevant factors that determine it today: the hazards of gold production, industrial consumption, hoarding and speculation, and/or the international financing of unpredictable United States and United Kingdom deficits through the incorporation of their resulting dollar and sterling IOUs in the monetary reserves of the rest of the world.

III.

Short-run predictions, however, remain far more hazardous than long-run predictions, for the orderly progress of this evolution depends on the adaptability of the institutional and legal framework within which it takes place. Conscious governmental and international action is needed at times to smooth its path, but may also make it far bumpier through misguided action or—as happens far more frequently—through excessive inertia and stubborn resistance to needed reforms.

The repeated financial crises that preceded, and finally impelled, the creation of the Federal Reserve System in the United States can be ascribed to the political resistance to centralized monetary management in this country. On the whole, however, the irrepressible evolution of *national* monetary systems from commodity-money to centralized credit-money encountered fewer legal and institutional obstacles than did the later and similar evolution of the *international* monetary system. The centralized supervision of national credit-money systems was part of the increasing role and powers assumed by national states in the direction of their economies. International agreements among theoretically sovereign states about the composition and management of international reserves were, and still are, far more difficult to achieve.

Numerous international conferences failed, over the last century, to elicit any such agreement. The actual composition of reserve assets shifted radically over this century from bimetalism to gold and later to the uneasy coexistence of gold, reserve-currencies (dollars and sterling), and claims on the International Monetary Fund (IMF). None of these changes—except for the creation of the IMF itself—was ever initiated by deliberate government planning. They were mostly the combined by-products of the absence of agreement and of the relative availability and attractiveness of alternative reserve assets.

The failure to reach international agreement as to what should constitute an internationally acceptable reserve asset at first ensured the survival of traditional commodity-moneys, even after they had lost this role within the national monetary systems themselves. The elimination of silver in favor of gold alone was belatedly ratified—rather than initiated—by the governments. The initial step in this direction can be traced back to the totally inadvertent slip of Great Britain into a de facto gold standard, as a consequence of the 1696 recoinage of outworn silver coins. Gresham's law that "bad money drives out good" was not enacted by the British Parliament, but explains why the new, full-bodied silver coins minted by a government intent on preserving the traditional silver standard quickly disappeared from circulation, as their increased silver content gave them a somewhat higher value on the commodity markets than the *legal* conversion ratio between silver and gold at the Royal Mint.

The other, and even more radical, shift from the gold standard to the gold-exchange standard, in the 1920s, was also a de facto reaction to the unplanned impact of the war upon the monetary and reserve systems of those days. Wartime operations and postwar reconstruction had been financed in large part by monetary inflation. This had drastically curtailed the ratio of monetary gold stocks to the vastly expanded volume of national paper moneys, and had created a "gold shortage" which became the subject of endless debates at gatherings of international experts and central bank meetings in Brussels (1920), Genoa (1922), and the Gold Delegation of the League of Nations (1929–1932). A broad consensus emerged at these meetings to recommend the expanded use of the "gold-convertible" currencies of major financial centers as a supplement to scarce gold. This solution was particularly favored and propagandized by British experts who rightly expected to see sterling—the most prestigious currency of the largest and oldest trading and financial center of the world—play the major role; they believed that it would enable the

United Kingdom to finance its deficits and/or strengthen its slender gold reserves through the acceptance of its own paper IOUs as international reserves by other central banks. Both expectations proved correct but involved a quasi-automatic financing by other countries of Britain's return to an overvalued rate for sterling and of the balance-of-payments deficits that ensued.

While none of the conferences produced any firm agreements and commitments in this respect, the major "gold-convertible" currencies—particularly sterling, first, and later the dollar—gained increasing acceptance as monetary reserves. Since reserve holders remained free to switch at any time from one currency into another, or into gold, a dangerous instability was built into the system.

The Gold Delegation was still debating the ways and means that would prevent an abuse of the system by the reserve centers and protect it against destabilizing switches by their creditors when these very defects prompted the collapse of the pound sterling in September 1931. For a while, this sounded the death knell of the gold-exchange standard, and signaled a generalized rush into gold reserves and a protracted period of beggar-my-neighbor devaluations and trade and exchange controls.

During and after World War II, the gold-exchange standard was revived on the same precarious basis, bringing back the same abuses and sources of instability that killed it in 1931. The financing of World War II and of postwar reconstruction entailed, as in the case of World War I, a new bout of inflation, curtailing once more the ratio of gold reserves to the increased volume of national paper moneys. The latter continued to rise with the unprecedentedly high rates of economic growth sustained in later years. The resulting "gold shortage" was again made up by huge acquisitions of sterling and dollar balances legally convertible at any time into gold. The day would inevitably come—as I pointed out as early as 1957—when a "liquidity shortage" would arise, either as a result of such conversions of overflowing dollar and sterling balances into scarce gold metal, or because the United States and the United Kingdom would seek—unsuccessfully—to protect themselves against such a danger by eliminating the balance-of-payments deficits that now fed most of the increases in world monetary reserves. This gloomy prognosis was scornfully dismissed at first by overcomplacent officials, but was later accepted by them, prompting in 1963 the opening of another marathon debate on the need for international monetary reform.

One may still hope, however, that the outcome will be less disastrous than it was in 1931. First of all, the world economy is in far better shape today than it was then, and the overall economic and financial position of the United States is far stronger than that of Britain in 1931. Even more important, the world's monetary and financial leaders are now keenly aware of the disastrous consequences of any repetition of the

1931 policies, or lack of policies, for the international monetary, economic, and even political fabric of the West. They have developed—particularly since the first flare-up of gold prices in London in October 1960—an unprecedented degree of international cooperation and an uncanny ability to cope with recurrent crises. They have also acquired an understanding of the basic problems and a sense of joint responsibility for their solution far greater than ever existed in the past.

IV.

Thus, history need *not* repeat itself. Our hope that it will not springs primarily from the unprecedented insight now gained by responsible officials regarding the functioning of the international monetary system and the consensus already reached by them regarding the shortcomings that must be remedied by the three major reforms now under negotiation:

> *1 The creation of international reserves should be deliberately oriented toward satisfying the requirements of feasible growth in world trade and production.*
>
> *2 The resulting reserve pool should be protected against destabilizing switches between reserve assets, and primarily between reserve currencies and gold.*
>
> *3 These reforms in the overall amount and composition of the world reserve pool must be accompanied by a strengthening of the adjustment mechanism, facilitating the financing of temporary, reversible disequilibria, but also ensuring more prompt correction of persistent disequilibria, rather than their perpetuation either by inflationary financing or by trade and exchange controls.*

This consensus should, and some day undoubtedly will, lead to agreement on the kind of reform suggested by past historical trends—that is, the development of a truly international credit-reserve standard aiming at the simultaneous fulfillment of all three of these objectives.

Indeed, the cornerstone of such a reform has already been laid by the unanimous Rio resolution on the creation of a new reserve instrument (the so-called Special Drawing Rights, or SDRs) to be issued by the IMF in the amounts deemed necessary by the international community itself to meet future reserve needs. This was undoubtedly the hardest hurdle that the negotiators had to surmount, and contrasted sharply with their earlier myopic denunciation of such a proposal as a dangerous and utopian dream—unattainable "today and for any foreseeable future"—the dream of setting up a "super-bank" with "no supporting super-government to make good on its debts or claims."[4]

The Rio negotiators showed rare vision and courage in creating this central piece of the international monetary machinery of the future, but

---

[4] The quotation is from [9].

unfortunately left for later determination the role to be played by the traditional components of the gold-exchange standard (that is, gold and the reserve currencies). The sterling, dollar, and gold crises that were soon to dampen the high hopes evoked by the Rio agreement arose from the inability of the negotiators to tackle with the same vision and courage the more urgent problems raised by the coexistence of overflowing dollar and sterling reserves with the dwindling gold stocks into which they were legally convertible under the rules of the ill-fated gold-exchange standard.

The basic conflict that has so far prevented full agreement on this issue reflects an unrealistic assessment by the reserve-currency debtors and creditors alike of their true national interests. The reserve-currency debtors—primarily the United States and the United Kingdom—welcome the new reserve asset as a supplement, or even an ultimate substitute, for scarce gold, but are understandably reluctant to renounce the privilege of financing a substantial portion of their deficits through other countries' accumulation of their IOUs as international reserves. The reserve-currency holders of continental Europe, on the other hand, still see in gold settlements their ultimate protection against the inflationary potential and surrender of national sovereignty entailed in the accumulation of dollar and sterling IOUs financing United States and United Kingdom policies in which they have no voice and which they may, at times, consider directly contrary to their own interests or those of the world community. This conflict has been exacerbated in recent years by the size and persistence of British and American deficits and the fact that they could be ascribed, at least in part, to the laxity of monetary and fiscal policies—particularly in the United Kingdom. The disagreement has been further aggravated by the inflationary pressures triggered in the United States by the escalation of the Vietnam war, and by what some Europeans regard as an excessive take-over of European enterprises by American capital.

V.

Paradoxically, the main hopes for a negotiated agreement spring from the very sharpness of this conflict and from the consequent realization in both camps that neither gold nor reserve currencies can expand, or even retain, their previous role in monetary settlements. This conclusion is being forced upon the United Kingdom and the United States by the resistance of other countries to the acquisition and retention of traditional sterling and dollar balances as growing components of their monetary reserves. These traditional "liquid" holdings of sterling and dollar IOUs by foreign central banks rose spectacularly from about $2 billion in 1937 to a peak of nearly $20 billion in 1963, but they have declined even more spectacularly since then to about $13 billion in 1968. Thus, the traditional reserve-currency role of sterling and dollar balances no longer assures Britain and the United States of special facilities for financing their current deficits. It exposes them, on the contrary, to the enormous and unbearable risk of sudden or massive repayment of the enormous short-term indebtedness accumulated by them over many years past.

The creditor countries, however, also realize that insistence on gold repayment would inevitably bring about another 1931, as neither the United Kingdom nor even the United States could actually stand such a drain on their gold reserves. The total amount of these ($11 billion as of the end of 1968) is considerably short of their gold-convertible obligations to central banks and the IMF ($28 billion).

Both groups of countries have thus been impelled by their own self-interest to negotiate new agreements based on the realities of the situation rather than on their previous hopes and expectations. The acquisition and retention of sterling and dollar assets by the major reserve holders of Western Europe, and even by the sterling-area countries, have become increasingly dependent upon such negotiated agreements. Gold or exchange guarantees against devaluation risks were grudgingly granted by the United Kingdom and the United States to deter their creditors from speculative switches of their reserve assets from sterling into dollars, or from both into gold. The creditor countries, on the other hand, agreed to retain a specific portion of their total reserves in sterling, and to convert part of their "liquid" dollar claims into longer-term obligations.

Taken together, these various agreements, negotiated since 1963, now cover about half of the combined dollar and sterling reserves ($24 billion) of foreign reserve holders. A further $3.3 billion of reserve credits have been extended to the United Kingdom and the United States through the mediation of the IMF. Finally, a vast array of reciprocal credit lines—in the form of so-called "swap" or "reciprocal currency" agreements—have been negotiated among major central banks to protect them against speculative attacks on any one of their currencies.

All these negotiations and arrangements testify to the death of the traditional "gold-exchange standard" and to a de facto gradual shift toward what might be called a "negotiated credit-reserves standard." The official negotiators should be congratulated for having been able to avoid, in this way, a total collapse of the international monetary order. The new system, however, remains highly precarious, for it depends on continuous negotiation and renegotiation of the short- or medium-term credit lines on which it rests. Some of the countries called upon to provide such financing also feel that it fails to provide adequate protection against the abuse of such facilities, primarily by the United States. They cling tenaciously to their legal right to gold conversion as their ultimate protection against such abuses and the total surrender of monetary sovereignty which might be imposed upon them if they were incorporated into a formal or informal "dollar area." The continuation of recent trends in that direction would be bound, sooner or later, to trigger a major breakdown, political as well as economic and financial, among the countries of the Atlantic Community. Responsible circles in the United States are keenly conscious of this danger, as is evidenced in the unanimous report of the Congressional Subcommittee on International Exchange and Payments in September 1968.

Gold, however, is incapable of providing a reasonable alternative to a "dollar-area" system of international reserves and settlements. The $3.7 billion losses experienced by the Gold Pool countries over a short period of six months (October 1967–March 1968) forced the liquidation of the pool and the hurried adoption of a precarious and ambiguously phrased agreement among its members—with the exception of France—that would, if faithfully and generally observed in the spirit as well as in the letter, freeze forever both the official gold price and the world monetary gold stock at their levels of March 18, 1968, irrespective of future developments in the private gold market.

This is most unlikely indeed to provide a long-term solution to the gold problem, as central banks can hardly be expected to remain forever indifferent to market developments regarding the price of a commodity in which they have invested close to $40 billion and which is still regarded by public opinion in many countries—no matter how erroneously—as the ultimate guarantee of their mounting issues of paper money.

If gold were the only alternative to a dollar-area system, governments would sooner or later have to resign themselves either to a fluctuating gold price, or to a substantial increase in its present price. In all probability, this would set the clock back to 1931, and postpone for many years to come the evolution toward rational reforms of the anachronistic and haphazard gold-exchange standard of yesteryear.

VI.

The way out of the present impasse lies in a comprehensive reform plan, inspired by the long-term historical evolution of the international monetary system. It should encompass all major aspects of the problem and thereby give adequate recognition to the convergent interests and feasible policy objectives of all countries concerned.

A unanimous agreement was reached in Rio de Janeiro in 1967 on the keystone of such a reform: the deliberate creation of centralized reserve assets in the form of internationally guaranteed claims on the IMF, usable and acceptable by all countries in all balance-of-payments settlements. A keystone, however, is not an edifice. The reform cannot stop with the mere superimposition of the new reserve asset upon the traditional ones. It must encompass the role of all three types of reserve assets—gold and reserve currencies as well as SDRs—in the orderly growth of world reserves and the improvement of the adjustment mechanism. The new reserve asset should be created by international agreement, in the amounts needed to substitute for—rather than merely add to—dwindling gold supplies and overflowing reserve currencies, and to adjust overall reserve growth to the requirements of an expanding world economy rather than to the vagaries of the gold market and of United States and United Kingdom balance of payments.

Surplus countries should accept such assets in settlement, retain them as reserves, and be able to use them at any time to settle later deficits in their own international payments. They would remain free, of course, to slow down—or even reverse—their reserve accumulation by taking action to reduce their surpluses through trade or exchange liberalization, more expansionist monetary and fiscal policies, and/or larger outflows of capital. They should not be entitled, however, to force deflation, devaluation, or restrictions upon the rest of the world by insisting on gold payments in excess of available supplies. Nor should they be allowed to arrogate to themselves the right to accumulate international reserves in any national currency they choose and then to switch at any time from one currency to another, or into gold. All countries should agree to deny each other a right which exposes them to political blackmail by the reserve debtors as well as by the reserve holders. Surpluses should be accumulated exclusively—except for working balances—in the new IMF reserve asset.

Such a commitment by the surplus countries would endow the IMF with the lending potential needed to finance the deficits that are the counterparts of the other countries' surpluses. The overall volume of such financing, however, would be limited by rules restricting the IMF's creation of reserves to the amounts needed to sustain feasible, but non-inflationary, growth of the world economy. A presumptive guideline of 4 to 5 percent per year would probably rally widespread agreement in this respect, but exceptions should be authorized, by qualified majority vote, to combat actual worldwide inflationary or deflationary pressures.

The use and allocation of this lending potential should be a matter for international decision, based on a collective judgment regarding the nature of the deficits. Temporary, reversible deficits, such as those triggered by speculative shifts of private funds among major financial centers, should be met by compensatory shifts of IMF investments from the countries in surplus to the countries in deficit. Persistent deficits calling for correction should be financed only as part and parcel of an agreed stabilization program, designed to eliminate deficits with a minimum of hardship to the deficit countries themselves as well as to their partners in world trade and finance. External deficits accompanied by internal inflationary pressures are a sign of "overspending," which should be corrected by changes in fiscal and monetary policies designed to equate expenditures with the country's productive capacity. On the other hand, the coincidence of deficits with deflationary pressures and unemployment would suggest that the root cause of the trouble lies in uncompetitive levels of prices and costs, for which a readjustment of exchange rates will often prove the most appropriate remedy.

If the deficit country feels unable to agree with its IMF partners on the action to be taken, it will, of course, retain its "sovereign" right to conduct its own affairs as it wishes, but not to obtain financing from other "sovereign" countries which disagree with its policies. The gradual depletion of its monetary reserves will, willy-nilly, force an adjustment of its exchange rate, though trade and exchange restrictions may postpone the day, if they are not made ineffective by other countries' retaliatory action.

More and more people now advocate a shift from stable to flexible exchange rates—whether or not they are limited to an agreed "band" or rate of "crawl"—as a way to strengthen the adjustment process in a nationalistic world. This would be an attractive solution for the disequilibria ascribable to international cost-price disparities, but might tend to foster unnecessary instability and actual distortions of exchange rates in the other two cases of deficits, which call instead for financing or for changes in monetary and fiscal policies.

The reforms outlined so far would, moreover, remedy only imperfectly the so-called "deflationary bias" of the international monetary system. They would force the surplus countries to finance, but not to eliminate, disequilibria caused by deflationary errors in their own policies or by an undervalued exchange rate. Ideally, an excessive rate of reserve accumulation, even in the form of claims on the IMF, should force them to enter into policy consultations with the IMF, just as an excessive rate of reserve losses already imposes such consultations upon the deficit countries. In the absence of agreement, they should be enjoined from preventing an appreciation of their exchange rate through further market interventions and excessive reserve accumulation.

Merely to allow exchange-rate flexibility would be insufficient for this purpose, as was amply demonstrated by the outcome of the Bonn conference called in 1968 to deal with the difficulties created for other countries by the obdurate surpluses of Germany and the rush of speculative capital into German marks. The United States, Britain, France, and presumably other countries felt strongly that the best solution to the problem was a revaluation of the German mark, but even their combined pressure failed to persuade the German leaders to accept such advice. One may sympathize with the German view that the over-competitiveness of the mark is the result of the inflationary policies of other countries rather than of any deflationary policies in Germany. Yet, after such a situation has been allowed to develop, price or exchange-rate adaptations by Germany itself may prove far more feasible and less damaging to all concerned than alternative deflationary action or devaluation by many other countries.[5]

VII.

Agreement on all aspects of such ambitious reforms will obviously take time and will have to deal with a number of transitional problems, particularly regarding gold and the bloated reserve-currency balances inherited from the past. Both problems could be met through the creation of an International Conversion Account that would convert into reserve deposits or certificates, identical with the SDRs, all reserve-currency balances in excess of those actually needed for daily interventions in the exchange market. The Account would also issue such deposits or certificates in exchange for the gold it needed to intervene in the gold market as its members jointly saw fit, in order to regain control over a market now abandoned to speculators by the two-tier decision of March 1968.

This proposal is no longer deemed so utopian and unnegotiable as it appeared to many when I first formulated it a few years ago. The abortive Maudling plan of 1962, but particularly the comprehensive sterling agreements of September 1968, demonstrate Britain's receptiveness to such a solution of the sterling problem. In the United States, its main features were unanimously endorsed in September 1968 by the Congressional Subcommittee on International Exchange and Payments. Concrete proposals for such a Conversion Account were also developed by Finance Minister Colombo of Italy, and forcefully advocated by him at the 1968 annual meeting of the IMF as an essential complement to the SDR agreement. Finally, France should logically welcome a plan that meets the two basic objectives repeatedly emphasized by former President de Gaulle: the elimination of the "exorbitant privilege" of the reserve-currency countries to pay their deficits with their own IOUs, and "the organization of international credit . . . on an indisputable monetary basis bearing the mark of no particular country."

De Gaulle, of course, proposed that this basis be gold, while most of my academic colleagues and congressional friends would, on the contrary,

---

[5] The 1969 French devaluation is the most recent example of the "devaluation bias" of the present system. Reserve losses inevitably force the deficit countries to devalue in the end, while reserve gains never force the surplus countries to revalue—upward—an overcompetitive exchange rate. The 1969 German revaluation represents a rare and long overdue exception to this "devaluation bias." One of the most serious results of this bias is that each successive devaluation leads to a further overvaluation of the United States dollar so long as it remains the "anchor" of the exchange rate system.

accelerate the "demonetization" of gold by converting all national gold reserves overnight into Conversion Account deposits or certificates. I would myself favor such a solution, but do not feel that it will be negotiable until familiarity and experience with the new system have demonstrated its practicability and developed sufficient trust in the wisdom and fairness of its management.

Such an abrupt transformation of ingrained institutions and habits of mind is, in any case, unnecessary. My own proposals would recognize the essential—but no longer determinant—role which national gold holdings will inevitably retain in the international monetary system for some years to come. All that is needed, and negotiable, at this stage is to agree on those initial steps which are indispensable to meet present-day problems and to reopen the door to the evolutionary process that will gradually improve man's control over this crucial basis of his economic life in an increasingly interdependent world.

VIII.

The worldwide reforms suggested above—and already under way—will increase considerably the responsibilities of the present IMF for international decisionmaking. A decentralization of these responsibilities will become even more necessary than it already is for the efficient management of a system previously left in part to haphazard factors and in part to British and American policies, or policy failures.

The world monetary system should be a more structured one, placing as much reliance as possible on the gradual development of regional— as well as worldwide—cooperation and integration. The protracted crisis of the so-called key currencies is bound to spur further efforts in this direction, particularly in Asia, where a plan developed by the Economic Commission for Asia and the Far East is under active study; in Latin America, following the example already set by the Central American Monetary Union; and in Western Europe.

The countries of the European Economic Community are becoming increasingly aware of the need to set up a European Reserve Fund to ward off their gradual absorption into a "dollar area" and to implement the joint monetary policies indispensable to the progress—and even to the survival—of their economic union. Such a Fund would also facilitate enormously the solution of the monetary problems raised by the accession of Britain to the European Economic Community [11].

Finally, a more decentralized IMF structure would greatly ease the reintegration of Eastern Europe into the international monetary community. Balance-of-payments problems *among* these countries could be handled regionally by the COMECON organization (Council of Mutual Economic Assistance), resort to the IMF being reserved to the handling of disequilibria between the COMECON countries as a group and the rest of the world.

In this matter as in others, however, the major factors that will determine the pace of future progress—or regress—are obviously far more political than economic. The past history of the international monetary system strongly suggests that its evolution will continue to be slowed down, or even reversed, temporarily by official policies or lack of policies, and that major advances will continue to depend on the crises triggered by the failure of our leaders to perceive or implement in time the reforms needed to adjust anachronistic institutions and habits of mind to the ever-changing world in which we live.

REFERENCES

1. *Annual Reports* of the International Monetary Fund (Washington, D.C., 1963 and following years).
2. CASSELL, FRANCIS. *Gold or Credit? Economics and Politics of International Money* (London: Pall Mall Press; New York: Praeger, 1965).
3. COOPER, RICHARD N. *The Economics of Interdependence: Economic Policy in the Atlantic Community* (New York: McGraw-Hill, 1968).
4. FELLNER, WILLIAM, et al. *Maintaining and Restoring Balance in International Payments* (Princeton, N.J.: Princeton University Press, 1966).
5. *International Monetary Arrangements: The Problem of Choice* (Princeton N.J.: Princeton University Press, 1964).
6. JOHNSON, HARRY G. *The World Economy at the Cross Roads: A Survey of Current Problems of Money, Trade, and Economic Development* (Oxford: Clarendon Press, 1965).
7. MACHLUP, FRITZ. "Plans for Reform of the International Monetary System," in *International Payments, Debts and Gold* (New York: Scribner's, 1964), pp. 276–366; and *Remaking the International Monetary System: The Rio Agreement and Beyond* (Baltimore: Johns Hopkins, 1968).
8. Reports and Hearings of the Subcommittee on International Exchange and Payments of the Joint Economic Committee (90th Cong., 1st Sess., Sept. 14, Nov. 22, and Dec. 7, 1967; 90th Cong., 2d Sess., Sept. 9 and Sept. 19, 1968; 91st Cong., 1st Sess., May 28 and Aug. 14, 1969).
9. ROOSA, ROBERT V. "Assuring the Free World's Liquidity," *Business Review*, Federal Reserve Bank of Philadelphia, September 1962; reproduced in *The Dollar and World Liquidity* (New York: Random House, 1967), p. 102.
10. TRIFFIN, ROBERT. *Gold and the Dollar Crisis* (New Haven, Conn., Yale University Press, 1960); *The World Money Maze: National Currencies in International Payments* (New Haven, Conn., Yale University Press, 1966); and *Our International Monetary System: Yesterday, Today and Tomorrow* (New York: Random House, 1968).
11. ———. *The Fate of the Pound* (Paris: Atlantic Institute, 1969).
12. YEAGER, LELAND B. *International Monetary Relations* (New York: Harper & Row, 1966).

16

ECONOMIC GROWTH AND DEVELOPMENT

*Jeffrey B. Nugent**

MANY of the other contributors to this volume have emphasized the difficulties and obstacles to be found in their particular areas of specialization. Presumably the difficulties provide convenient excuses for lack of progress. We economists in the field of economic development need excuses, too, and, as will be seen momentarily, we also suffer from many kinds of limitations, often of even greater severity than those confronting our colleagues in other specialized areas. Nevertheless, I should like to open my comments on the status of current research in economic development on the positive side by mentioning some of its special advantages.

The field of economic development touches each of the specialized areas in the discipline of economics. Consumption, investment, welfare, and trade theory are important areas not only for their intrinsic value but also for their relation to economic development. Economic history and comparative economic systems are primarily, although not entirely, concerned with economic growth. The policy-oriented fields of fiscal and monetary economics are likewise concerned with economic growth.

Furthermore, the problems of economic development have captured the imagination and interest, not only of the present generation of economists, but also of several centuries of political economists dating back to the mercantilists.

* University of Southern California.

What else were the schemes of the mercantilists and physiocrats if not strategies for economic development? Adam Smith's *The Wealth of Nations* [28] and Karl Marx' *Das Kapital* [19] are but two of the many major contributions of the classical school to economic development. Likewise, after the unfortunately long neoclassical and early Keynesian period, dominated by concern with microeconomic and short-term macroeconomic problems, the postwar period has seen a great renaissance in the study of economic development.

Despite this central position within the discipline of economics and the fact that the goal of economic growth claims a high priority among the resources of almost every society in the world, it is clear that few of the secrets of economic development have yet been learned. This can be seen in the extremely poor growth performance of a majority of the world's countries and in the great variety of approaches to development currently employed by countries facing similar kinds of development problems throughout the world.[1] Presumably, if there were substantial agreement on the explanation of causes of economic development, we should expect to find somewhat greater similarity of approach.

On the positive side, it can be said that in the past few years there has been a prodigious amount of research activity on various aspects of the development process. The outlook is bright for rapidly expanding our knowledge about the fundamental building blocks of the theory of economic development.

Before going further, I should point out that the field of development economics is normally divided into two subfields—*economic growth*, where attention is largely confined to the developed countries, and *economic development*, where study is largely restricted to the problems of the "less-developed" or "developing" countries.[2] Part of the explanation for the distinction between growth and development lies in the common (though untested) presumption that the requirements for generating growth in developed countries are easier to fulfill and narrower in scope than those for the development of the less-developed countries. It is sometimes asserted that one can have growth in less-developed countries without development.[3] Even if development of a certain less-developed region or country should be attainable, the cost of development in some cases might be so high as to make development of the region a strategy

---

[1] Consider how very different are the development strategies in the following countries (paired by the similarity of their resource endowments and stage of development): Yugoslavia and Greece, Chile and Brazil, Mexico and Venezuela, Senegal and Guinea, China and India.

[2] In many less-developed countries, stagnation is so characteristic that the term "developing" is less appropriate than the term "less-developed."

[3] For example, Clower [5] has depicted Liberia as a case of a country that has had rapid growth but not development.

inferior (or second-best) to the alternative strategy of moving the people, and perhaps other resources, to areas in which conditions are more favorable to development. Consider the tremendous cost of irrigating deserts or settling Arctic regions.

Despite their differences, these subfields share much of the same methods, subject matter, and (to a lesser extent) theories. We shall for this reason discuss them together, only later distinguishing some special characteristics of the economics of less-developed countries.

Theory and Measurement of Growth and Development One of the tasks of growth and development theory is to explain the level of development attained by a particular society at a point in time, and the rate at which that level changes between any two points in time.

To make any progress in explaining development, we should have some generally acceptable criterion for measuring development. How is development to be measured? Although any number of ways have been suggested, none is so comprehensive or so generally accepted as gross national product (or national income) per capita. This index requires the existence of national accounts statistics, which are not yet available for all countries in the world. Even in countries where such statistics exist, they may cover only a very limited period of time—in many cases only a part of the postwar period. Our poverty of information—even as to the very definition or measure of development—has undoubtedly contributed to our embarrassing inability to identify more precisely the factors most closely associated with rapid growth and high levels of development.

Despite difficulties in applying the per-capita-income criterion to certain countries—such as Kuwait, where the largest economic activity consists of exporting a natural resource—the quest for "broader" indexes of development has been quite unsuccessful,[4] and per capita income remains the best index available. It is relatively free of bias as to a society's specific goals (such as improved consumption, employment, investment, leisure, or national defense) and is fairly neutral with respect to taste, climate, location, and the like.

Factors Affecting Economic Growth Almost all growth and development theorists start from the point of view that income Y at any point in time depends upon the stocks of physical resources K, of human resources H, and of technical knowledge T, and upon the ability of society to use these stocks, which we might call "efficiency" E.

Also, it is generally agreed that the role of the development or growth

[4] Note, however, the sophisticated approach to an index of development followed by Adelman and Morris [1].

theorists does not stop with explaining the relative expected impact of these factors, or the expected effect of *changes* in these factors, on the level of income. If the growth theorist went only this far, his explanation of growth would indeed be superficial, and his analysis would hardly be in demand by policymakers and planners. Therefore, it is also part of the growth theorist's job to explain how these immediate explanatory factors—K, H, T, and E—are themselves determined, until everything that (in the theorist's opinion) needs to be explained is explained. These factors, which combine the characteristics of having the greatest impact on income and being the most manipulable, may be said to be the most important factors in the development process.

Therefore, the theorist must specify a functional relationship between income and its factors

$$Y = f(K,H,T,E)$$

as well as between each factor and its determining subfactors

$$K = g(U) \qquad H = h(V) \qquad T = i(W) \qquad E = j(X)$$

and perhaps for other variables, in order to include explanations of each important element in the development process.[5]

As one might imagine, the correct formulation of such a system is a most formidable endeavor. The earlier economists of the so-called classical and preclassical schools probably went as far as anyone has in constructing such systems by formulating growth as an interdependent system of "laws"—laws of capital formation, population growth, and technological change. Unfortunately, despite their valuable efforts and insights, these grand constructions have largely been scrapped because of their glaring failure to predict events. Note, for example, how overly pessimistic the gloomy predictions of Malthus and Ricardo on output and wage rates have proved to be, and how little evidence has been accumulated to date in support of the Marxian predictions of a falling rate of profit and increasing "immiserization" of the working class in capitalist countries. In view of these disastrous failures on the part of even the most brilliant classical economists, it is no wonder that all but a few subsequent economists have tended to recoil from the construction of large and complete models of economic growth—at least until more is known about the individual pieces and connecting links of which these complete models are composed.[6]

---

[5] U, V, W, and X should be thought of as sets of individual variables, including some of the previously defined variables—Y, K, H, T, and E.

[6] A notable exception is the work of Trygve Haavelmo [12], who has suggested the superimposition of random variables on an otherwise deterministic system such as that of Adam Smith [28].

Modern Growth Theory and the Role of Technological Change The inspiration for much of modern growth theory was the work of Harrod [14] and Domar [8, 9], which provided a simple and easily understood marriage of Keynesian macroeconomics and standard equilibrium theory. The following comment from Domar characterizes the motivation behind the new approach.

> *Like a not-too-honest schoolboy who cannot solve his problem, I would prefer to look up the answer in the back of the book and then try to fix up the solution to satisfy the answer. Let us assume that the economy is growing. If we can learn something about the character, perhaps we shall be able to come back and get a glimpse of the causes of its growth, or at least the conditions that should be satisfied to make this growth possible* [10, pp. 29–30].

Note that in the quest for simplicity much of the power of growth theory has been sacrificed. The search for the *causes* of growth by early growth theorists has been given up in favor of the less ambitious quest for the *conditions* under which growth may take place.

Specifically, the growth model proposed by Harrod and Domar contains (1) a Keynesian savings function, $S = sY$; (2) a simple production function in which potential output Y_P is determined by the stock of capital K and a fixed technological parameter, the capital-output ratio—that is, $Y_P = K/v$; and (3) the equilibrium condition $Y = Y_P$, which implies that savings S equals investment I. In the dynamic context of growth, if it is assumed that s and v remain constant, the equilibrium rate of growth $\triangle Y/Y$, at which

$$\frac{\triangle Y}{Y} = \frac{\triangle Y_P}{Y_P}$$

turns out to be given by the ratio of s to v. Thus, if $s = 0.12$, or 12 percent of income, and the capital-output ratio is 4,

$$\frac{\triangle Y}{Y} = \frac{\triangle Y_P}{Y_P} = \frac{s}{v} = \frac{0.12}{4} = 0.03$$

or 3 percent per annum.

More recent growth formulations have extended the analysis by (1) using more realistic production functions, in which more than one factor of production would appear—for example, K and H, or K, H, and imports M (as in the recently popular two-gap models[7]), with some specified degree of substitution possibilities between them; (2) relaxing the

---

[7] See, for example, Chenery and Strout [4], who argue quite convincingly that a scarcity of foreign exchange, and hence the inability to import the raw materials, intermediate goods, and capital goods required in the production process, acts as a significant obstacle to more rapid growth in less-developed countries.

constancy of the technical and behavorial parameters, such as s and v; and (3) explicitly introducing technology and technological change T and efficiency E. Thus it is that growth theory has slowly made its way to the general formulation of the aggregate production function given above, in which $Y = f(K,H,T,E)$.

Even if this general formulation of growth—in which the rate of growth in income (output) depends on the rates of growth of physical capital, human resources, technology, and efficiency—is widely accepted, the specific formulation of the interactions of these variables is still most unsettled, and the use of alternative specifications seems at this point to be largely a matter of taste. Consider for a moment some of the issues that remain open questions. What is technological change? Does it depend on the installation of new physical capital (capital-embodied technological change) or improved human resources (labor-embodied technological change)? Or does it depend only on time or "learning-by-doing"? What is the effect of technological change on the rate of accumulation of physical and human capital? Does technological change have a labor- or a capital-displacing bias? Why or why not? Similar questions could be raised concerning efficiency and its role in the growth process.

While some empirical work has been undertaken in an effort to sort out the relative importance of some of these factors and relationships,[8] it is obvious that the empirical results are sensitive to the theoretical formulation. For this reason, extensive tests of the numerous alternative hypotheses would be required before any such results could really be trusted.

Some Special Features of Growth and Development Theory In an entertaining essay Kenneth Boulding [2] has called attention to some common properties of growth theories in a number of disciplines. One of the most interesting and universal of these properties is the concept of structure and structural change in economic growth. In economic-growth theory the emphasis on structural change takes several forms. One recurring theme is what Boulding calls the "nucleation principle." The idea is that up to a certain threshold level, a certain influence will have only a negligible effect, but above that threshold, it will have a sizable influence. Harvey Leibenstein [16] has made use of this principle in his "critical minimum effort" hypothesis, arguing that movements away from the "low-level equilibrium trap," in which most less-developed countries find themselves, must be large and sustained to more than offset the various reversal factors that make that state a quasi-stable equilibrium.

---

[8] See, for example, the detailed framework used by Denison [6, 7] in some of the more-developed countries and the much simpler procedures that have been applied to less-developed countries, as by Bruton [3].

While Leibenstein has emphasized the relationship between income and population growth in this process, Nurkse [22] and Rosenstein-Rodan [25] have emphasized the relationship between investment and market size in their complementary theories of "balanced growth" and "big push."

A second theme of structural change which recurs in the literature of economic growth and development is that, for growth to take place, the relationship among the parts, and of the parts to the whole in the economic structure, must change in some fundamental way. Marx [19] pointed out certain technical relationships between the capital-goods and consumer-goods sectors, while Feldman (as interpreted by Domar [10]) and Mahalanobis [18] have shown that under certain conditions (most particularly an economy with *no* foreign trade) the rate of growth of income (or income per capita) is a function of the proportion of capital-goods output allocated to the capital-goods sector. A number of statistical studies have attempted to test the empirical validity of the well-known Fisher-Clark hypothesis, which states that the process of development is characterized by a gradual change in sector dominance from primary (agriculture, fishing, forestry, and mining) through secondary (manufacturing), to tertiary (services) industries as income and population size increase. What is remarkable about the results of these statistical studies is the apparent universality of such structural changes in the process of development in many different countries.

Does this mean that one can project a certain less-developed country's population and income into the future, and compute a sectoral pattern that would be consistent with (or "cause") the projected level of development? More specifically, does the rise in the industrial share in national income as income increases imply that industrialization causes economic development? Some excellent economists have advocated this position, but the existence of a correlation between industrialization and economic development does not necessarily mean causality.

Structural change is also implicit in the various "stage theories," which attempt to characterize the process of growth as one of moving from one stage to another. The stages are presumably distinguished by supposing that different factors are more important at one level of development than at another. Marx [19], Rostow [27], and Adelman-Morris [1] are advocates of this stage-theory approach, which dates from the German historical school of the nineteenth century.

Doubts about the Usefulness of Economic Theory and the Market Mechanism in Growth and Development Many (but certainly not all) development and growth economists distrust both traditional economic theory and the allocative efficiency of the market mechanism in the dynamic context of economic growth. Their distrust is greatest in the context of the less-developed countries. What lies behind their doubts about the applicability of much of economic theory to the problems of growth and development, particularly in the less-developed countries?

One explanation for lack of confidence in free-market forces in the growth process in general, and in the less-developed countries in particular, is the supposed importance of external economies and diseconomies in the growth process. Another is the supposed greater imperfection of markets in the less-developed countries than in the advanced countries—as a result both of the presence of monopolistic elements in industry and the lack of sufficient information about market conditions and investment opportunities. Another, and perhaps more basic, explanation is the supposed insensitivity (or even perversity) of important kinds of behavior, for example, the poor investment and production decisions of farmers—hacienda owners and peasant farmers alike.

The result of these various suppositions is a pessimism about the ability of the market mechanism to provide an efficient, let alone an optimal, allocation of resources either in the short run (the static case) or more especially in the long run (the dynamic case)[9] in today's less-developed countries. Various signs of the inability of market prices to reflect social opportunity costs and social marginal productivity are likely to be present, such as black markets, smuggling, high wage rates along with large-scale unemployment (or disguised unemployment), and rationing of foreign exchange, credit, and other scarce resources.

Even though it could probably be shown that a substantial proportion of these deficiencies in free-market forces are due to misguided government interference, some economists would contend that more careful use of development theory and techniques should allow planners to interfere with, supplement, or substitute for market forces in more beneficial ways in the future. Increasingly sophisticated and powerful tools, such as linear and dynamic programming models, have been applied to various phases of national economic planning. Some of these models can provide the planner with an alternative set of prices supposed to be more representative than market prices. Where it has been impractical to apply such sophisticated models, development economists have suggested certain rules of thumb—such as investment criteria, broad planning strategies, and the like—that would enable weak economies to avoid some of the deficiencies of complete reliance on "free" market forces.

I do not mean to imply that planning-oriented development economists (of which there are many kinds and degrees) have convinced anybody

---

[9] It may be useful to distinguish between the more static concept of allocational efficiency—operating at a given point—and dynamic efficiency, which shows how the production-possibility curve is shifted outward over time.

(except possibly themselves) that the models they build, or the criteria and strategies they suggest, would provide better results than would market forces. On the contrary, in recent years there has been a strong counterattack by market-oriented economists, who have attempted to show the following: (1) that farmers, even very poor and uneducated ones, are quite efficient in allocating their very limited resources; (2) that the appealing panacea of shifting agriculture's disguised unemployment to industry is neither practical, possible, nor desirable; (3) that economic behavior in a variety of institutional settings is remarkably sensitive to differing penalty-rewards, once these differing settings are correctly understood; and (4) that satisfactory planning methods would require much more time and technical-administrative skills than less-developed countries can spare. Perhaps the most valuable contribution of these counterrevolutionaries has been their willingness to challenge the new orthodoxy in development on strictly empirical grounds. The result has been a long-overdue concern for developing operational theories and for testing alternative theories.

The Role of Monetary Factors in Growth and Development In a number of the growth theories formulated for studying the problems of developed countries, monetary factors have been integrated with nonmonetary factors in such a way that monetary factors can affect the "real" (nonmonetary) variables, and vice versa. Keynes and a number of post-Keynesian economists have done a great deal to steer growth theory in this direction. On the other hand, in development economics the role of monetary factors has been severely limited to determining the price level and little else. Aside from the lively, but somewhat barren, controversy between the *monetarists* and the *structuralists*,[10] the field of economic development has remained backward in its treatment of monetary factors.

Some Special Features of Development Theory in the Context of Less-developed Countries It will be noticed that we have said little thus far about foreign trade. It may be appropriate to omit foreign-trade considerations from the theory of economic growth in large developed countries such as the United States, the U.S.S.R., and Germany, where it plays a relatively minor role in the overall economy. However, the omission of foreign trade in discussing small, less-developed countries would

---

[10] The *monetarists* place the blame for inflation on government fiscal and monetary policies, and claim that price stability is a necessary condition for growth. The *structuralists* call the monetarists naïve for thinking they can cure the disease by treating the symptoms. They attribute inflation and lack of growth to basic structural weaknesses and market deficiencies.

be dangerous, in view of the vital role that exports and imports play in overcoming the disadvantages of their small domestic markets and in promoting benefits from trade by inducing greater efficiency and building up capital stock. The early postwar views of Nurkse [23] and numerous others that (1) trade can no longer be expected to play an important role in the development process, and that (2) exports (and hence imports) are largely, if not totally, beyond the control of policymakers in the less-developed countries, are being debunked by the accumulating empirical evidence.[11] As a result, we can expect that the conspicuous absence of trade from development theory will soon be a thing of the past.

We have already noted (in our reference to the Harrod-Domar growth model) the large influence that equilibrium theory has exerted on modern growth theory. The existence of obviously distorted and disorganized markets in the less-developed countries, and of disequilibrium in many areas of life there, has brought *disequilibrium economics* into the analysis of growth in such countries. One manifestation of this fact has been the building of an entire strategy of economic development on a series of planned disequilibria, as set forth in a popular book by Albert Hirschman [15]. Another manifestation of the introduction of disequilibrium economics is the popularity of a number of surplus resource models in the development field. For example, there is the *labor surplus* model of Lewis [17], Nurkse [22], and Rosenstein-Rodan [26], which has been extended by Fei and Ranis [11] into a theory of economic growth in which a less-developed country may, under certain conditions, take advantage of its surplus resources—in this case, unemployed or underemployed labor. In other kinds of surplus models, land or even capital may be the surplus resource.

Finally, it is especially characteristic of the economics of less-developed countries that important influences are often attributed to noneconomic factors such as cultural heritage, religion, and structure of (and mobility within) social groups, family size, and the like.

It is perhaps unfortunate that demonstration of the importance of noneconomic factors in economic development is often based on what I would call the "before-after" technique. Like the magazine advertisement which displays to the reader the ugly profile of Fat Jane *before* taking Joe's Massage alongside the beautiful profile of Slim Jane *after* taking Joe's Massage, the "before-after" technique is often used to contrast the value orientation of a poor society with that of a rich society. Just as the reader of the magazine never knows whether Fat Jane became Slim Jane by using Joe's Massage or by starving herself, or even whether the photographs are genuine or fraudulent, we are seldom given a well-documented and careful explanation of just how the value orientation of

---

[11] See, for example, Nugent [21].

a poor society gives way to the value orientation and development of a rich society. When we *are* given explanations, the theory is generally such that the various factors—both social and economic—are so interdependent as to make it extremely difficult to choose among alternative explanations.

The theory of *n-achievement*, or need for achievement, as developed by McClelland, Atkinson, and others[12] is an exception, both because it provides a moderately complete explanation and because it can be quantified, thereby permitting one to test its explanatory power in predicting subsequent economic development. Unfortunately, the measures of n-achievement motivation are so primitive and the results so sensitive to alternative indexes of economic development that the theory they support is still open to challenge.

Thus, whether the importance attached to noneconomic factors reflects anything but the failure of existing economic theory, or our inability to apply that theory, remains to be seen. Nevertheless, a strong intuitive, and perhaps empirical, case can be made, especially in the early stages of economic development, for the greater relative importance of noneconomic factors in the less-developed countries [1]. The development field's most important journal, *Economic Development and Cultural Change*, and certain influential development texts[13] reflect not only the strong interest of economists in noneconomic factors, but also the beginnings of what may eventually become a multidisciplinary approach to economic development.

REFERENCES

1. ADELMAN, IRMA, and CYNTHIA TAFT MORRIS. *Society, Politics and Economic Development: A Quantitative Approach* (Baltimore: Johns Hopkins, 1967).
2. BOULDING, KENNETH E. "Toward a General Theory of Growth," *Canadian Journal of Economics and Political Science*, 19:3 (August 1953).
3. BRUTON, HENRY J. "Productivity Growth in Latin America," *American Economic Review*, 58:5 (December 1967), pp. 1099–1116.
4. CHENERY, HOLLIS B., and ALAN M. STROUT. "Foreign Assistance and Economic Development," *American Economic Review*, 56 (September 1966), pp. 679–733.
5. CLOWER, ROBERT W., and others. *Growth without Development: An Economic Survey of Liberia* (Evanston, Ill.: Northwestern University Press, 1966).
6. DENISON, EDWARD F. *The Sources of Economic Growth in the United States and the Alternatives before Us* (New York: Committee for Economic Development, 1962).

---

[12] David McClelland, a social psychologist at Harvard University, is the leader of this group. His most important book is [20].
[13] See, for example, Everett E. Hagen [13].

7 ——— (assisted by Jean-Pierre Poullier). *Why Growth Rates Differ* (Washington, D.C.: Brookings, 1967).

8 DOMAR, EVSEY D. "Capital Expansion, Rate of Growth and Employment," *Econometrica*, 14 (1946), pp. 137–147.

9 ———. "Expansion and Employment," *American Economic Review*, 37 (March 1947), pp. 34–55.

10 ———. *Essays in the Theory of Economic Growth* (New York: Oxford University Press, 1957).

11 FEI, J. H., and GUSTAV RANIS. "A Theory of Economic Development," *American Economic Review*, 51 (1961), pp. 533–564.

12 HAAVELMO, TRYGVE. *A Study in the Theory of Economic Evolution*, 3d ed. (Amsterdam: North-Holland, 1964).

13 HAGEN, EVERETT E. *On the Theory of Social Change: How Economic Growth Begins* (Homewood, Ill.: Dorsey, 1962).

14 HARROD, ROY E. "An Essay in Dynamic Theory," *Economic Journal*, 49 (1939), pp. 14–33.

15 HIRSCHMAN, ALBERT O. *The Strategy of Economic Development* (New Haven, Conn.: Yale University Press, 1958).

16 LEIBENSTEIN, HARVEY. *Economic Backwardness and Economic Growth* (New York: Wiley, 1957).

17 LEWIS, W. ARTHUR. "Economic Development with Unlimited Supplies of Labor," *The Manchester School*, May 1954.

18 MAHALANOBIS, P. C. "Some Observations on the Process of Growth of National Income," *Sankhya*, 1953.

19 MARX, KARL. *Capital, the Communist Manifesto, and Other Writings by Karl Marx* (New York: Modern Library, 1932).

20 McCLELLAND, DAVID. *The Achieving Society* (Princeton, N.J., Van Nostrand, 1961).

21 NUGENT, JEFFRY B. "Exchange Rate Policy and Export Performance: A Comparative Study of Less Developed Countries on the Silver and Gold Standards in the Late Nineteenth Century," Center Discussion Paper No. 69, Yale University, Economic Growth Center, 1969.

22 NURKSE, RAGNAR. *Problems of Capital Formation in Underdeveloped Countries* (New York: Oxford University Press, 1953).

23 ———. *Patterns of Trade and Development* (New York: Oxford University Press, 1961).

24 PAPANDREOU, ANDREAS G. *A Strategy for Greek Economic Development* (Athens: Center of Planning and Economic Research, 1964).

25 ROSENSTEIN-RODAN, P. N. "Notes on the Theory of the Big Push," in *Economic Development for Latin America*, Howard S. Ellis, ed. (London: Macmillan, 1951).

26 ———. "Problems of Industrialization of Eastern and South-Eastern Europe," *Economic Journal*, June–September 1943.

27 ROSTOW, WALT W. "The Stages of Economic Growth," *The Economic History Review*, August 1959, pp. 1–5.

28 SMITH, ADAM. *The Wealth of Nations* (New York: Modern Library, 1937).

17

CONTINUITIES AND DISCONTINUITIES IN ECONOMIC DEVELOPMENT

Robert Lekachman *

ONE of the perennial issues that enliven historical argument concerns the extent of continuity in human affairs. Each identification of an epoch such as the Renaissance, the Reformation, or the Enlightenment amounts to the claim that in some significant way the events occurring during these periods relate uniquely to the time studied. To believe in historical periods is to believe at once in discontinuity and the impact of great events and great ideas upon human affairs. In good part the stuff of historical investigation is the thrust and parry between the partisans of discontinuity and the exponents of slow, incremental change in the conduct of economic and political institutions.

I.

In Western Europe's long nineteenth century, stretching from the French Revolution in 1789 to the onset of World War I in 1914, one idea that resonated and continues to resonate even in our own day is that of the Industrial Revolution. What was different about the Industrial Revolution? Why have such devotees of slow, unsensational change as the English economic historian T. S. Ashton[1] come to accept the label as meaningful? If we believe Friedrich Engels, before the Industrial

---

* State University of New York at Stony Brook.
[1] By thus entitling his magisterial survey of the period [1], Ashton conceded a good deal to the partisans of discontinuity in English economic history.

Revolution "the workers enjoyed a comfortable existence. . . . Their standard of life was much better than that of the factory worker today" [4, p. 10]. So judged Engels in 1845. Although G. R. Porter reached a much more cheerful conclusion, he too accepted the idea that the Industrial Revolution was a break with the past:

> *If we look back to the condition of the mass of the people as it existed in this country even so recently as the beginning of the present century, and then look around us at the indications of great comfort and respectability that meet us on every side, it is hardly possible to doubt that here, in England at least, the elements of social improvement have been successfully at work, and that they have been and are producing an increased amount of comfort to the great bulk of the people* [8, p. 532].

Early and late the historians have quarreled over the significance of the Industrial Revolution. Arnold Toynbee, great uncle of his modern namesake, had no doubt in 1884, when he coined the term Industrial Revolution, that he was examining a cataclysmic change: "We now approach a darker period—a period as disastrous and as terrible as any through which a nation ever passed; disastrous and terrible because side by side with a great increase of wealth was seen an enormous increase of pauperism" [12, p. 14]. The argument about what happened to the ordinary Englishman in extraordinary times is by no means resolved, nor is it my object to pass judgment upon the contending sides. Instead I shall seize upon one point of agreement, upon the fact that the Industrial Revolution involved what economists are prone to call a transformation of production functions, or what a possibly legendary student referred to as a wave of gadgets. The new inventions and the new modes of using them which invaded English life between 1780 and 1830 shaped the country's subsequent history and, as the new industrialism spread, influenced the history of the rest of the world.

The key economic institution of the new era was the factory, a central location where relatively large bodies of workers, directed by a common discipline, operated machines energized by steam power. The ideology of the new era was one of progress, opportunity, and self-improvement. For the French philosophes of the eighteenth century, progress was in the improvement of the mind and the spirit. As the Manchester proprietor of a spinning mill saw it, progress was defined by growing profits founded upon efficiency, low wages, and large foreign markets. Although the classical economists who followed Adam Smith were pessimists, the likes of Thomas Robert Malthus and David Ricardo did not really speak for the practical men of business, who all around them rejoiced in profitable soot, profitable slums, and profitably docile laborers.

How did England take off, to use W. W. Rostow's provocative metaphor [9]? A fortunate coincidence of suitabilities rather than a single overwhelming superiority over other candidates seems the best explanation. Physically separated from the continent of Europe, England was spared the financial burden of standing armies and the devastation of invasion. At a time when roads were everywhere wretched, her extensive coastline and efficient canal network facilitated cheap and rapid communication. In the eighteenth century England was an exceptionally productive agricultural society. Moreover, she was richly endowed in the resources strategic to early industrialization: coal, iron, and falling water.

Although *The Wealth of Nations* appeared in 1776 at the outset of the Industrial Revolution, its doctrines of free trade and domestic laissez faire did not win many immediate converts. The official doctrine of British politicians remained mercantilist. Nevertheless, England was lucky in her possession of the next best alternative to an enlightened official ideology, the weak and ineffective administration of an unenlightened doctrine. The mercantilist restrictions were delightfully inefficacious. Smuggling resembled an organized industry; its participants included many of the pillars of English society. The Laws of Settlement in theory impeded the free movement of men and women from parishes where jobs were few to parishes where new factories meant new opportunities; in practice, administration was so weak that the Laws of Settlement were dead letters long before Parliament thought to repeal them.

None of these advantages would have sufficed if England had not been blessed with an unusually large number of vigorous entrepreneurial types, upstarts like Samuel Arkwright, who began his thrusting life as a barber and dealer in wigs and ended it as a knight of the shire and the very model of the hero as industrial magnate. The period abounded in improving dukes, converted yeomen like Samuel and Aaron Walker, prudent Quakers, Independents, and Congregationalists, and more than one canny clergyman, all united in a yearning for wealth. Many of the inventions that removed spinning and weaving from the home and relocated these processes in the factory were the contributions of self-educated artisans. As Wesley Clair Mitchell memorably put it, in eighteenth-century England individual initiative became a mass phenomenon.

By 1830 England was the workshop of the world. Her factories poured out an endless stream of cheap cotton goods, woolens, cutlery, tools, and equipment. What her capitalists did not invest at home, they dispersed in the finance of French reparations, the construction of railroads and canals in the United States and Europe, the financing of Latin American governments, and the development of Egypt. As a profitable corollary of these activities, the City of London, England's financial district, became the world center of international lending, securities flotation, brokerage, and marine insurance. English technicians and experts traveled the civilized world, advising, installing machines, and frequently managing the factories and railroads that English capital had financed.

Full of pride at their country's success, British economists were not slow to advance the British example as the model for lesser breeds. Conventional opinion held that free trade and free competition were the twin pillars upon which the British achievement rested. Government was very nearly limited to defense, enforcement of contract, and a very small amount of public construction, the three legitimate functions allowed government by Adam Smith. Unions were weak and scarcely legal. Unemployment was high enough to tame the spirits of workers.

Indeed, as few contemporary writers cared to note, until the 1860s English economic success brought small rewards to the ordinary Englishman. And today's radical historians identify a restiveness and a radicalism in the English proletariat which casts serious doubt on the alleged tranquility of the simple working man. Nevertheless, when revolution swept over much of Europe in 1848, England was spared, and English society has today, as yesterday, been spared violent change.[2]

England's last revolution was in the seventeenth century. A patriotic Englishman might well have read his country's record as a demonstration of the intelligence of the governing classes in yielding repeatedly to the demands of the lower classes well before the flash point of violence was reached. The Reform Act of 1832 extended suffrage to the middle classes. The Reform Act of 1867, Disraeli's "leap into the dark," gave the vote to male workers. The first decade of the twentieth century witnessed the beginnings of unemployment compensation, old age pensions, and health insurance. If these and like measures did not necessarily prove that the rich had developed compassion for the poor, or the educated empathy for the ignorant, the pliability of the privileged did at least imply a keen instinct for survival.

Whatever life was like in 1810 or 1830, whether people were happier on the farms of the eighteenth century or not, there is no doubt that by any statistical indicator available, standards of life were higher, working conditions better, hours shorter, and the social provision against personal disaster much more extensive in 1914 than they had been at the start of the Industrial Revolution. Just as the economists had said, innovation, division of labor, freedom of contract, mobility of resources, and free trade had produced their undismal consequences. Other countries need only do likewise.

---

[2] The radical case is best made in [11], an amply documented and persuasively reasoned case for the strength of working class radicalism during and after the Industrial Revolution. See also [6].

II.

From the incrementalist's standpoint, then, even the Industrial Revolution in England was a break in just a part of society's slow, orderly, adjustment to new circumstances. Manufacturing no doubt was transformed, but the traditional crafts lingered on and the social, cultural, and political life of the land changed scarcely more rapidly than before.

Did other countries imitate England's experience? Consider the United States. In 1880 the American consul in Birmingham, on a comparison shopping tour of the towns in the area, discovered to his delight an American success story: "Canned meats, hominy in sacks, scissors and small tools, sewing machines and watches, fresh meat and salted meats, peaches and other tinned fruits, and apples in barrels are to be found everywhere."[3] How did it happen that the brash Americans who only a few decades earlier were cheerfully defaulting on railroad and canal loans made by trusting British investors were now challenging the British not only abroad, which was bad enough, but at home as well? Had the United States simply copied the English model of devotion alike to innovation and tradition? Scarcely. The American path to industrial success was dotted with violence. The expropriation of Indian lands, the American Revolution, the Mexican War, and the Civil War: these are events disjunctive enough to make the point. The War for Independence shook the thirteen colonies loose from the shackles of a feeble and declining British mercantilism. Westward expansion opened sources of raw materials, generated railroad and canal booms (and busts), and created new markets for Eastern manufacturers. The Civil War made it unequivocally plain that the interests of the Northern capitalists were to prevail over the free-trade preferences of Southern planters. These were the events that widened the American market and harvested the traditional rewards of specialization and division of labor.

By the 1880s the Germans were alarming patriotic Englishmen nearly as much as the Americans were. Yet there had been no Germany and accordingly no German challenge until 1871. War, as Engels memorably phrased the matter, is the midwife of social change. Certainly war was the occasion of the German industrial and commercial thrust in the 1880s and after. Bismarck's three wars—against the Danes, the Austrians, and finally the French—produced a united Germany under Prussian hegemony and completed the move toward economic unity begun with the Zollverein four decades earlier. Once more force widened markets, encouraged specialization, promoted division of labor, and rewarded innovation after a fashion impossible to the collection of small, weak states that constituted the Germanies at the start of the century.

[3] Quoted by [2, p. 29].

As for Japan, it was Commodore Perry's gray ships in Tokyo harbor which exemplified for the Japanese the weakness of an ancient, tradition-bound society confronted by the brute machines of modern technology. Their response to the demonstration was a determined, concerted national effort to reshape Japanese political, economic, and educational institutions in ways calculated to equip Japan to compete successfully in world markets and hold the national head up among the arrogant westerners. The Russo-Japanese War of 1905 and the destruction by yellow sailors of a Russian fleet were violent events that signalized the policy's success as well as the destruction of the myth that technology was the white man's game.

A final leap to our own time: In 1945 Europe was in disarray. Italian and French Communists were numerous and powerful enough to make real the possibility of electoral triumph and peaceful takeover. Industrialized Germany was in ruins. Half-industrialized France and sketchily industrialized Italy were uncompetitive in world markets. Yet twenty years later, half the gold stock of the United States had ended in the central banks of France, Italy, West Germany, Switzerland, and Japan.

Is Western Europe about to perform upon Americans an operation similar to the one Americans performed upon the British? Such a judgment is premature, to say the least. Europeans remain frightened of the power of American technology. The distance that they have come toward parity with the United States is no matter of gradual, incremental change. Large events like the Marshall Plan, the cold war, and the NATO alliance have had profoundly energizing effects upon Europe.

The most significant of the institutional leaps taken by Western Europeans was the creation of the Common Market. Who could have imagined that Frenchmen, Germans, and Italians could have sunk enough of their very recent animosities and their ancient cultural differences to sign the Treaty of Rome in 1958, a handful of years after the Second World War ended? Whether, with the departure of de Gaulle, this treaty portends, as Europeans like Jean Monnet hope, the political as well as the economic unity of the six partners, no man can sensibly predict. But during the twelfth anniversary year of the treaty, it is evident at the least that internal trade barriers have been lowered, external tariffs reduced, and a market potentially bigger than the American one created. It is a market that has proved itself a magnet for American investors and a source of apparently permanent prosperity for European businessmen.

But this is once more no imitation of earlier models of free trade and small government. Andrew Shonfield has persuasively argued [10] that by itself the Common Market could not have generated Western Europe's spectacular postwar economic growth. The complementary institutional shift that was essential was the spread of the technique of indicative planning, particularly in France.[4] In its Gallic version, indicative planning is a highly flexible affair of intensive consultation between public officials and industrialists, reconciliation of private plans and public objectives, and deployment of a bewildering array of techniques of control and direction, among them the familiar tools of fiscal and monetary policy, direct controls over investment and imports, preferential financing, and selective variation of tariff rates. Possibly most important of all is the maintenance of a steady climate of economic optimism based upon confidence in the government's intention and ability to maintain prosperity.

In France, as in most other European countries, the sphere of government ownership and control is considerably broader than it is in the United States or even in England. The circumstance is still another index of how very much postwar Common Market countries differ in ideology as well as institutional arrangement from their American and English exemplars. Success has involved the sinking, at least partially, of nationalistic animosities: it has not demanded either free trade or laissez faire in domestic policy.

III.

As for England, it is now possible to perceive with all the acuity of hindsight that economic decline has been the British experience continuously from the 1880s onward. The English share of world trade has been falling. Financial leadership has shifted decisively from London to New York. The English standard of life, once the highest in Europe, is now matched or surpassed by that of several of the Common Market countries, not to mention Scandinavia and Switzerland. Persistent balance-of-payments deficits caused devaluation of the pound, first in 1949 and again in 1967. East of Suez, the residual burdens of empire have proven too heavy to be borne. With resentment and bewilderment, Englishmen face the possibility that their future is that of a larger Sweden, unhappily minus Swedish efficiency and living standards.

Why has this long decline occurred? Prudence suggests a certain care in framing easy answers. As one English economist has put it:

> *Our understanding of the nature and causes of economic growth remains very limited. Some people have been tempted to attribute this unsatisfactory state of affairs to the stupidity or perversity of economists, but unfortunately* [sic!] *this simple diagnosis is at fault [5, p. 15].*

But one feature of the explanations currently in vogue is striking. Even economists tend to identify England's trouble outside the realm of economics.

Thus it is often said that despite a new emphasis upon education for

[4] The best short account of French planning is [3].

more people and the growth of what Englishmen term meritocracy, the class system still operates to waste human resources and discourage talented youngsters from working-class families. No doubt Americans squander resources upon the attempt to provide something called higher education for nearly half the population [7]. But the English practice of offering good secondary school education to only a small minority, and limiting university opportunities to a still smaller fraction of the eligible population, absolutely ensures a shortage of the skills essential to successful competition in international trade—those of the engineer, computer programmer, and applied scientist.

And in England the impact of the shortage is all the greater because even those youngsters who survive rigorous early screening and attain university degrees seem to prefer the traditional arts subjects, among them history, English, and the classics. Such studies may make life beautiful, but it is science and technology that make life efficient. Really able university graduates disdain business careers and prefer government service or university teaching. Thus it is that British industry gets too small a share of too small a number of highly trained young Englishmen and Englishwomen.

On the critics' little list, also, are the unions and the managers. The unions are hostile to technical change, prone to strike over minor alterations in working conditions, and obsessed by a fear of unemployment, which derives from the memory of the 1920s and the 1930s, when unemployment was a central problem. For their part, the managers are notably unprogressive (some honorable exceptions aside), unwilling, as the ancient joke has it, to invest in new equipment when times are bad, because trade is slack, and equally unwilling to buy new machines when times are good, because they are able to make good profits with old equipment.

This standard (though not necessarily accurate) diagnosis of the British malaise has very little to do with the fact that England is now deficient in most important minerals. So she is, but Switzerland does nicely with still fewer natural resources. One of the virtues of the Common Market is its size, but the Japanese have been flourishing within a market only a bit larger than the English one. No, the theme running through the litany of lament is a criticism of excessive continuity. The persistence of tradition, affection for the past, fondness for the ceremonial rather than the efficient, which have done much to make England a stable society blessed by a gentleness of public manners and a tranquility of political life which an American in the 1960s must envy, have also had the less happy effect of slowing economic change, discouraging necessary adjustments in education, managerial training, and industrial relations, and accelerating England's steady decline in the international economic league standings.

Admirers of England may hope that the trend is reversible. If they are realists, they will identify as a necessary condition of such a reversal the need for more discontinuity in contemporary British experience than she has experienced possibly since the impetus of the Industrial Revolution wore itself out. Harold Macmillan's and then Harold Wilson's attempts to enter the Common Market amounted to a tacit quest for discontinuous change, for a plunge into the icy bath of the competition of efficient Europeans. For the time being this door is closed. Englishmen must, without external aid, set about to transform their education, unions, and business managements.

England's brief time of economic domain was founded upon the sweeping events of the Industrial Revolution. English political and cultural institutions proved themselves strong enough to absorb the economic discontinuities of the experience. Will these institutions be resilient enough to withstand other leaps and discontinuities in the 1970s?

REFERENCES

1. ASHTON, THOMAS S. *The Industrial Revolution: 1760–1830* (London: Oxford University Press, 1948).
2. AUSUBEL, HERMAN. *In Hard Times* (New York: Columbia University Press, 1960).
3. BAUCHET, PIERRE. *Economic Planning: The French Experience* (London: Heineman, 1964).
4. ENGELS, FRIEDRICH. *The Condition of the Working Class in England* (1845), translated and edited by W. O. Henderson and W. H. Chaldner (New York: Macmillan, 1958).
5. HENDERSON, PATRICK D. (ed.). *Economic Growth in Britain* (London: Weidenfeld and Nicholson, 1966).
6. HOBSBAWN, ERIC J. *Labouring Men: Studies in the History of Labour* (London: Weidenfeld and Nicholson, 1964).
7. JENCKS, CHRISTOPHER, and DAVID RIESMAN. *The Academic Revolution* (Garden City, N. Y.: Doubleday, 1968).
8. PORTER, GEORGE R. *The Progress of the Nation: In Its Various Social and Economical Relations, from the Beginning of the Nineteenth Century to the Present Time* (London: C. Knight, 1836).
9. ROSTOW, WALT W. *The Stages of Economic Growth: A Non-Communist Manifesto* (Cambridge: Cambridge University Press, 1960).
10. SHONFIELD, ANDREW. *Modern Capitalism: The Changing Balance of Public and Private Power* (New York: Oxford University Press, 1965).
11. THOMPSON, EDWARD P. *The Making of the English Working Class* (New York: Pantheon, 1963).
12. TOYNBEE, ARNOLD. *The Industrial Revolution* (1884) (Boston: Beacon Press, 1956).

18

CONTINUITIES AND CHANGE IN CENTRALLY PLANNED ECONOMIES

Gregory Grossman *

THE fourteen countries ruled today by communist parties[1] account for about one-third of the population of the globe and one-quarter of its land area. They include two giants, the U.S.S.R. and China, and a country as small as Albania. Culturally, they are as diverse as Cuba and Korea, or Czechoslovakia and China. Ethnically, some are homogeneous (Hungary or Bulgaria), and others are multinational (the U.S.S.R. or Yugoslavia). Geographically, they range from the tropics to the Arctic. Mongolia contains fewer than 0.3 persons per square mile, East Germany, over 60. Some of the countries are very poor in natural resources, while others are very rich; for these and other reasons, most depend strongly on foreign trade, although a few, notably the two giants, do not. They include some of the economically least developed and some of the most developed countries of the world. And while their economic institutions are not entirely identical, the surprising thing is perhaps not how much they differ on this score, but how little.

Since the communist regimes took over, nearly all of the countries have grown greatly in productive (especially industrial) capacity. In the U.S.S.R. itself, in the forty years since forced industrialization began

---
* University of California at Berkeley.
[1] These countries are (listed by their colloquial, rather than official, names): the Soviet Union; in Eastern Europe—Albania, Bulgaria, Czechoslovakia, East Germany, Hungary, Poland, Rumania, and Yugoslavia; in Asia—China, North Korea, (Outer) Mongolia, and North Vietnam; and Cuba.

at the end of the twenties, and despite a most destructive war, industrial output has increased something like 20 times, and the gross national product, around 7 times.[2] But the economic *institutions* of the Soviet Union have changed very little in these four decades. The same is true of most of the other communist countries since their adoption of the Soviet economic system (which in the case of Eastern Europe occurred in the late forties).

There are, of course, good reasons for these uniformities and continuities. The economic system established in the Soviet Union by Stalin—the "centrally planned economy," or "command economy" as it is often called in the West—was exported to other communist countries either by force of Soviet arms or by the (initially) unquestioning imitation of the Soviet prototype by local communist regimes. This economic system has remained in force in most communist countries until now. Yet today, in virtually all these countries, the U.S.S.R. included, there is much criticism of the command economy; and in nearly all of them some steps have already been taken to modify it. Often these changes are only minor, although in some communist countries significant systemic changes are under way.

Three important exceptions should be noted—countries where the Soviet-type model either was abandoned at a relatively early point or never quite took root at all. In Yugoslavia, after little more than half a decade's experience with it, the command economy was dismantled and replaced with a distinctive system, the Yugoslav version of the socialist market economy. China, after following the Soviet example for a decade, struck out in a radically different direction that we shall have occasion to note below. Cuba's economic institutions have never followed too closely the Soviet model since Castro's seizure of power in 1959. It should be noted that these three are the only countries (in addition to North Vietnam) where the communist regime came to power without significant assistance on Moscow's part, and that in Yugoslavia and China the restructuring of the economic system followed a decisive political break, in the one case, or paralleled the emergence of a major political dispute with Moscow, in the other.

The Command Economy To understand the command economy, we must first understand the objectives for which, and the conditions under which, the Soviet economic system was established. The ultimate goal of the Soviets is, and has been from the start, to bring about in their country (and everywhere else in the world, but this we may overlook for the moment) a society that would correspond to the Marxist ideal of "full

---

[2] These are rough estimates based on Western computations at constant Soviet 1937 prices.

communism"—that is, one in which there would be an abundance of material goods and, thanks to this (in the Marxian view) social harmony, no political coercion or economic exploitation of man and full development of man's intellectual and moral capacities. But this is the *ultimate* goal; much more important for an understanding of Soviet institutions and policies are the short- and medium-term objectives. Among these we should list:

Rapid industrialization, with particular emphasis on heavy industry.
Maximization of military power.
Rise in consumption levels (though this objective did not enjoy much priority until the mid-fifties).
Autarky (national economic self-sufficiency).
Achievement of scientific and technological preeminence.
In the earlier years, socialization in the sense of the elimination of private enterprise, including even the smallest-scale private productive activity.

In striving for these objectives, the Soviet leaders have felt an enormous sense of urgency. Much of what they have done cannot be understood except with reference to a "logic of haste." They have been in a hurry because of what they perceived, rightly or wrongly, to be the menace from a hostile and aggressive capitalist world without, and from various dangers within—both of which could be staved off only by the most determined and rapid industrialization. In addition, they have regarded themselves to be competing economically with the leading Western powers, especially the United States, for mastery of the future.

It is also important to note the conditions under which rapid industrialization began in the late twenties in the U.S.S.R. Stalin had already consolidated his absolute dictatorship. The country was overwhelmingly agrarian and on the whole very poor—that is, average incomes were low—by Western standards (though not by Asian standards). The average level of skills and education was low, but not so low as in most of the underdeveloped world. The ratio of population to natural resources (including those to be discovered in subsequent decades) was on the whole a favorable one, although the agricultural resource base was (and is) belied by the vastness of the country. Industrial production *per capita* was small, though in the aggregate it was quite large—indeed, the fifth largest in the world—and much of it was in the heavy industries. There was also a small but often very competent nucleus of scientists, engineers, and other specialists. This physical and human capital, the result of swift industrialization and modernization between the 1880s and World War I, was to prove of inestimable value to the Soviets in pursuing their major objectives. All in all, when the five-year plans began in 1928, the Soviet Union was still an underdeveloped country, but one far more favorably endowed for rapid industrialization than most other underdeveloped countries then or since.

Given these conditions and the aforementioned urgent objectives, at the end of the twenties and the beginning of the thirties Stalin fashioned what might be called the classic Soviet model of a command economy. Political and social control was centralized in an all-powerful state run by a monolithic, all-powerful party. Terror suppressed every glimmer of opposition and every spark of dissent, except deep in the hearts and minds of men, where, as we now know, they were never quite extinguished. Public expression was either entirely suppressed or closely controlled. It was in this political and ideological climate that Stalin's economic policies were pursued and his economic model given shape.

In the economy, too, all decisions—both short- and long-term—were highly centralized, although absolute centralization was, of course, impossible. The whole economy constituted a huge formal hierarchy, almost entirely socialized (in the sense of public ownership of means of production). Down this hierarchy flowed orders ("commands") for positive acts ("produce so much of such and such a good") and permits for the use of resources ("you may pay out up to so much in wages per year"); up flowed requests for permits ("give us more of this, that, and the other") and reports on compliance with the commands (sometimes deliberately titivated to create a good effect). Compliance was usually measured in crude and aggregate terms, such as the value of the total output of an enterprise or the physical amount of a commodity produced. Almost everything needed for production—from wages to fuel—was doled out by central authorities, supposedly according to exactly determined production needs. The economy was "planned," a term with a dual meaning as well as an almost sacred significance in Soviet usage. Planning refers to the steering of economic development toward intended objectives and goals. But it also refers to the coordination of all the producing units of the economy in the short run, and to the issuance of corresponding commands to these units—an indispensable, if not infallible, activity in the absence of a market mechanism.[3]

If we think of the economy's surplus as the difference between national product and household consumption (minimal consumption throughout most of the Soviet period, at that!), then under the Stalinist model nearly the whole of the surplus was either concentrated directly in the hands of the central authorities or subject to their indirect but effective control.

---

[3] For a fuller but still succinct account of the model, see Alan A. Brown and Egon Neuberger, "Basic Features of a Centrally Planned Economy," in [2, pp. 405–416]. See also the bibliography attached to that essay. Another brief account of the Soviet economy can be found in [8, Chap. 6]. A fuller treatment can be found in [11].

This was accomplished by keeping real wages low (and levying sales taxes mostly on consumer goods) and by giving state-owned enterprises little power of disposal over their net profits and depreciation reserves. In agriculture, this was done even more bluntly by virtually requisitioning produce from collective farms at minimal prices, and at the same time employing coercive measures (as well as paltry material incentives) to force the peasants to work for the farms.

As a result, a very high proportion—some 25 to 30 percent or more—of the gross national product was typically allocated to gross investment. And of this, in turn, the overwhelming proportion went into sectors that enjoyed high priority in view of the regime's objectives, mostly heavy industry. In addition large resources were directed into education and training (chiefly for modern industrial skills), into scientific research and related work, and into other growth-inducing activities. A vast and highly organized system of "borrowing" foreign technology was set up. And last, millions of persons moved, or were moved, from villages to cities and towns.[4] These and other factors go far to explain the swift growth of the Soviet economy as a whole, and of its industry in particular.[5]

The relationship of the household sector to the hierarchical production organization is quite complex and has varied a good deal in Soviet history. Under what might be called more normal conditions—referring primarily to the post-Stalin period—the individual household is autonomous, in the sense that it possesses considerable freedom of choice of jobs and of consumer goods. Like the typical household in a Western-style industrial country, the Soviet (nonpeasant) household is faced with given wages attaching to employment alternatives, and with given retail prices for consumer goods and services; it chooses among these so as to maximize its utility. Legal bars to the quitting of jobs, directed assignment to jobs, other forms of coercion over labor, and rationing of consumer goods—all common during much of the Stalin era—have been the exception rather than the rule since Stalin's death. Private economic activity is, of course, another matter; it is illegal outside a narrowly defined range or where it involves employing others.

A major exception to this picture of relative freedoms is the collective-farm peasant, who possesses a considerably narrower choice of work options than do "workers and employees" in the labor force. But even peasants may engage in farming on their own account, though their so-called household plots may be very small.

An important aspect of the household sector in relation to the production sector is the material incentives used to elicit the former's effort and

---

[4] The proportion of the urban population in the total population rose from 18 percent in 1928 to 55 percent in 1967.

[5] For a summary presentation and analysis of this growth, see [13].

cooperation. These incentives are chiefly monetary, although some nonmonetary incentives may also be significant. (Examples of nonmonetary incentives are the availability of housing, the variety of consumer goods purchasable in the retail market, and the availability of vacations or of trips abroad. Again, an exception must be made for collective-farm peasants, who are still remunerated to a considerable extent *in natura*.) Soviet workers choose their occupations, levels of skill, jobs, and places of residence largely—though obviously not entirely—in response to the economic advantage they expect to derive from them, primarily better money wages and salaries. In other words, the incentives to which Soviet workers and employees respond are not fundamentally different from those affecting persons employed in other industrial societies, always remembering that the prospect of becoming "one's own boss" has little part in the Soviet picture. Since Stalin's death, coercion has played a relatively minor role in distributing and motivating labor. The same is true of ideologically based appeals, despite the all-penetrating and ever-present nature of Soviet official propaganda.

While this economic system has brought impressive industrial growth and equally impressive military strength to the Soviet Union, its accomplishments on other scores leave much to be desired. Shortcomings are cited in what is now a large critical literature, much larger in the East even than in the West. Briefly, overcentralization leads to "bureaucracy" (in the pejorative sense), to slow communications, and to tardy and often faulty decisionmaking; in production, quality and variety are often sacrificed for quantity; supply of and demand for individual goods are poorly articulated, leading to waste; in general, there is waste of resources in the production and distribution of goods; many managers resent the short tether on which they are kept; labor has little opportunity to express significant grievances; the consumer's share of total resources is small and inefficiently managed; collectivized agriculture suffers from many ills and on the whole performs poorly; management has little incentive to introduce innovations, so that technological progress is slow; much of the all-embracing planning is of dubious rationality and worth; the country's exports are not competitive (for many of these reasons) in world markets, an especially serious matter for those communist countries that depend heavily on foreign trade and have few crude commodities to export; and so forth. The list could be considerably extended and detailed. But what should be noted is that in the minds of many people, particularly those most directly affected, a *command economy* is intimately linked with a *totalitarian polity*. While the connection between the two is complex, it is probably true that a command economy cannot be maintained for long without a highly authoritarian political structure.

The command economy has been in effect in the U.S.S.R. since the early thirties—that is, for almost forty years—with little significant change in its institutional characteristics. Even the much-publicized economic reform of 1965 has not altered the command-economy system; somewhat more attention is now paid to profit within enterprises, but basically physical planning, physical production targets, and physical allocation of materials still dominate the picture. In agriculture there has been perhaps more meaningful reform than in industry: the abolition of the machine-tractor stations in 1958, greater certainty regarding the collective farms' obligatory deliveries to the state since 1965, successive—and cumulatively very important—increases in material incentives to peasants, and the introduction of pensions and guaranteed minimal incomes to the collectivized peasants in the mid-sixties. Forced labor on a mass scale was abolished in the mid-fifties, as were the oppressive laws aimed at reducing labor's mobility and maximizing its obedience to management and to the state. And yet today the overall features of the Soviet economic system, its strengths and weaknesses, are strikingly similar to what they were twenty or thirty years ago.

As we look at other countries of Eastern Europe—except Yugoslavia—we find, till the late sixties, only a few significant deviations from the Soviet prototype. The most important such deviation is to be seen in Polish agriculture, where six-sevenths of the arable land is privately farmed, a direct result of the Polish revolution of October 1956. In East Germany there is an appreciable amount of private activity in nearly all major sectors of the economy, as there is also in Hungary; on the other hand, in Czechoslovakia private activity has been almost totally eliminated outside agriculture (and even there it is minimal). In the late sixties, Czechoslovakia and Hungary embarked on major economic reform; more on this below.

What we have described is a model of the command economy as it was established in the U.S.S.R. in the early thirties and maintained there since, and as it was exported to Eastern Europe and China after World War II. But the half-century-long experience of communist regimes provides us with two other types of economic system: what we call here "siege communism," and "market socialism." Of these, the latter is considerably more important, both as a historical experience and as a model toward which present-day command economies may evolve. But the siege-communism model, once regarded as merely a brief interlude in the early history of Soviet Russia, has reappeared in a milder form in the Cuban economy.

Siege Communism The typical setting of siege communism is a condition of dire political or military emergency to a communist regime and society—no matter whether correctly or exaggeratedly perceived by the regime. The economic response to this situation is characterized by greater centralization than in a command economy; egalitarian distribution of income (except with regard to members of the formerly privileged and now repressed classes) combined with great reliance on ideological appeals and mass mobilization by the party;[6] even greater disparagement of the market and of money than in a command economy; and strong ideological rationalization of the system as the dawn of a brave new world.

The first—and in a sense the classic—case of siege communism is the so-called War Communism that held sway in Soviet Russia for approximately three years, 1918–1921, coinciding roughly with the civil war. For a good part of this period the Soviet regime was faced with the direst of military and economic emergencies, and its very survival hung in the balance. The economy was operating at an extremely low level; indeed, toward the end of the period it was almost paralyzed. All produce above their own bare consumption needs was confiscated from the peasants, often at the point of a gun. Consumer goods in minimal quantities were physically doled out to nonpeasants. Industry and other nonagricultural sectors of the economy were managed in a highly centralized way, more like an army than an economy. Both production and distribution of goods took place on direct command from a central authority. Money virtually disappeared from use—in addition to being astronomically inflated—and with it disappeared accounting and calculation in money terms. In the absence of material incentives, labor was controlled through appeals to revolutionary and patriotic fervor and by coercion.[7]

In 1921, to avoid complete economic collapse Lenin turned the economy sharply in the other direction and introduced a socialist market economy known as the New Economic Policy (NEP). But while War Communism was in effect, its institutions—particularly its rejection of the market and of money, together with its rejection of material incentives—were seriously discussed by leading communist theoreticians as the rightful institutions of the postcapitalist (though not yet socialist) society.

The Cuban economy lies, systemically, somewhere between War Communism and the Soviet-type command economy—probably closer to the latter than to the former. But it still differs sufficiently from the Soviet prototype to be seen as a latter-day version of siege communism. What concerns us especially in this instance is the high degree of egalitarianism in income distribution (buttressed by the rationing of many

---

[6] The qualification following the parentheses is important. Thus, in Czechoslovakia, until recently very much a Soviet-style command economy, there has been a high degree of egalitarianism, but relatively little reliance on ideological appeals or mass mobilization for production purposes.

[7] For an extensive discussion of War Communism, see [3, pp. 57–128].

consumer goods); the relatively low reliance on material incentives to elicit work performance and to redeploy labor; and the correspondingly high reliance on ideological (revolutionary and patriotic) appeals, mass mobilization, "socialist emulation," and coercion. Siege communism in Cuba is thus theoretically legitimated with reference to communist morality and justice, but its practice is facilitated by an all-pervading sense of revolutionary and national emergency, particularly under the threat from the colossus to the north. In other words, Cuba sees itself as being virtually under siege.

Moreover, a large part of Cuban industry—specifically, the part subordinated to the Ministry of Industry, which was then headed by Che Guevara—has operated since early 1964 (and on a lesser scale since 1960) under the system of "budget finance," which is reminiscent of the organization of industry under Soviet War Communism. The stress in this instance is on highly centralized decisions, transmitted to the firm through the so-called consolidated enterprises, which are product-line groupings of firms somewhat like trusts in Soviet history. The term "budget finance" refers to the procedure whereby all the receipts of an individual enterprise are turned over to the state budget (the treasury), and funds for expenditures are drawn from the state budget. That is to say, the firm has virtually no financial autonomy; it is not the keeper of its own purse, with all that this implies for its economizing behavior. Under this procedure, there is no need for financial relations in the conventional sense, nor is the firm amenable to control by financial instruments. The analogy with the Soviet firm under War Communism is quite close on this score.

While the bulk of Cuban industry operates under budget finance, some firms operate under an alternative procedure, "self-finance," which gives them considerably more financial autonomy and responsibility, and which seems to be closely similar to the Soviet system of "business-like management" (*khozraschet*). In recent years there has been considerable debate in Cuba between partisans of these two systems. When Cuban economists speak of decentralizing reforms, they tend to mean the supersession of budget finance by self-finance—that is, a movement toward Soviet-style *khozraschet* rather than a movement away from *khozraschet* to an even more decentralized arrangement, as the East European reform measures would have it.

Guevara's preference for budget finance as against *khozraschet* was based on ideological premises. He seemed to prefer the highly centralized arrangement as a way of maintaining close social control over economic activity. But, even more, he was concerned with the implications for man. He feared that under greater financial autonomy the enterprise would require financial incentives to exercise its autonomy properly. This in turn, he held, would necessitate greater reliance on material incentives for the individual and would promote particular economic interests—a solution incompatible with his vision of the socially conscious, responsive, unacquisitive socialist man. He severely criticized the Soviet Union for having embarked, as far back as the twenties, on the path of dispensing individual material incentives as stimuli for building socialism. Even the minimal devolution of managerial power implicit in the *khozraschet* system was to him, for this reason, a serious mistake. Although he did not rule out material rewards entirely, Guevara insisted that "moral" stimuli are the proper ones for socialism.[8]

Another possible example of siege communism is the period of the Great Leap Forward in China, 1958–1960. True, the political setting of this example is rather different from the settings of the first two, but there may be some psychological likeness in that the Chinese Communist leadership may have felt a sensation of isolation and emergency stemming from the realization that *both* superpowers were now its enemies. The Great Leap Forward was too complex a phenomenon to summarize here. Suffice it to say that material incentives were downgraded and nonmaterial ones upgraded to a greater extent than has been practiced in China before or since. Understandably, this was combined with equality of remuneration (especially among peasants) and with mass mobilization by the Party.[9]

Market Socialism If siege communism is the institutional expression of a high pitch of revolutionary fervor and ideological commitment, inflamed by imminent danger to the regime's survival, then market socialism, lying at the other end of the spectrum, reflects the quest for economic improvement and social stability by enlisting for the collective good the individual's and the group's material interests. Of course, the good must be so defined—or redefined—as to exclude precisely those values of extreme social solidarity and spartan egalitarianism that provide siege communism with much of its philosophical justification. Market socialism relies, if not on Adam Smith's invisible hand, then at least (in Professor

---

[8] Guevara's views on this question are presented at some length in [6, chap. 24]. For briefings on the institutions of the Cuban economy, I am much indebted to Professor Roberto M. Bernardo of the University of Guelph (who is, of course, not responsible for what I say here).

[9] The pre-1958 institutional patterns of the Chinese economy are conveniently presented in [10]. For the later period, the reader is referred to the near-encyclopedic work by Audrey Donnithorne [4]; the more analytical book by Dwight H. Perkins [12]; and the collection of papers in [14]. On incentives under the Great Leap Forward, see [9, *passim*].

Neuberger's phrase) on the "visible hand" of a planned and regulated market mechanism—rather than on the clenched fist of economic command or the authoritarian finger of indoctrination.

There are three major historical instances of market socialism under communist auspices. The first is that of the NEP in the U.S.S.R., which spanned the period between War Communism and the beginnings of the Stalinist command economy, say, from 1921 to 1928. Its historical mission was to lift the economy from near-paralysis to complete recovery at the earlier high levels; this much it accomplished with distinction. Its institutional structure was rather complex (cf. [1]). Essentially, it was a mixed economy with nearly all agriculture, and much small-scale activity in other sectors, in private hands and conducted in a traditional manner. Some production was cooperatively organized. But nearly all large-scale activity, especially finance and foreign trade, was in state hands. The state enterprises, however, did dispose of a good deal of autonomy and were in large measure motivated by profit-making. For its part, the government exercised considerable control over both the private and the socialist sectors of the economy in many ways, such as credit policy, investment allocations, exchange control, and (often) price control.

The Yugoslav variant of market socialism came into being in the early fifties, soon after the political break between Tito and Stalin. The thumbnail sketch of the NEP in the preceding paragraph can be made to apply to Yugoslavia also if we add a few significant facts. First, the Yugoslavs have seen their system not merely as a transitional one, designed to bring about economic recovery from a depressed level, but also as a long-term mechanism for attaining a high rate of growth. Second, local political authorities (say, municipalities)—and, more recently, the six republics—have played an important active economic role, especially by way of initiating new enterprises. Third, and most importantly, the Yugoslav system—unlike the NEP—combines the market mechanism with a fundamentally new kind of structure of power *within* the enterprise, called *workers' self-management*.

Under the Yugoslav system of workers' self-management the ultimate decisionmaking power in an enterprise theoretically rests with the workers as a group, who exercise this power through a structure of assemblies and councils. Management is ultimately responsible to workers. With this power also go rewards and penalties in the sense that a certain portion of the firm's net income is disposed of—or, in case of failure, forgone—by the workers and their representatives. Such funds go to the workers as their remuneration for both labor and collective entrepreneurship, but a portion may be plowed back to augment the firm's capital and hence future earning capacity. In sum, the system of workers' self-management thus provides at once a locus of authority within the firm and an incentive to exercise this authority in a (more or less) profit-maximizing way. In the view of its designers, it also represents an effective form of industrial democracy, overcoming that "alienation" of the worker that the Yugoslavs allege exists as much in the Soviet as in the capitalist economies.

There is some question as to how close to its own model the Yugoslav economy has hewn. On the whole, there has been considerably more central control and intervention than the model would theoretically seem to call for. Some of this control, especially price and foreign-exchange control, has been occasioned by the economy's strong proneness to inflation. Nor has workers' self-management operated without serious shortcomings. The Yugoslav economy has had its share of major problems: inflation, unemployment, sharp fluctuations in the rate of growth. But at the same time it can claim a high average rate of growth and a more flexible economic mechanism than that in the command economy. Finally, there has been a concomitant loosening of political controls and some suggestive steps toward democratization, quite apart from (but not unrelated to) workers' self-management, on which the advocates of the system place much stock on philosophical grounds.

The Yugoslav experience has pointed up the feasibility and viability of a socialist market economy—as well as its possible political benefits—in comparison to the economy of other communist countries. It is hardly surprising, therefore, that it received growing attention as the East European countries became increasingly concerned with reforming their economic institutions during the sixties. So far only two countries, Hungary and Czechoslovakia, have carried their reform blueprints far enough to be said to have opted for market socialism, albeit qualified on many scores. As this book goes to press (mid-1970), the Czech reform has been stopped and reversed in the wake of that country's invasion by the U.S.S.R. and its allies in August 1968 (though the reform was probably not a major cause of the invasion). However, the Hungarian reform, put into effect at the beginning of 1968, seems to be working out reasonably well; it represents our third instance of market socialism. All in all, the question of institutional reform remains very much on the agenda, not only in Eastern Europe, but in the U.S.S.R. as well. And if, to paraphrase Marx, there is today a specter haunting socialist Europe, it is the specter of market socialism.

Let us briefly look at five major issues in the problem of reforming the command economy.[10]

1. Decentralization The ills of the command economy which we

---

[10] The literature on East European economic reforms is already very large, even in the English language. A convenient introduction is [5]. A succinct (but less up-to-date) summary and analysis may be found in [7].

briefly noted above derive in large measure from the overcentralization of its organizational structure and decisionmaking process. Everywhere the command economy is under attack on this score. But the issues under the general rubric of "decentralization" are highly complex. The basic question is whether decentralization should stop short of abolishing the command economy, or go on to replace it with some sort of socialist market economy. In either case there are numerous questions of institutional and even systemic redesign. How far down should decisionmaking powers be delegated? How coarsely or finely should the organizational structure be partitioned? Should the major organizational components be territorial or sectorial (industrial)? How should prices be formed, and who should form them? What objectives should the enterprise pursue? What should be the role of financial institutions? What kind of planning should there be? And so forth, virtually ad infinitum.

2. *Prices* Should prices be administratively set—and if so, according to what economic principles? Or should they be left to be formed freely in the market in the event of the establishment of a market economy? This issue is closely tied to the preceding one. Clearly, the more decentralization, the less administrative control of the economy from the center, and the more must the task of coordinating economic activity be left to the price system. How should prices be formed in a command economy to permit reasonable efficiency in resource allocation (which requires a good deal of price flexibility in response to changing conditions); to avoid inflation (which may call for administratively imposed inflexibility); to exercise administrative control over industries and enterprises; or to permit the smooth functioning of a market mechanism if the command principle should be substantially abandoned?

3. *Incentives* If more decisions are to be made in a decentralized way, then those who will make them, especially managers, must be given financial incentives to do so. Moreover, these incentives must almost necessarily be tied in with the new prices, or with the profits that derive from them. In addition, in countries like Czechoslovakia and Hungary, where the wage and salary scales have been overcompressed for the sake of egalitarianism, it may be necessary to spread the scales again in the interest of productive performance. There is also a trend in many countries toward greater material rewards to peasants to alleviate the shortages of agricultural products. All in all, the problem of incentives ties in closely with those of decentralization and price-wage policy and raises a host of economic, social, political, and even ideological questions.

4. *Workers' Councils* This issue is closely related to the three preceding ones. Not only is the lodging of significant discretionary power with the workers of an enterprise in itself a major decentralizing move, but workers' councils cannot exercise meaningful power within society

unless the individual enterprise has meaningful autonomy—that is, unless the economy's organizational structure is itself significantly decentralized. As the Yugoslavs have insisted, only within a market structure is there enough scope for workers' self-management to operate. Although pressures for "marketization" in the East European countries at this juncture probably derive little force from a desire to pave the way for workers' councils—as often as the two have been linked in discussion—it is likely that successful transition to a socialist market economy in a country such as Hungary would quickly bring the issue of workers' councils to the forefront.

5. *Planning* Clearly, the purposes, methods, and instruments of planning bear an intimate relationship to other major institutions of the economy. The "imperative" planning in a Soviet-type economy is very different from the "indicative" planning in a relatively decentralized economy such as socialist Yugoslavia or capitalist France. In addition, there is also the issue of the best methods of planning with *given* institutions and for given objectives. For instance, even within its existing command economy, could the Soviet Union plan better than it does—in the sense of producing more internally consistent plans, taking fuller account of feasible alternatives, using the economy's resources more efficiently, responding more quickly to changing conditions, committing fewer resources to the task, and so forth? (Mathematical planning models and electronic computers readily suggest themselves in this connection; these are much discussed but so far little used in the U.S.S.R. in actual planning.)

There are many reasons why these issues have come to the forefront in the past ten or fifteen years, particularly since the middle sixties. To begin with, a much wider range of expression of opinion is now possible in the East European countries and the U.S.S.R., thanks to the diminution of terror and the weakening of internal political controls. But greater latitude for expression of opinion is not a sufficient condition; there must also be dissatisfaction with the state of affairs and a conception (or many conceptions) of how things might be otherwise. The dissatisfaction focuses on the waste of resources, on the low quality and poor variety of goods, and especially on the disproportionately small return to the consumer after decades of privation.

There is also widespread appreciation that economic conditions today are not what they were in the U.S.S.R. when the command economy was first established there. The Soviet economy then was still relatively backward and technologically simple. Its institutions were designed to mobilize resources to the utmost and to concentrate them on a comparatively small number of high-priority objectives. It paid little attention either to the consumer or to the foreign market. Today, in most of the countries in question, such crude means no longer suffice. Technology is more advanced, the economy is more complex, and the consumer is not easily satisfied with skimpy resources shoddily proferred to him. All the countries except the U.S.S.R. are heavily dependent on foreign trade. They are especially short of convertible (Western) foreign exchange. They find that the command economy is at a serious disadvantage in producing goods that can compete on world markets. One could go on.

True, the relevant conditions vary from country to country. Some relatively less advanced (for example, Rumania and Bulgaria) find that their economies are not yet very complex; they still have resources left to mobilize in the accustomed ways, their exports to the West still consist of relatively simple commodities, and their consumers on the whole are less demanding. In other East European countries the economic arguments for reform are more pressing—especially when driven home by serious economic setbacks, as in Czechoslovakia in the first half of the sixties. Moreover, the idea of economic reform is associated in many minds with the idea of political liberalization; in this regard, too, the intensity of aspiration in the various countries probably differs according to cultural forces, past experience, and other factors. In all these countries there is much resistance to economic reform: from vested interests, from fear of change, from ideological dogma, and the like. The intensity of antireform forces also varies from country to country. All these reasons help explain why economic reforms advance at very different speeds—and in some cases hardly at all—in different communist countries.

Concluding Remarks Because most of the centrally planned economies at one time had essentially the same economic system—the Soviet model of the command economy—when we speak of "continuity and change" in such economies we necessarily mean the comparative study of communist economic systems as we observe them at different points of time and in different countries. Comparative communist economic systems is a field of study within economics which has interested many specialists in North America, Western Europe, and the communist countries themselves. Yet it is a very young field, as young as any within the broad region of economics. It barely existed at the beginning of the sixties, and would probably have been regarded as a contradiction in terms by competent observers in the early fifties, when Stalin's rigid economic model was in effect wherever his authority reached.

The comparative study of communist economic systems is a subfield of the more general comparative study of economic systems. Professor Neuberger's observations in the present volume, then, apply here as well. Take, for example, the goals toward which economic activity is directed, and the values by which it is appraised by an outside observer. Although we are dealing here with communist regimes, all professing unwavering allegiance to the ideology of Marxism-Leninism, we still cannot assume the value basis of economic policy and institutions to be invariant from country to country. As we saw in the preceding section, the major economic issues at stake in the communist world today rest on essentially divergent conceptions of the nature and purpose of socialism, of the role of conflict in society, and of the relationship between man and society. All these divergent views are nominally socialist and Marxist, but to designate them in these general terms today is to say very little about them. The ideological differences between a Red Guardsman in Peking and a reformer in Prague are as great as any differences across the "East-West" line. This ideological evolution and differentiation in the communist countries—pertaining perhaps more to the open *expression* of different ideological positions and their influence on policy than to individually held views, which no doubt were always there in some variety but whose expression was until recently suppressed—is one of the more interesting aspects of the current fluid scene in the communist world, an aspect that the economist overlooks at his peril.

This brings us to a broader point. The study of continuity and change in centrally planned economies is also a study of contemporary economic history. To be sure, for the professional economic historian "contemporary history" is virtually a contradiction in terms. What kind of definitive historical perspective can the scholar have on something that is happening before his eyes? But if we are to study the subject—and study it we must, if only because of its intellectual appeal—we must see it as a historically conditioned process. We must apply to it, among other approaches, that of economic history. Once we accept this much, we enter upon the methodological ground sketched out in this volume by Professor Gerschenkron (Chapter 2). The students of continuity and change in centrally planned economies, like Gerschenkron's economic historians, "must at all times start by asking economic questions.... But when it comes to providing answers ... it cannot be taken for granted that those answers will be primarily economic answers." Thus, it would be impossible to study the economic reforms in Eastern Europe, or even a specific aspect of reform in a specific country, without reference to the role of the communist party and the problem of power in a communist society, the question of political democratization, the ideological conflicts within present-day communism, and the Soviet Union's attempts to preserve political hegemony over the region. Herein lies much of the appeal and the challenge of comparative studies of communist economies; herein—as in the case of economic history, noted by Gerschenkron—also lie difficulties for the young economist whose training, thanks to the remarkable technical progress of his discipline, has typically not prepared him to look in other disciplines for answers to economic questions.

Of course, the "technically" trained economist does have room to apply his tools when he turns his attention to the communist economies. Enough reasonably reliable quantitative data are now available to keep computers humming for (at least) minutes. (In this regard, the situation has changed strikingly from the not-so-distant days of the first postwar decade when simply to determine, say, the size of Soviet steel output to no more than two significant digits required patient detective work of many months.) Though the two should not be confused, quantitative empirical findings may well be important grist for the mill of comparative systems study. More may be possible along this line in the future. The builder of rigorous models of the behavior of firms or of planning systems, too, can keep himself busy in the field of comparative study of communist economies—provided he is prepared to live with the ideological, political, and other noneconomic assumptions on which his models must necessarily rest.[11]

It is these extraeconomic entanglements that make the comparative study of communist economies part of yet another latter-day, and rapidly growing, intellectual pursuit: the study of comparative communism. This last, like its economic subdivision, was born a few years ago in the swift process of differentiation of the various communist societies, polities, ideologies, parties, and movements. It is of necessity an interdisciplinary pursuit in which the economist plays a key role—in a sense the reverse of what he does within his own discipline—by offering economic explanations for political, sociological, and other noneconomic aspects of that process. His efforts will not remain unrequited, for in employing his tools to help answer other people's questions he is likely to gain new insights into the efficacy of his own tools and the relevance of his own questions.

REFERENCES

1. BANDERA, V. N. "The New Economic Policy (NEP) as an Economic System," *Journal of Political Economy*, 71:3 (1963), pp. 265–279.
2. BROWN, ALAN A., and EGON NEUBERGER. *International Trade and Central Planning* (Berkeley: University of California Press, 1968).
3. DOBB, MAURICE. *Soviet Economic Development since 1917*, 6th ed. (London: Routledge, 1966).
4. DONNITHORNE, AUDREY. *China's Economic System* (New York: Praeger, 1967).
5. GAMARNIKOW, MICHAEL. *Economic Reforms in Eastern Europe* (Detroit: Wayne State University Press, 1968).

[11] A good example is [15].

6. GERASSI, JOHN (ed.). *Venceremos! The Speeches and Writings of Ernesto Che Guevara* (New York: Macmillan, 1968).
7. GROSSMAN, GREGORY. "Economic Reforms: A Balance Sheet," *Problems of Communism*, November–December 1966, pp. 43–55.
8. ———. *Economic Systems* (Englewood Cliffs, N.J.: Prentice-Hall, 1967).
9. HOFFMAN, CHARLES. *Work Incentive Practices and Policies in the People's Republic of China, 1953–1965* (Albany: State University of New York Press, 1967).
10. HUGHES, T. J., and D. E. T. LUARD. *The Economic Development of Communist China, 1949–1960*, 2d ed. (London: Oxford University Press, 1961).
11. NOVE, ALEC. *The Soviet Economy: An Introduction*, 3d ed. (New York: Praeger, 1969).
12. PERKINS, DWIGHT H. *Market Control and Planning in Communist China* (Cambridge, Mass.: Harvard University Press, 1966).
13. POWELL, RAYMOND P. "Economic Growth in the USSR," *Scientific American*, December 1968, pp. 17–23.
14. U.S. CONGRESS, JOINT ECONOMIC COMMITTEE, *An Economic Profile of Mainland China*, 2 vols. (1967).
15. WARD, BENJAMIN. *The Socialist Economy: A Study of Organizational Alternatives* (New York: Random House, 1967).

19

COMPARATIVE ECONOMIC SYSTEMS

Egon Neuberger [*]

COMPARATIVE economic systems, as indicated in the first chapter of this volume, is by far the broadest field of study in all of economics, and therefore the most appropriate one with which to conclude our survey of economic perspectives. Its method of comparative analysis may be applied profitably to the particular economic problems covered in the various chapters of this book as well as to the problems of economies in their totality. The study of comparative economic systems treats not only all characteristics of a given economic system, using every tool of economic analysis, but also the contrasting features, actual or theoretical, of different economic systems—and even noneconomic issues in such areas as ideology, political science, and psychological and social dynamics. It must take into account historical background, natural endowment, and changing levels of technology.

The economic system is that part of a total social system which allocates scarce economic resources among competing ends. Thus, the study of economic systems consists of a description, analysis, and comparison of different institutional mechanisms designed to answer the basic economic questions of *what* to produce, *how* to produce it, and *for whom* to produce it. Students of this field face the difficult problem of having to evaluate the relative merits not only of different economic

---

[*] State University of New York at Stony Brook.

organizations in various corners of the world but also of different theoretical systems. Thus, the study of comparative economic systems requires an understanding of alternative approaches to economic theory, acquaints us with the institutions of countries with which we may not be familiar, improves our understanding of our own economic system, and gives us insights into the strengths and weaknesses of various analytical tools and the institutional assumptions upon which they are based.

GOALS

The first, and possibly most difficult, problem in the study of economic systems is to determine the goals that various countries are, or should be, pursuing. A knowledge of goals is helpful in describing a system, and absolutely essential in evaluating its relative merits. Three major obstacles may be encountered in determining the goals of a set of economic systems: (1) it is usually difficult to pinpoint them exactly (some goals also serve as means); (2) it is virtually impossible to attach proper weights to each of them in a given country; and (3) it is not simple, if we make comparisons between countries, to decide whose goal structure should be chosen as an unbiased standard. In assessing the performance of any system, the economist tries to avoid injecting his own value judgments, but he must decide whether the goals of the leaders of the country or the goals of its inhabitants (as consumers or as producers) should be used. It does not imply our approval of a system when we assume as "given" the goals of the decisionmaker. It is the frequent failure to draw these essential distinctions, and to acknowledge that there are no "correct" solutions, that has befogged attempts to evaluate particular economic systems or to compare the merits of two or more economic systems.

To facilitate his analysis of the relative desirability of different systems, the economist finds it necessary to identify, as precisely as possible, the most important goals pursued by leaders of various economic systems. Although clearly no short list will include all possible goals, and while some may legitimately argue in favor of expanding this list, we shall select the following set: (1) the ability of the system to foster rapid and sustainable economic growth; (2) the efficient use of economic resources (at given points in time); (3) a "desirable" distribution of benefits among participants in the system; (4) control over the system by its leaders, or freedom of choice for all participants; and (5) the ability to maintain full employment, price stability, and balance-of-payments equilibrium.

In a broad sense, this list implicitly includes many other goals, such as security for individual participants and support for nonmaterial values such as political freedom, national pride, and beauty.

There are, of course, numerous secondary goals. An economic system should react flexibly to changes in the underlying technology and demand conditions; it should provide conditions conducive to technological and other innovations; it should assure a steady and adequate flow of investment; it should develop the necessary superstructure, including an informational subsystem that supplies all decisionmakers with reliable information at a reasonable cost; and it should offer proper incentives to the system's participants.

CLASSIFICATION

The next question is how to classify various economic systems. What criteria should be applied? The criterion most generally used is property relationships—that is, one asks who owns the means of production. Any good Marxist will tell you that, once you have the answer to this crucial question, you can easily place any system into its proper pigeonhole. A difficulty with this approach is that all twentieth-century economic systems would have to be squeezed into either of two categories: capitalism (means of production owned by private capitalists) or socialism (means of production owned by society, or by the state as its representative). An insistence on using the single criterion of property relationships would force us to lump the United States, France, Denmark, and Nazi Germany under capitalism, and the Soviet Union, Communist China, Yugoslavia, and Albania under socialism. This would make for some very uncomfortable bedfellows indeed.

We must seek a less Procrustean classification of economic systems. Surely, a multidimensional approach is needed. Let us consider the following four key structures in any economic system: decisionmaking, motivational, informational, and coordination structures.[1] This will enable us to focus on four questions: (1) What is the locus of decisionmaking? (2) What motivates a decisionmaker to reach a particular decision? (3) What information does he need to reach a decision? (4) What mechanism coordinates the decisions of several decisionmakers? Let us note that decisionmaking, not property, has been moved to the center of the stage.

The Decisionmaking Structure In dealing with the locus of decisionmaking power, one must consider the level of the economy at which decisions are made, the types of decisions made there (for example, the decision

[1] This classification, which is being developed more fully by the author in a forthcoming book, does not represent a consensus among students of comparative economic systems. Classification of economic systems is one of the issues at the frontier of the study of methodology in this field.

on how many houses are to be built in a tract is more important than the decision on the colors to be used for interior decoration), and the legal or extralegal sanctions (property rights, tradition, or bureaucratic position) provided to protect the right of a decisionmaker, or a group of decisionmakers, to make decisions.

What is our reason for placing ownership in a secondary position, making it merely one of several sanctions provided to protect the right of a decisionmaker to make a decision? The answer is that ownership rights, in themselves, may signify very little. They may mean anything from complete control over the owned object to virtually no control at all. For example, they may range from the almost absolute control you have in the decision to save or spend the dollar in your wallet to the almost zero control a child of three has over the same dollar deposited in his name by his parents in a savings bank. In addition, ownership is by no means the sole sanction behind a decisionmaker's right to dispose freely of some object. The native chieftain who rules a tribe by virtue of tradition may have both the decisionmaking power and the ability to reap many benefits from the tribe's property without having actual ownership over anything. The same can be said of a high functionary in a socialist state, or of a top executive in many United States corporations.

The most important question concerning a decisionmaking structure is the degree of its centralization or decentralization. While much has been written about this question, no fully satisfactory treatment exists. Of the many important issues here, we shall attempt to clarify only two. Instead of the simple dichotomy between centralization and decentralization, we shall deal with four basic types of decisionmaking structures—complete centralization, administrative decentralization, manipulative decentralization, and complete decentralization. And we shall discuss shifts in decisionmaking in cases where there are more than two levels in a hierarchy.[2]

It is easy to define *complete centralization* in the abstract. This exists when a unique, central, monolithic authority in an economic system makes all the decisions. No national economic system based on such complete centralization has ever existed. The cost and difficulty of obtaining the necessary information and the problem of assuring that everyone in the economic system does what he is told provide effective barriers against such centralization. The only conceivable way such a system could be made to operate is by means of a cybernetic revolution, where the information and control problems are solved by information technology and automation.

Administrative decentralization provides for the formulation of basic

[2] These ideas are based on [13], which develops other aspects of this chapter in greater depth and deals with many issues that could not be included here.

decisions by the central authority, but for the delegation of the responsibility to implement the decisions and the right to make the necessary subordinate decisions to lower-level authorities. The control over the actions of lower-level authorities is achieved by placing limitations on their freedom of action—for example, by commanding them to do something, forbidding them to do something else, or setting rules by which they must guide their decisions. A textbook case of administrative decentralization is the army. The army clearly represents the ultimate in a hierarchical, command organization, with all the important decisions being reached at the top of the pyramid, and so may appear to represent complete centralization. However, no commander worth his salt spells out for his subordinates the precise manner in which his commands are to be implemented—for example, a division commander is not likely to tell the company commander which squad to send out on patrol.

For the third type of decisionmaking structure we have coined the name *manipulative decentralization*. This is similar to administrative decentralization, but in this case the central authorities do not place explicit limitations on the freedom of action of lower-level authorities. Instead, they control their actions by affecting the environment within which these actions take place. For example, they may manipulate prices, bonuses, taxes or subsidies, or access to credit.

The fourth type of decisionmaking structure is *complete decentralization*. This provides for the dispersal of basic decisionmaking power among a number of independent decisionmaking centers. In the extreme case—again virtually nonexistent—each of these centers would have complete freedom of decision. The textbook case of complete decentralization is pure competition, where each entrepreneur has complete freedom to make his decisions and there is no higher organ to control his actions in any way. Paradoxically, in the case of pure competition it is obvious that all this freedom actually amounts to very little real power. This is because the invisible hand of the market serves as a demanding taskmaster. Thus, situations of oligopoly—where a few sellers divide the market—or of "countervailing power"—where strong buyers face strong sellers across a market—offer better examples of complete decentralization in the economic sphere.

The fundamental difference between administrative and manipulative decentralization, on the one hand, and complete decentralization, on the other, is between the delegation of authority to lower echelons merely to make decisions that implement the basic decisions reached by higher echelons, in the former, and the dispersal of decisionmaking power among independent decisionmaking organs, in the latter. In the one case, circumscribed rights are granted to subordinates and can be taken away at the discretion of the superior. In the other case, by rights of ownership, custom, or law many independent organs possess power which they cannot be deprived of, except by major changes in these sanctions. In view of this, we would argue that the most significant watershed lies between complete decentralization and administrative or manipulative decentralization, rather than between centralization and decentralization.

Another crucial issue arises when we consider shifts in decisionmaking power in a system that has more than two levels of authority. In a three-level hierarchy, the definition of decentralization, whether administrative or manipulative, is no longer clear. In this case, there are twelve possible shifts in decisionmaking power:

	1 2 3	4 5 6	7 8	9 10	11 12
Central units	− − −	+ + +	−	+	− +
Intermediate units	− +	− +	− +	+ −	+ −
Primary units (enterprises)	+ + +	− − −	+	−	− +

Let us define *decentralization* as a shift of decisionmaking power from the top toward the bottom of the hierarchy (that is, where the power of the highest unit decreases (−) and the power of the lowest unit increases (+)). It should be clear that there are three kinds of decentralization (columns 1, 2, and 3), the most thorough being seen in column 1 and the least thorough in column 3. *Centralization* is, of course, defined by the reverse process, as in columns 4, 5, and 6. The most thorough centralization appears in column 4, the least thorough in column 6.

Semidecentralization occurs when there is a downward shift in decisionmaking power between any two adjoining levels. The two cases of semidecentralization are seen in columns 7 and 8. *Semicentralization* is the reverse phenomenon and is pictured in columns 9 and 10.

Positive-intermediation occurs when the intermediate decisionmaking units gain power at the expense of the highest and lowest units, as in column 11. *Negative-intermediation* occurs when the intermediate units lose power at the expense of the highest and lowest units, as in column 12.

The Motivational Structure A decisionmaker bases his decisions, either consciously or subconsciously, on his perception of the circumstances surrounding the particular choice facing him; the goals he is pursuing; the incentive structure linking his goals and the various alternative decision outcomes available to him; and the type, amount, and quality of information at his disposal or obtainable with further effort and expense.

There exists no generally acceptable theory of human motivation. By combining elements of many different theories of motivation, we can indicate some of the important aspects of this problem. At very low levels of income, physiological needs, such as hunger and thirst, and a desire for security against natural or man-made disasters are likely to be the dominant motivational variables. The economic system must satisfy these needs or use coercion as a substitute. As income rises, material incentives, in their role of satisfiers of physiological needs, and coercion will begin to decrease in importance. Their place is taken by the desire for self-esteem and recognition, for furthering the goals of the organization to which one belongs or for exercising influence over the goals and operation of the organization. To the extent that material incentives represent recognition of the individual's importance and of the significance of his contribution to the organization, they remain crucial motivational elements even at very high income levels. How else is one to explain the extremely high salaries paid to executives in some United States companies when the lion's share of the additional $100,000 of income ends up with the Internal Revenue Service?

Given this range of possible motivational variables, the economic system may be structured in such a way as to accept the objectives of the participants as given or to try to remold them. Most economic systems, including those of the United States and Soviet Union, use the first approach. The motivational structure of the system is adapted to providing the participants in the economic process with appropriate incentives, principally in the form of positive material benefits, but also in the form of ego-satisfying, nonmaterial rewards. Negative incentives in the form of coercion have been used in systems such as the antebellum South or slave labor camps under Hitler and Stalin. However, no modern economic system has been based primarily on coercion.

While most economic systems accept the objectives of the participants as given, some systems use the second approach. They attempt to remold the value structure of the participants in such a way as to make them place a low value on selfish motives, particularly with respect to material benefits. Mao Tse-tung's attempt in the Great Proletarian Cultural Revolution to remold the value structure of the Chinese people is an extreme example.

The Informational Structure Another major input into decisionmaking is information. Information has been gaining importance recently because of changes both in economic systems and in information technology. We will define information very broadly to include the collection, transmission, processing, storage and retrieval, and analysis of economic data; the communication of orders or other signals; and the feedback necessary for evaluating decisions taken as a result of the signals. As we move from a subsistence economy to a traditional economy, from that to a market economy or centrally planned economy, or even to the extreme of a cybernetic economy, the importance of information in the economic system rises very greatly. The larger the number of participants in the economic process, the greater the division of labor, the more complex the technological processes, and the wider the assortment of goods and services an economic system produces, the more information-intensive the economic process becomes. Information becomes more essential not only for the system as a whole but for every participant in the economic process.

The amount of information entering into the decisionmaking process varies greatly among decisionmakers in the same economic system, with those nearer the center of economic power requiring and obtaining more information than those at the periphery. It also varies greatly among decisionmakers with similar positions but operating under different economic systems.

The three major types of informational signals are prices; data on physical units of inputs, outputs, capacities, and the like; and commands. Data on physical units and commands are hallmarks of Soviet-type central planning, while prices are hallmarks of the market system. However, each type of informational signal can be found in both centrally planned and market systems.

Information may be generated within a given organization or received from outside the organization. It may be obtained by horizontal channels—for example, from customers or rival businesses—or by vertical channels—for example, as commands from higher echelons or as data on levels of output and unused capacities transmitted from a firm to its ministry. Information may consist merely of scattered bits of data used to support an action based on intuition, or it may be generated by a well-established system of information collection and analysis, using the latest instruments of information technology.

Three indirect indicators of the degree of informational centralization may be found in an economic system: (1) horizontal channels of information; (2) reliance on price changes, manipulation of incentives, and generalized monetary and fiscal policy; and (3) limitations on the types of messages that can be demanded by the center and sent from the center to the enterprises. All three correspond to informationally decentralized systems.

The way an economic system is organized with respect to the demand it places on informational inputs to decisionmaking, the channels of information that are established, and the ability of decisionmakers to obtain high-quality information in a reasonable time and at a reasonable cost—these are important factors in determining the efficiency of the system.

The Coordination Structure Decisions of many separate decisionmaking units are coordinated in three ways: by tradition, by a market, or by a plan.

TRADITION This coordinating mechanism may be best explained by the following description of the Trobriand Island economic system:

> *Every man knows what is expected from him, in virtue of his position, and he does it, whether it means the obtaining of a privilege, the performance of a task, or the acquiescence in a status quo. He knows that it has always been thus, and thus it is all around him, and thus it always must remain. The chief's authority, his privileges, the customary give and take which exist between him and the community, all that is merely, so to speak, the mechanism through which the force of tradition acts. For there is no organized physical means by which those in authority could enforce their will in a case like this. Order is kept by direct force of everybody's adhesion to custom, rules and laws, by the same psychological influences which in our society prevent a man of the world doing something which is not "the right thing." The expression "might is right" would certainly not apply to Trobriand society. "Tradition is right, and what is right has might"—this rather is the rule governing the social forces in Boyowa, and I dare say in almost all native communities at this stage of culture [12, pp. 158–159].*

A MARKET The "invisible hand," as the coordinating mechanism in the market, consists of three major elements: every individual is motivated by self-interest; he obtains the commodities and services he requires through exchange with others; and by his pursuing his self-interest, in competition with others, the welfare of society is maximized. Some quotations from Adam Smith illustrate these points:

> *It is not from the benevolence of the butcher, the brewer, or the baker that we expect our dinner, but from their regard to their own interest. We address ourselves, not to their humanity but to their self-love, and never talk to them of our own necessities but of their advantages [16, p. 13].*

While humans obtain most of what they need by means of exchange— "Give me that which I want, and you shall have this which you want"— this does not happen with other species: "Nobody ever saw a dog make a fair and deliberate exchange of one bone for another with another dog" [16, pp. 12–13]. The most important, but by no means most obvious, aspect of the market is that, according to Smith, a man pursuing his own self-interest is

> ... led by an invisible hand to promote an end which was not part of his intention. Nor is it always the worse for the society that it was no part of it. By pursuing his own interest he frequently promotes that of the society more effectually than when he really intends to promote it [16, p. 400].

Or again,

> Every individual is continually exerting himself to find out the most advantageous employment for whatever capital he can command. It is his own advantage, indeed, and not that of the society, which he has in view. But the study of his own advantage naturally, or rather necessarily, leads him to prefer that employment which is most advantageous to the society [16, p. 398].

A PLAN   The third major coordinating mechanism is a plan. One of the earliest examples of planning is told in the Biblical story of Joseph, who prepared Egypt for seven lean years by gathering grain and storing it in the warehouses of the Pharaoh during seven fat years. A more recent example is the centrally planned economic system introduced by another Joseph, Joseph Djugashvili, better known as Stalin.

According to its adherents, the major advantages of a plan as the coordinating mechanism are (1) the possibility of ex ante coordination, which enables a given objective to be attained more smoothly and more speedily, and (2) the reduction of uncertainty as to the actions of competitors, suppliers, and buyers, which makes for more rational investment decisions and may help in internalizing external economies.

In addition to requiring a coordination mechanism, an economic system must provide mechanisms for assuring that decisions are implemented. Implementation in a traditional society is based on voluntary adherence to custom, or, if need be, on the enforcement of custom by such means as ostracism. In a market system, implementation takes place through the operation of the price system. In a planned system there are many possible mechanisms for enforcing the decisions of the planners. The usual one is by informational messages in the form of commands from superiors to inferiors. But this role could theoretically be performed by a cybernetic system transferring information from one machine to another, by the setting of prices by planners, by the use of coercion, or possibly even by the willing cooperation of all the participants. All of these implementing mechanisms, of course, contain motivational or informational components, and could be dealt with as aspects of the motivational and informational structures. Closely connected with implementing mechanisms are the economic policies—monetary, fiscal, or antitrust—adopted by the government in any given economic system.[3]

---

[3] We will not discuss these or other government policies here, since they are treated in Chaps. 6 to 18. The fact that so many of the present chapters deal with govern-

TWO EXTREME MODELS

It is easy to describe, by the classification scheme above, the economic system at either end of the scale, but difficult to classify the many economic systems that fall somewhere in between. At one extreme, we find the centrally planned command economy,[4] where (1) virtually all important decisions are made by the leadership by virtue of their political power and position in the bureaucratic hierarchy; (2) decisionmaking by lower-level bureaucrats is controlled by rules set for them from above, motivation takes the form of obtaining approval from their superiors (with attendant material benefits and chances of promotion), and the major information flows consist of commands going down the line and information about fulfillment of the commands going back up the line; and (3) decisions are coordinated by a central plan and implemented by bureaucratic command.

At the other extreme is the pure laissez faire free-enterprise system, consisting of innumerable small firms owned by individuals, either directly or as shareholders. The chief characteristics of this system are familiar enough: (1) Decisionmaking power is in the hands of consumers and the owners of economic resources, including capital, land, and labor. Consumers and managers of enterprises play a dominant role, the managers making decisions by their right as owners of the capital of the firm, or as representatives of the owners. (2) Managers of firms are highly motivated by profit. The information on which they act consists primarily of price signals obtained from the marketplace. (3) Competition operating in the free market provides a coordinating mechanism, while changes in the prices both of products and of factors of production stimulate market participants to act in their own self-interest, thereby assuring the maximum satisfaction for all (Adam Smith's "invisible hand").[5]

SYSTEM COMPARISONS

Neither of these economic systems exists in its extreme form today—if, indeed, it ever existed—so the task of the student of comparative economic systems is to study the many economic systems that lie between

---

mental policies indicates clearly the importance of this subject matter for economics. Comparative economic systems deals with problems of a country's environment, such as its human and natural resources; of the country's goals; of the institutional structure of its economic system; and of its economic policies. In this chapter we concentrate on the institutional structure and, to a lesser extent, on the goals of economic systems.

[4] See [4] for a more detailed discussion of this system.
[5] See Chap. 4 for a more detailed discussion of this system.

them and combine their distinctive features in various ways. He can approach this task by attempting to describe each economic system as fully as possible—analyzing its goals, its locus of decisionmaking power, its motivational and informational structures, and its coordinating and implementing mechanisms, thereby drawing as complete a picture of the system as possible—and then showing how the system copes with basic economic problems. Or he may select the most important problems that any economic system is called upon to solve—such as assuring a balance between the demand and supply of resources and final products, determining the level and allocation of investment resources, and distributing the income among the various productive agents—and then analyze the way in which they are solved by the several systems. Neither of these approaches can be said to be clearly superior to the other. Possibly the best way to proceed is to start with a description of each of the economic systems, in which one attempts to explain how institutions and policies operate to make the system function, and then to follow through by showing how selected economic systems solve certain important economic problems in different ways. The first part of this two-part approach teaches us how various countries' economic systems operate, while the second improves our understanding of comparative-system solutions.

In examining an economic system, the student may either abstract the essential elements of the system and use them to build a system model, or study the actual economic system in all its complexity. Since, however, no investigator can possibly cope with the myriad details that make up a complete economic system, he is forced to be highly selective in analyzing the operation of the economic system. In the process of selection, he is better off to state explicitly what he is doing, and why, than to build an implicit theory of the system. The classification scheme described earlier represents an attempt to select key variables, but it is not a full-fledged theory of economic systems; it does not provide behavioral or other relationships among the variables.[6]

Pinning down the essential characteristics of an economic system is a difficult task. Descriptive models of an economic system or its components are only imperfect representations of the actual thing. With the passage of time an economic system may change, while "cultural lag" may delay changes in the model.

SYSTEM CHANGES

Models of the two extreme types of economic systems described above may have conformed to historical reality at one time, but they do so no longer. The centrally planned command economy faithfully represents

[6] A similar problem is faced by economic historians; see the discussion in Chap. 2.

the dominant features of the Soviet and Eastern European economies during Stalin's reign, and of the Yugoslav economy until the early 1950s. It does not fit the Soviet economy quite so well now; it fits the Eastern European economies undergoing economic reforms even less well; and it is completely unsuitable for describing the present Yugoslav economy. The trend in these countries is away from the earlier, virtually complete neglect of consumer desires; away from the centralization of all decision-making powers in a small group at the top; and away from the stress on rules to be followed, and commands to be obeyed, by lower echelons. The shift is not toward capitalism, as some Western writers would like to believe, but toward a type of guided market system—a "visible hand" system. The locus of decisionmaking power for all but the most crucial decisions is being shifted to lower echelons (enterprises or associations of enterprises); the importance attached to incentives in influencing the decisions of lower-level decisionmakers has grown considerably; and the role of the market and price mechanism for implementing (but not necessarily for coordinating) decisions is increasing.[7]

At the other extreme, the model of laissez faire free enterprise has significant descriptive power for middle nineteenth-century United States and England. However, it portrays present-day free-enterprise countries even less faithfully, perhaps, then the central-planning model portrays present-day socialist countries. Among many important historical changes in the free-enterprise system, we draw attention to two: the changing nature of business enterprise and the changing role of the government. The economies of the United States, the United Kingdom, and other Western industrial countries no longer consist of many small firms competing freely and trying to maximize their profits, thereby contributing unwittingly to national welfare. Instead, there are a relatively small number of large, powerful monopolistic or oligopolistic firms dominating some industries and coexisting with a larger number of small firms in other industries. The large corporations are not simple profit-maximizers, and they do not accept market prices as immutable facts. Instead, they influence prices and attempt to fulfill goals—by such means as increasing their share of the market, maintaining good public and labor relations, and avoiding government interference. Their size relative to the economy in which they operate makes it both possible and necessary for such firms to engage in long-range planning. Their absolute size creates significant internal organizational problems. Thus, corporation executives face problems of much the same sort as leaders of centrally planned economies. After all, the value of the output of General Motors is much greater than the value of the output of all Albanian industry.

The concept of the proper role of government in the economy has

---

[7] For a more complete discussion of this topic, see Chap. 18.

altered greatly in the past century, especially since the onset of the Great Depression of the 1930s. Instead of playing a laissez faire role and abstaining from interference with the operation of the economy, most governments now accept the obligation of exerting considerable economic control. The use of government fiscal and monetary policy aimed at maintaining full employment and stability, and more recently growth, is now accepted by virtually every national government.[8] Similarly, most governments continually interfere in the operation of the economy by such measures as antitrust legislation, farm subsidies, tariff policies, minimum wages, and the like. Some Western governments go much further and engage in various degrees of national planning; for example, the French, who have always had an etatist disposition, accept considerable government planning of the economy, in what has been called a system of "indicative planning."

CONVERGENCE?

The changes that have taken place in both centrally planned and free-enterprise economies naturally raise the question of whether all systems are not converging toward one optimal economic system. The matter of the degree of convergence which has already taken place and which may be expected to occur in the near future lies at the frontier of the study of comparative economic systems, as does the relative merit of the mixed systems toward which we are moving vis-à-vis systems closer to the extremes. No simple answers are possible, so let us merely suggest that, although differences between economic systems are smaller today than they were in the past, there is no sign that all economic systems will converge toward one specific mixed system. Rather, it is likely that the trend away from the extreme economic systems will continue, but that future systems will combine various institutions and policies in many different ways and no single blueprint will be followed.

It is interesting to note that the Eastern European countries all started with a slavish imitation of the Soviet model after World War II, but each of them is now developing its own version of socialism. Thus, within the Soviet bloc it is quite clear that there is divergence and not convergence.

We feel fairly confident in predicting for the short run a continuation of the movement away from the extremes of pure market and pure central planning, toward systems that combine these two coordinating mechanisms. Similarly, these two mechanisms are likely to be combined differently in different countries. The result should be divergence in the degree of centralization of decisionmaking and in the composition of the informational and motivational structures adopted.

However, to predict the nature of economic systems far into the future

[8] See Chaps. 5, 6, 7, and 16.

would require information on many difficult points, such as the prospect for nation states and political systems in the world, changes in social customs and values, and possible scientific and technical breakthroughs. One event that could easily change the basic nature of future economic systems is the advancing revolution in information technology and control mechanisms. It is conceivable that in the more distant future all economic systems will converge toward some type of cybernetic system, and that students of economic systems will have to be electronic engineers, mathematicians, and students of artificial intelligence as well!

REFERENCES

1. AMES, EDWARD. *Soviet Economic Processes* (Homewood, Ill.: Irwin, 1965).
2. BERGSON, ABRAM. *The Economics of Soviet Planning* (New Haven, Conn.: Yale University Press, 1964).
3. BORNSTEIN, MORRIS (ed.). *Comparative Economic Systems: Models and Cases*, revised ed. (Homewood, Ill.: Irwin, 1969).
4. BROWN, ALAN A., and EGON NEUBERGER. "Basic Features of a Centrally Planned Economy," in *International Trade and Central Planning* (Berkeley: University of California Press, 1968).
5. CAMPBELL, ROBERT W. *Soviet Economic Power: Its Organization, Growth and Challenge*, 2d ed. (Boston: Houghton Mifflin, 1966).
6. ECKSTEIN, ALEXANDER. *Communist China's Economic Growth and Foreign Trade* (New York: McGraw-Hill, 1966).
7. FRIEDMAN, MILTON. *Capitalism and Freedom* (Chicago: University of Chicago Press, 1962).
8. GALBRAITH, JOHN K. *The New Industrial State* (Boston: Houghton Mifflin, 1967).
9. GROSSMAN, GREGORY. *Economic Systems* (Englewood Cliffs, N.J.: Prentice-Hall, 1967).
10. HALM, GEORGE N. *Economic Systems: A Comparative Analysis*, 3d ed. (New York: Holt, 1968).
11. LOUCKS, WILLIAM N., and WILLIAM G. WHITNEY. *Comparative Economic Systems*, 8th ed. (New York: Harper & Row, 1969).
12. MALINOWSKI, BRONISLAW. *Argonauts of the Western Pacific* (New York: Hutton, 1961).
13. NEUBERGER, EGON, and FREDERIC L. PRYOR. *A New Conceptual Framework for Analyzing Economic Systems*, unpublished paper, International Development Research Center, Indiana University, 1969.
14. SCHUMPETER, JOSEPH A. *Socialism, Capitalism and Democracy* (New York: Harper, 1947).
15. SHONFIELD, ANDREW. *Modern Capitalism: The Changing Balance of Public and Private Power* (London: Oxford University Press, 1965).
16. SMITH, ADAM. *The Wealth of Nations* (London: Dent, 1910). First published, 1776–1778.
17. SOLO, ROBERT A. *Economic Organizations and Social Systems* (Indianapolis: Bobbs-Merrill, 1967).